Family Spending

2007 edition

Editor: Ed Dunn

Office for National Statistics

palgrave
macmillan

First published 2008 by
PALGRAVE MACMILLAN
Houndmills, Basingstoke, Hampshire RG21 6XS and 175 Fifth Avenue, New York, NY 10010, USA
Companies and representatives throughout the world.

PALGRAVE MACMILLAN is the global academic imprint of the Palgrave Macmillan division of St. Martin's Press, LLC and of Palgrave Macmillan Ltd. Macmillan® is a registered trademark in the United States, United Kingdom and other countries. Palgrave is a registered trademark in the European Union and other countries.

ISBN 978-0-230-54561-8
ISSN 0965-1403

This book is printed on paper suitable for recycling and made from fully managed and sustained forest sources. Logging, pulping and manufacturing processes are expected to conform to the environmental regulations of the country of origin.

A catalogue record for this book is available from the British Library.

10 9 8 7 6 5 4 3 2 1
17 16 15 14 13 12 11 10 09 08

Printed and bound in Great Britain by
Hobbs the Printers Ltd,
Totton, Hampshire,

A National Statistics publication

National Statistics are produced to high professional standards set out in the National Statistics Code of Practice. They are produced free from political influence.

About the Office for National Statistics

The Office for National Statistics (ONS) is the government agency responsible for compiling, analysing and disseminating economic, social and demographic statistics about the United Kingdom. It also administers the statutory registration of births, marriages and deaths in England and Wales.

The Director of ONS is also the National Statistician and the Registrar General for England and Wales.

Contact points

For enquiries about this publication, please contact: Expenditure and Food Survey
Tel: 01633 455282
email: efs@ons.gsi.gov.uk

For general enquiries, contact the National Statistics Customer Contact Centre.

Tel: 0845 601 3034 (minicom: 01633 812399)
email: info@statistics.gsi.gov.uk
Fax: 01633 652747
Post: Room 1015, Government Buildings,
           Cardiff Road, Newport NP10 8XG

You can also find National Statistics on the Internet at:
www.statistics.gov.uk

CORRECTION

Family Spending
2007 edition

ISBN 978-0-230-54561-8

Pages 3 & 4 'Celebrating 50 years of Family Spending'

Unfortunately there are minor errors on pages 3 and 4 of Family Spending 2007. These minor errors affect text references to rankings in table C 'Household Expenditure 2006' and to the labels for the percentage shares given in Figure B 'Percentage of total weekly household expenditure in the UK in 1957' and Figure C 'Percentage of total weekly household expenditure in the UK in 2006.'

A corrected version of both pages is attached.

The PDF version of this publication on the National Statistics website is correct.

The Office for National Statistics apologises for any inconvenience caused.

Office for National Statistics
January 2008
Palgrave Macmillan: Basingstoke

Table A Household expenditure based on the FES classification, 1957 to 2006
2006 Prices[1]

Year	1957	1967	1977			1987[2]	1996–97	2006
Weighted number of households (thousands)[3]							24,310	24,790
Total number of households in sample	2,840	7,390	7,200			7,400	6,420	6,650
Total number of persons	8,720	22,140	19,890			18,740	15,730	15,850
Weighted average number of persons per household	3.1	3.0	2.8			2.5	2.5	2.4
Commodity or service	Percentage of total expenditure			Commodity or service		Percentage of total expenditure		
Housing	9	12	14	1 Housing (Net)		16	16	19
Fuel, light and power	6	6	6	2 Fuel and power		6	4	3
Food	33	27	25	3 Food and non-alcoholic drinks		19	18	15
Alcoholic Drink	3	4	5	4 Alcoholic drink		5	4	3
Tobacco	6	5	4	5 Tobacco		2	2	1
Clothing and footwear	10	9	8	6 Clothing and footwear		7	6	5
Durable Household goods	8	6	7	7 Household goods		7	9	8
Other Goods	7	7	7	8 Household services		4	5	6
Transport and Vehicles	8	12	14	9 Personal goods and services		4	4	4
Services	9	10	10	10 Motoring		13	13	14
Miscellaneous	0	0	1	11 Fares and other travel costs		2	2	2
				12 Leisure goods		5	5	4
				13 Leisure services		10	11	15
				14 Miscellaneous		0	1	0
All expenditure groups	100	100	100	1–14 All expenditure groups		100	100	100

1 Figures have been deflated to 2006 prices using the RPI all items index.

2 In 1986 groupings changed to align with the categories recommended for the RPI. The 11 categories were extended to 14.

3 Non-response weighting introduced in 1998/1999.

• Since 1957 the proportion of our average weekly expenditure spent on food and non-alcoholic drinks has halved from 33 per cent to 15 per cent in 2006.

• Weekly expenditure on the four categories 'Food', 'Transport', 'Housing' and 'Leisure' has become more equivalent over the past 50 years.

• As a proportion of total expenditure, the amount spent on 'Clothing and footwear' and 'Fuel, light and power' has halved since 1957.

• Expenditure on leisure remained fairly stable until 1977. From 1977 until 2006 the expenditure has increased at a greater rate than in the twenty years between 1957 and 1977.

Top 50 items of expenditure in 1957 and 2006

Tables B and C list the top 50 categories of expenditure in 1957 and 2006. In 1957 expenditure data were classified using the FES classification, since the introduction of the EFS in 2001-02 expenditure data have been classified using the Classification of Individual COnsumption by Purpose (COICOP). These data are presented solely for the purpose of historical comparisons and it should be stressed that it is not possible to directly compare

the FES data presented in 1957 with the COICOP data presented in the 2006 top 50. Nevertheless, highlights include:

• Housing related expenditure is number one on both the 1957 and 2006 top 50 list. The remainder of the top 10 look very different.

• The 1957 top ten included four food and beverage items, 'meals bought away from home, milk (fresh), poultry and other undefined meat. In 2006 the top ten items of expenditure included a single food item – which was restaurant and café meals.

• Cigarettes accounted for almost 6 per cent of total expenditure and was item two in the top 50 in 1957. Since then the proportion of weekly income spent on cigarettes has decreased to just under 1 per cent and is ranked as item 30 in the 2006 top 50.

• Gambling payments did not appear in the 1957 top 50. However, in 2006 the proportion spent on these payments was placed in 33rd place in the top 50.

• Fresh vegetables were listed in 34th place in 2006 but did not appear in the top 50 in 1957.

Some items remained in similar places in the top 50, these include:

- The proportion of expenditure spent on running a vehicle was very similar in 1957 and 2006. In 2006 Petrol, diesel and other motor oils were third, in the top 50 and in 1957 just one place below at fourth.

- In 2006 package holidays (abroad) are ranked in sixth place, in 1957 subscriptions and donations, hotel and holiday expenses, miscellaneous other services were also in seventh place (although these categories are not directly comparable).

- Finally, in 2006 – hair products, cosmetics etc. and hairdressing were at places 39 and 40 in the top 50. In the 1957 top 50, toilet requisites, cosmetics etc. are in 40th place.

Note

1 OPCS merged with Central Statistical Office (CSO) in 1996 to form the Office for National Statistics (ONS).

Figure **A**

Percentage of total expenditure on selected categories 1957 to 2006 (based in FES classification)

Per cent

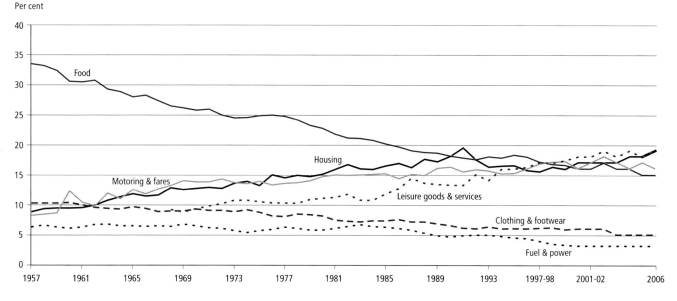

Figure **B**

Percentage of total weekly household expenditure in the UK in 1957 (2006 prices)

Percentages

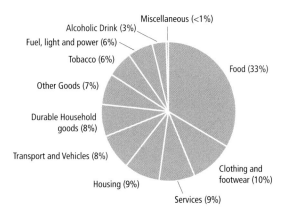

Figure **C**

Percentage of total weekly household expenditure in the UK in 2006

Percentages

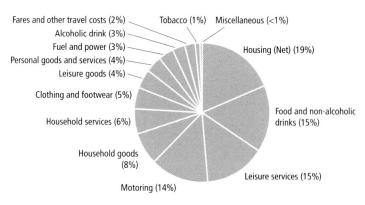

Contents

List of tables

4: Trends in household expenditure over time

Appendix A

List of figures

Page

Equivalised income

Symbols and conventions used in this report

[ ]	Figures to be used with extra caution because based on fewer than 20 reporting households.
..	The data is suppressed if the unweighted sample counts are less than ten reporting households
Rounding:	Individual figures have been rounded independently. The sum of component items does not therefore necessarily add to the totals shown.
Averages:	These are averages (means) for all households included in the column or row, and, unless specified, are not restricted to those households reporting expenditure on a particular item or income of a particular type.

Period covered: Calendar year 2006 (1 January 2006 to 31 December 2006).

List of contributors

Editor:	Ed Dunn
Authors:	Deborah Curtis
	Steven Dunstan
	Rebecca Gatward
	Joseph Hawthorne
	Sian-Elin Wyatt
EFS Team:	Karen Carter
	Linda Cording
	Cathy Gibbins
	Kay Joseland
	Tony King
	Jo Monger
	Martina Portanti
	Angela Potter
	Melanie Richard
	Gareth Rusgys
	Rachael Salmon
	Tim Samuels
	Lloyd Shemwell
	Grant Symons
	Karen Watkins
	Field Team and Interviewers
	Coders and Editors
Reviewers:	Ann Harris
	Francis Jones
	Bev Botting

Acknowledgements

A large scale survey is a collaborative effort and the authors wish to thank the interviewers and other ONS staff who contributed to the study. The survey would not be possible without the co-operation of the respondents who gave up their time to be interviewed and keep a diary of their spending. Their help is gratefully acknowledged.

This edition of Family Spending celebrates 50 years of results from the Expenditure and Food Survey and, its predecessor, the Family Expenditure Survey which began in 1957. It is appropriate at this time to acknowledge the efforts and contributions of everyone that has been involved with both surveys over the last 50 years, and to thank the 320,000 households that have taken part since 1957.

Introduction

This report presents the latest information from the Expenditure and Food Survey (EFS) for the 2006 calendar year (January to December) and celebrates 50 years of results from a continuous household expenditure survey in the UK.

The current EFS is the result of the amalgamation of the Family Expenditure and National Food Surveys (FES and NFS). Both surveys were well established and important sources of information for government and the wider community, charting changes and patterns in Britain's spending and food consumption since the 1950s. The Office for National Statistics (ONS) has overall project management and financial responsibility for the EFS while the Department for Environment, Food and Rural Affairs (DEFRA) sponsors the specialist food data.

For the 2006 results the survey has moved onto a calendar year basis from the previous financial year basis in preparation for its integration to the Continuous Population Survey (CPS). As a consequence, the January 2006 to March 2006 data are common between the 2005/06 financial year results (as published in the 2006 Edition of Family Spending) and the 2006 calendar year results.

The design of the EFS is based on the FES and the same questions were asked of the respondents. The survey continues to be primarily used to provide information for the Retail Prices Index; National Accounts estimates of household expenditure; the analysis of the effect of taxes and benefits, and trends in nutrition. However, the results are multi purpose, providing an invaluable supply of economic and social data.

The 2006 survey

In 2006 6,650 households in Great Britain took part in the EFS. The response rate was 55 per cent in Great Britain and 54 per cent in Northern Ireland. The fieldwork was undertaken by ONS and the Northern Ireland Statistics and Research Agency.

Further details about the conduct of the survey are given in Appendix B.

The format of the *Family Spending* publication changed in 2003-04 so that the tables of key results which were found in the main body of the report are now in Appendix A. This year's report includes an overview chapter outlining key findings, two detailed chapters focusing upon expenditure on housing and the impact of equivalising income when calculating results, and a fourth chapter looking at trends in household expenditure over time. Also included in this publication is a chapter celebrating 50 years of results from the Family Expenditure and Expenditure and Food surveys in Great Britain.

Data quality and definitions

The results shown in this report are of the data collected by the EFS, following a process of validation and adjustment for non-response using weights that control for a number of factors. These issues are discussed in the section on reliability in Appendix B.

Figures in the report are subject to sampling variability. Standard errors for detailed expenditure items are presented in relative terms in Table A1 and are described in Appendix B, section B6. Figures shown for particular groups of households (e.g. income groups or household composition groups), regions or other sub-sets of the sample are subject to larger sampling variability, and are more sensitive to possible extreme values than are figures for the sample as a whole.

The 2006 results are the first to be based on a calendar year since the EFS was introduced in April 2001. In January 2006 the EFS switched from a financial to calendar year basis in anticipation of the introduction of the CPS (of which the EFS will be part) in January 2008. As a result, tables that have previously been based on data collected across two or three financial years, are now presented based on one year's data and, therefore, should be interpreted with care since they may be subject to greater variability than if based on two or three years as previously.

The definitions used in the report are set out in Appendix B, section B4, and changes made since 1991 are described in section B5. Note particularly that housing benefit and council tax rebate (rates rebate in Northern Ireland), unlike other social security benefits, are not included in income but are shown as a reduction in housing costs.

Related data sources

Details of household consumption expenditure within the context of the UK National Accounts are produced as part of Consumer Trends (http://www.statistics.gov.uk/statbase/Product.asp?vlnk=242). This publication includes all expenditure by members of UK resident households. National Accounts figures draw on a number of sources including the EFS: figures shown in this report are therefore not directly comparable to National Accounts data. National Accounts data may be more appropriate for deriving long term trends on expenditure.

More detailed income information is available from the Family Resources Survey (FRS), conducted for the Department for Work and Pensions. Further information about food consumption, and in particular details of food quantities, is available from DEFRA, who are continuing to produce their own report of the survey (http://statistics.defra.gov.uk/esg/publications/efs/default.asp).

In Northern Ireland, a companion survey to the GB EFS is conducted by the Central Survey Unit of the Northern Ireland Statistics and Research Agency (NISRA). Households in Northern Ireland are over-sampled so that separate analysis can be carried out, however these cases are given less weight when UK data are analysed. Results from this sample will be published in a separate report, The Northern Ireland Family Expenditure Survey Report for 2006. Further information and copies of this report can be obtained from:

Northern Ireland Statistics and Research Agency,
Central Survey Unit
McAuley House
2-14 Castle Street
Belfast BT1 1SY
Tel: 02890 348 214

Additional tabulations

This report gives a broad overview of the results of the survey, and provides more detailed information about some aspects of expenditure. However, many users of EFS data have very specific data requirements that may not appear in the desired form in this report. ONS can provide more detailed analysis of the tables in this report, and can also provide additional tabulations to meet specific requests. A charge will be made to cover the cost of providing additional information.

The tables in *Family Spending* 2007 are available as Excel spreadsheets (with unrounded data).

Anonymised microdata from the Expenditure and Food Survey (EFS) and the Family Expenditure Survey (FES) are available from the United Kingdom Data Archive. Datasets available include the 1961 FES. Details on access arrangements and associated costs can be found at www.data-archive.ac.uk or by telephoning 01206 872143.

Celebrating 50 years

Family Spending 2007 marks 50 years of results from a household expenditure survey. From 1957 to March 2001, the Family Expenditure Survey and National Food Surveys (FES and NFS) provided information on household expenditure patterns and food consumption. In April 2001 these surveys were combined to form the Expenditure and Food Survey (EFS). The National Food Survey (NFS) is the longest-running continuous Government social survey having originally been set up in the 1940's to monitor the diet of the urban 'working class' population during the war years. In 1950 it was extended to cover all households in the general population and to collect data on food consumption and expenditure. In 1953 Social Survey Division of the Office of Population Censuses and Surveys (OPCS)[1] became involved in the Household Expenditure Survey, designed to provide up-to-date weights for the Retail Price Index. The Government wanted to expand the survey's coverage, so that spending could be related to family circumstances and income. The Ministry of Labour wanted to use its local office staff for the fieldwork, but after much discussion the Treasury decided that Social Survey's trained researchers would provide more reliable data. The Division subsequently played a large part in developing the survey and, in January 1957, it was re-launched as the Family Expenditure Survey (FES). A continuous household expenditure survey has been conducted each year since 1957.

Survey Timeline

- 1953 OPCS becomes involved in the Household expenditure survey.

- 1957 Household expenditure survey re-launched as the Family Expenditure Survey (FES), the survey was designed by William Kemsley, of the Social Survey Division of OPCS.

- 1961 Electronic computers first used in the processing of the FES data, leading to changes to the design of the interview schedule.

- 1967 The sample is doubled. Number of Primary sampling Units (PSUs) increases to 168 each quarter and arranged so that each calendar quarter is representative in itself.

- 15th February 1971 Decimalisation Day in the UK. For the first year the FES schedule designed to cater for old and new currency.

- July 1971 The token payment given to each household member for cooperation increases from £1 to £2.

- 1977 The 'Meals out' column is expanded and divided to include a 'Take-away meals' category.

- 1980 Merging the National Food Survey and FES is first suggested as a result of a Government Statistical Service review overseen by Sir Derek Rayner, of the Government Efficiency Unit.

- 1983 Men's and boys' shirts are classified as outerwear rather than underwear.

- 1986 Expenditure on holidays is shown separately in the main tables for the first time.

- 1987 Expenditure on air fares is shown separately in the main tables for the first time.

- 1994–95 'Gambling payments' and 'Mortgage protection payments' are added as expenditure items.

- 1995–96 The geographical coverage of the Family Expenditure Survey is extended to mainland Scotland north of the Caledonian Canal.

- 1995–96 Two week expenditure diaries for 7 to 15 year olds are introduced.

- 1996–97 Information on cable and satellite subscriptions and mobile telephones now collected via the household questionnaire rather than via the Diary.

- 1997–98 Information on access to the Internet now collected.

- 1998–99 Three new expenditure codes are introduced to cover children's income, pocket money to children, money given for specific purposes and cash gifts to children.

- 1998–99 Non response weighting is introduced.

- April 2001 the Family Expenditure Survey and National Food Surveys (FES and NFS) are merged to form the Expenditure and Food Survey (EFS).

- 2001–02 Classification of Individual COnsumption by Purpose (COICOP) is introduced as a new coding frame for expenditure items.

Pattern of expenditure – change over the last 50 years

Our pattern of expenditure has changed over the last 50 years. In 1957, food and non-alcoholic drinks accounted for the highest proportion of our average weekly household expenditure. In the fifty years since 1957 the proportion we spend on food has decreased, and, based on the original FES expenditure classification, housing now accounts for the highest proportion of our expenditure. Other main trends in expenditure (based on the original FES classification) over the past 50 years include:

Table **A** Household expenditure based on the FES classification, 1957 to 2006
2006 Prices[1]

Year	1957	1967	1977			1987[2]	1996–97	2006
Weighted number of households (thousands)[3]							24,310	24,790
Total number of households in sample	2,840	7,390	7,200			7,400	6,420	6,650
Total number of persons	8,720	22,140	19,890			18,740	15,730	15,850
Weighted average number of persons per household	3.1	3.0	2.8			2.5	2.5	2.4
Commodity or service	Percentage of total expenditure				Commodity or service	Percentage of total expenditure		
Housing	9	12	14	1	Housing (Net)	16	16	19
Fuel, light and power	6	6	6	2	Fuel and power	6	4	3
Food	33	27	25	3	Food and non-alcoholic drinks	19	18	15
Alcoholic Drink	3	4	5	4	Alcoholic drink	5	4	3
Tobacco	6	5	4	5	Tobacco	2	2	1
Clothing and footwear	10	9	8	6	Clothing and footwear	7	6	5
Durable Household goods	8	6	7	7	Household goods	7	9	8
Other Goods	7	7	7	8	Household services	4	5	6
Transport and Vehicles	8	12	14	9	Personal goods and services	4	4	4
Services	9	10	10	10	Motoring	13	13	14
Miscellaneous	0	0	1	11	Fares and other travel costs	2	2	2
				12	Leisure goods	5	5	4
				13	Leisure services	10	11	15
				14	Miscellaneous	0	1	0
All expenditure groups	**100**	**100**	**100**	**1–14**	**All expenditure groups**	**100**	**100**	**100**

1 Figures have been deflated to 2006 prices using the RPI all items index.

2 In 1986 groupings changed to align with the categories recommended for the RPI. The 11 categories were extended to 14.

3 Non-response weighting introduced in 1998/1999.

- Since 1957 the proportion of our average weekly expenditure spent on food and non-alcoholic drinks has halved from 33 per cent to 15 per cent in 2006.

- Weekly expenditure on the four categories 'Food', 'Transport', 'Housing' and 'Leisure' has become more equivalent over the past 50 years.

- As a proportion of total expenditure, the amount spent on 'Clothing and footwear' and 'Fuel, light and power' has halved since 1957.

- Expenditure on leisure remained fairly stable until 1977. From 1977 until 2006 the expenditure has increased at a greater rate than in the twenty years between 1957 and 1977.

Top 50 items of expenditure in 1957 and 2006

Tables B and C list the top 50 categories of expenditure in 1957 and 2006. In 1957 expenditure data were classified using the FES classification, since the introduction of the EFS in 2001-02 expenditure data have been classified using the Classification of Individual COnsumption by Purpose (COICOP). These data are presented solely for the purpose of historical comparisons and it should be stressed that it is not possible to directly compare the FES data presented in 1957 with the COICOP data presented in the 2006 top 50. Nevertheless, highlights include:

- Housing related expenditure is number one on both the 1957 and 2006 top 50 list. The remainder of the top 10 look very different.

- The 1957 top ten included four food and beverage items, 'meals bought away from home, milk (fresh), poultry and other undefined meat. In 2006 the top ten items of expenditure included a single food item – which was restaurant and café meals.

- Cigarettes accounted for almost 6 per cent of total expenditure and was item two in the top 50 in 1957. Since then the proportion of weekly income spent on cigarettes has decreased to just under 1 per cent and is ranked as item 32 in the 2006 top 50.

- Gambling payments did not appear in the 1957 top 50. However, in 2006 the proportion spent on these payments was placed in 35th place in the top 50.

- Fresh vegetables were listed in 36th place in 2006 but did not appear in the top 50 in 1957.

Some items remained in similar places in the top 50, these include:

• The proportion of expenditure spent on running a vehicle was very similar in 1957 and 2006. In 2006 Petrol, diesel and other motor oils were third, in the top 50 and in 1957 just one place below at forth.

• In 2006 package holidays (abroad) are ranked in seventh place, in 1957 subscriptions and donations, hotel and holiday expenses, miscellaneous other services were also in seventh place (although these categories are not directly comparable).

• Finally, in 2006 – hair products, cosmetics etc. and hairdressing were at places 41 and 42 in the top 50. In the 1957 top 50, toilet requisites, cosmetics etc. are in 40th place.

Note

1   OPCS merged with Central Statistical Office (CSO) in 1995 to form the Office for National Statistics (ONS).

Figure **A**

Percentage of total expenditure on selected categories 1957 to 2006 (based in FES classification)

Per cent

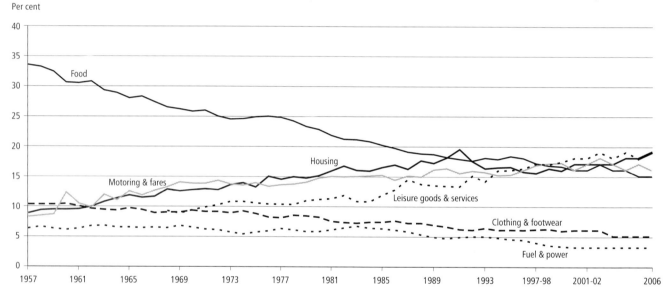

Figure **B**

Percentage of total weekly household expenditure in the UK in 1957 (2006 prices)

Percentages

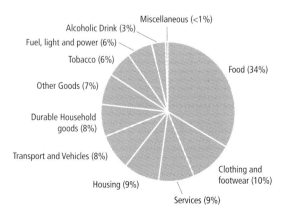

Figure **C**

Percentage of total weekly household expenditure in the UK in 2006

Percentages

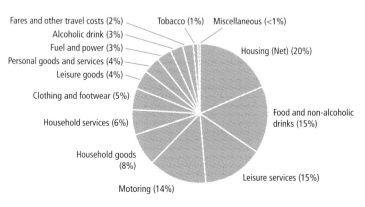

Table **B** Household Expenditure 1957
Top 50 commodities or services

Top 50	Commodity/Service	% of average weekly expenditure
1	Housing	8.7
2	Cigarettes	5.6
3	Meals bought away from home	3.1
4	Maintenance and running of motor vehicles	2.8
5	Milk, fresh	2.7
6	Poultry; other and undefined meat	2.7
7	Subscriptions and donations; hotel and holiday expenses; miscellaneous other services	2.7
8	Coal and manufactured fuels (exc. Coke)	2.6
9	Bus fares	2.2
10	Beer, cider, etc.	2.2
11	Women's outer clothing	2.0
12	Biscuits,cakes, etc.	2.0
13	Bread, rolls etc.	1.9
14	Footwear	1.9
15	Fruit	1.8
16	Other and undefined vegetables	1.8
17	Furniture, including repairs	1.8
18	Beef and veal	1.8
19	Net purchase of motor vehicles and accessories	1.7
20	Books, magazines and periodicals	1.6
21	Men's outer clothing	1.5
22	Radio, television and musical instruments, inc. repairs	1.5
23	Electricity, and hire of electric appliances	1.4
24	Matches, soap, cleaning materials, etc.	1.4
25	Gas and hire of gas appliances	1.3
26	Eggs	1.3
27	Tea	1.2
28	Sweets and chocolates	1.2
29	Bacon and ham (uncooked)	1.2
30	Women's underclothing and hoisery	1.1
31	Gas and electric appliances, including repairs	1.1
32	Other foods; food not defined	1.1
33	Mutton and lamb	1.1
34	Butter	1.1
35	Hats, gloves, haberdashery, etc.	1.0
36	Girls' and Boys' clothing	1.0
37	Soft furnishings and household textiles	0.9
38	Potatoes	0.9
39	China, glass, cutlery, hardware, ironmongery, etc.	0.9
40	Toilet requisites, cosmetics, etc.	0.9
41	Floor coverings	0.9
42	Sugar	0.9
43	Fish	0.8
44	Men's underclothing and hoisery	0.8
45	Toys and stationery goods, etc.	0.8
46	Footwear and other repairs not allocated elsewhere	0.8
47	Leather, travel and sports goods; jewellery; fancy goods, etc.	0.7
48	Wines,spirits etc.	0.7
49	Animals and pets	0.7
50	Railway fares	0.7

Table C Household Expenditure 2006
Top 50 commodities or services

Top 50	Family Spending 2007 category	Commodity/Service	% of average weekly expenditure
1	13.1.1	Mortgage interest payments	7.1
2	4.1.1	Gross rent	6.1
3	7.2.2	Petrol, diesel and other motor oils	4.0
4	13.1.3	Council tax, domestic rates	3.8
5	7.1.2	Purchase of second hand cars or vans	3.2
6	9.6.2	Package holidays - abroad	2.9
7	11.1.1	Restaurant and café meals	2.8
8	5.1.1	Furniture and furnishings	2.7
9	13.3.1	Money spent abroad	2.7
10	13.4.2	Cash gifts and donations	1.9
11	3.1.3	Women's outer garments	1.9
12	11.1.2	Alcoholic drinks (away from home)	1.8
13	7.1.1	Purchase of new cars and vans	1.8
14	12.4.3	Vehicle insurance including boat insurance	1.7
15	4.4.1	Electricity	1.7
16	4.4.2	Gas	1.6
17	7.2.3	Repairs and servicing	1.3
18	9.4.3	TV, video, satellite rental, cable subscriptions, TV licences and Internet	1.3
19	9.4.1	Sports admissions, subscriptions, leisure class fees and equipment hire	1.3
20	8.3.1	Telephone account	1.2
21	4.3.1	Water charges	1.2
22	7.3.4	Other travel and transport	1.2
23	12.4.1	Household insurances	1.1
24	4.2.2	House maintenance etc.	1.1
25	1.1.10	Other meats and meat preparations	1.1
26	9.1.2	TV, video and computers	1.0
27	3.1.1	Men's outer garments	1.0
28	1.1.1	Bread, rice and cereals	0.9
29	11.1.4	Other take-away and snack food	0.9
30	2.2.1	Cigarettes	0.9
31	5.1.2	Floor coverings	0.9
32	11.1.3	Take away meals eaten at home	0.9
33	9.4.6	Gambling payments	0.8
34	1.1.23	Fresh vegetables	0.8
35	8.3.3	Mobile phone account	0.8
36	9.3.5	Pets and pet food	0.8
37	11.2.2	Holiday abroad	0.8
38	2.1.2	Wines, fortified wines (brought home)	0.7
39	12.1.5	Hair products, cosmetics and electrical appliances for personal care	0.7
40	12.1.1	Hairdressing, beauty treatment	0.7
41	12.5.1	Moving house	0.7
42	1.1.19	Fresh fruit	0.6
43	1.1.3	Buns, cakes, biscuits etc.	0.6
44	6.2.1	Out patient services	0.6
45	13.2.3	Motor vehicle road taxation payments less refunds	0.6
46	11.2.1	Holiday in the UK	0.6
47	9.3.4	Horticultural goods, garden equipment and plants etc.	0.6
48	7.2.4	Other motoring costs	0.5
49	10.1.2	Secondary education	0.5
50	5.6.1	Cleaning materials	0.5

Note: The commodity and service categories are not comparable with those in publications before 2001-02
The numbering is sequential, it does not use actual COICOP codes

Overview

Chapter 1

This chapter presents the key findings of the 2006 Expenditure and Food Survey (EFS). The chapter is structured to provide an overview of general household expenditure, the variation in household expenditure by different types of household and by region and, finally, of the ownership of a limited range of durable goods.

All of the tables (except Table 1.1) referred to in this chapter can be found in Appendix A of the report (page 73).

Household expenditure

Table 1.1 shows total weekly household expenditure in the United Kingdom (UK) and expenditure by the twelve COICOP[1] categories. Average weekly household expenditure in the UK in 2006 was £455.90. As in previous years, spending was highest on transport at £62.00 a week with the next highest expenditure on recreation and culture at £58.50 a week. This was followed by housing, fuel and power at £47.60. The average weekly expenditure on food and non-alcoholic drinks was £46.90 a week.

Table **1.1** Expenditure by COICOP category and total household expenditure

COICOP category	£ per week
Transport	62.00
Recreation and culture	58.50
Housing, fuel and power	47.60
Food and non-alcoholic drinks	46.90
Restaurants and hotels	37.90
Miscellaneous goods and services	36.00
Household goods and services	30.30
Clothing and footwear	23.20
Communication	11.70
Alcoholic drinks, tobacco and narcotics	11.10
Education	7.20
Health	5.90
Total COICOP expenditure	378.30
Other expenditure items	77.60
Total expenditure	455.90

Totals may not add due to the independent rounding of component categories.

Of the £62.00 spent on transport each week, close to half (46 per cent) was spent on operating personal transport (£28.60 a week), the majority of which was spent on petrol, diesel and other motor oils (£18.20 a week). Households spent £10.00 a week on average on transport services, including rail, tube and bus fares (see Table A1).

Almost a quarter (24 per cent) of the expenditure on recreation and culture each week was spent on package holidays (£14.10

per week), most of which were holidays outside of the UK (£13.20). Spending on sports admissions, subscriptions, leisure class fees and equipment hire accounted for £5.80 a week, £2.00 was spent on admissions to the cinema, theatre and museums, and £3.60 was spent on gambling payments (Table A1).

Of the £46.90 spent on food and non-alcoholic drinks each week, £12.50 was spent on meat, £3.60 on fresh vegetables, £2.90 on fresh fruit, and £4.10 on non-alcoholic drinks (Table A1). Close to three quarters (71 per cent) of food and non-alcoholic drinks were purchased from large supermarket chains, £33.40 per week (Table A3).

Alcohol bought and consumed on licensed premises accounted for slightly more than half (£8.40, 56 per cent) of all expenditure on alcoholic drink (£14.90 per week). The remaining £6.50 was spent on alcohol bought at large supermarket chains or off-licence outlets (Table A2).

Household expenditure by income

Average gross household income in 2006 was £642 a week (Table A40). Household incomes have been ranked in ascending order and divided into deciles, with households with the lowest income in the first decile, in order to examine expenditure patterns between different income groups. Household expenditure ranged from £155.60 a week on average in the lowest of the ten income deciles to £964.40 a week in the highest (Figure 1.1, Table A6).

Figure **1.1**

Household expenditure by gross income decile group, 2006

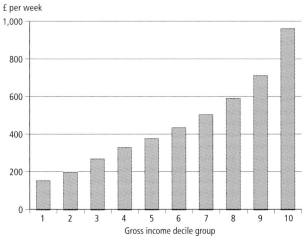

£ per week

Households in the lowest income groups spent a larger proportion of their expenditure on housing, fuel and power, and food and non-alcoholic drinks, than those in the higher income groups. The proportion of expenditure on housing, fuel and power, and food and non-alcoholic drinks was 21 and 16 per cent respectively among households in the lowest income group compared with 8 and 7 per cent respectively among households in the highest group (Table A7).

Households in the highest income group spent a larger proportion of their expenditure on transport than those in the lowest gross income group, 16 per cent compared with 9 per cent (Table A7).

Household expenditure by age

Average weekly expenditure varied by the age of the household reference person (HRP). Households whose HRP was aged 30 to 49 years had the highest average expenditure (£554.10 per week) while those with an HRP aged 75 years or over had the lowest average household expenditure (£211.80 per week). It should be noted that households with an HRP aged 30 to 49 years contained an average of three people, compared with 1.4 among households with a HRP aged 75 years or over (Table A11).

The proportion of spending on food and non-alcoholic drinks increased with the age of the household reference person, from 8 per cent among households with an HRP aged less than 30 years to 15 per cent among households with an HRP aged 75 years or over. The pattern was reversed for spending on restaurants and hotels: the proportion of spending fell from 9 per cent of all weekly expenditure among households with an HRP aged less than 30 years to 6 per cent among households with an HRP aged 75 or over. Expenditure on recreation and culture, as a proportion of total spending, increased from 11 per cent among households with an HRP aged less than 30 years to 16 per cent among households with an HRP aged 65 to 74 years, after which the proportion fell again to 12 per cent among those with an HRP aged 75 years or over (Figure 1.2, Table A12).

Figure **1.2**

Expenditure on selected items as a proportion of total spending by age of the HRP, 2006

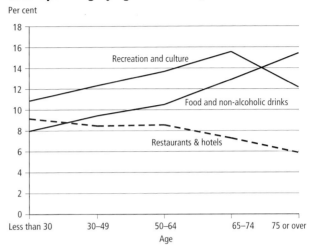

Per cent

Household expenditure by economic activity and socio-economic classification[2]

Average weekly expenditure of households where the HRP was in employment (£569.70 per week) was more than twice that of households where the HRP was unemployed or economically inactive (£236.00 and £282.00 per week respectively) (Table A19).

The items which households spent the most on also varied by the economic activity of the HRP. In households where the HRP was in employment, spending was greatest on transport, and recreation and culture, at £80.40 and £71.60 per week. Among households where the HRP was unemployed, spending on housing, fuel and power was highest (£45.50 per week) followed by transport (£33.00 per week). In households with an economically inactive HRP, spending was greatest on food and non-alcoholic drinks followed by recreation and culture, (£38.90 and £38.70 per week respectively) (Table A19).

Average weekly expenditure was greater among households where the HRP was in the 'large employers and higher managerial' occupational group, at £822.40 per week. This compared with £410.50 in households where the HRP was in the 'routine' occupational group (Table A24).

Household expenditure by household composition

As would be expected, household expenditure was generally higher in larger households. Thus, average weekly household expenditure was highest among households with three or more adults with children (£700.50) and lowest among one person retired households who were mainly dependent on the state pension (£138.10) (Table A25).

Household expenditure by region

Overall, average household expenditure in the UK was £455.90 per week for 2006. There were three regions in which expenditure over this period was higher than the UK average: London, where expenditure was greatest at £538.00 per week; the South East (£511.80); and the East (£487.20). Spending was lowest among households in the North East (£359.50 per week) (Figure 1.3, Table A35).

Figure 1.3

Household expenditure by region, 2006

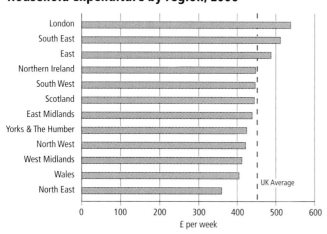

Table A37 shows spending on transport was highest among households in the South East (£77.30 per week) and lowest among those in the North East (£43.60 per week). In both regions spending on transport services, including rail, tube and bus fares, accounted for 14 per cent of transport expenditure: £6.00 a week in the North East and £11.00 a week in the South East. The remaining 86 per cent of transport expenditure was spent on vehicle purchases and the operation of personal transport (for example, petrol, diesel, oil, repairs and servicing): £37.60 a week in the North East and £66.30 a week in the South East.

Households in London spent the most on housing, fuel and power, £70.00 a week, which compared with the UK national average of £47.60 a week (Table A37). Housing expenditure is looked at in more detail in Chapter 2.

Households in Northern Ireland and Scotland reported the highest expenditure on cigarettes at £8.10 and £5.80 a week respectively (Table A37).

Households in rural areas had higher overall expenditure (£494.20) than those living in urban areas (£446.70 per week respectively). Those living in both rural and urban areas had the highest expenditure on transport (£71.40 and £59.70 per week

respectively) and recreation and culture (£65.40 and £57.10 respectively) (Table A38).

Ownership of durable goods

Households in the higher income groups were much more likely to have a home computer and internet connection than those in the lower income groups. Whilst overall just over half (59 per cent) of all households had an internet connection and 67 per cent had a home computer, among households in the highest income group, 96 per cent had a home computer and 94 per cent an internet connection, compared with 31 and 21 per cent of households in the lowest income group. A similar pattern was observed for mobile phone ownership, with 92 per cent of households in the highest income group owning a mobile phone compared to 56 per cent in the lowest income group. Households with children were more likely to own a home computer and have an internet connection than those without (Table A51).

Connection to the internet was lowest among households in the North East (51 per cent) and highest in the South East and East Midlands (66 per cent each). Ownership of a mobile phone was lowest among households in Northern Ireland (48 per cent) and highest in the East Midlands, West Midlands and Yorkshire and The Humber at 86 per cent (Table A53).

Just over three-quarters (76 per cent) of all households owned a car or van, with 32 per cent owning two or more. Ownership of at least one car or van varied from 31 per cent in the lowest income group, to 94 per cent in the highest (Table A52).

Ownership of a car or van was highest among households in the East and the South West (84 and 83 per cent respectively), and lowest among those in the North East (65 per cent) and London (63 per cent) (Table A53).

Notes

1 From 2001–02, the Classification of Individual COnsumption by Purpose (COICOP) was introduced as a new coding frame for expenditure items. COICOP is the internationally agreed classification system for reporting household consumption expenditure. Total expenditure is made up from the total of the COICOP expenditure groups (1 to 12) plus 'Other expenditure items (13)'. Other expenditure items are those items excluded from the narrower COICOP classifications, such as mortgage interest payments, council tax, domestic rates, holiday spending, cash gifts and charitable donations.

2 This analysis uses the National Statistics Socio-Economic Classification (NS-SEC), see Section B1, page 182.

Housing expenditure

Chapter 2

Housing expenditure

This chapter presents an analysis of all housing-related costs, including rent, mortgage payments, council tax, home improvement, maintenance and house insurance. Data relating to fuel and power consumption are excluded.

Most household expenditure is classified using the Classification Of Individual COnsumption by Purpose (COICOP) system. The COICOP categories cover net rent; household maintenance and repair; water and other service charges; and household insurances. However, COICOP does not provide a comprehensive definition of housing expenditure. For this reason, an 'other expenditure items' category has been included in the tables within Family Spending, which includes: mortgage interest payments, mortgage protection premiums, council tax, domestic rates for only or main residence, council tax, mortgage and insurance for second dwelling. In addition, certain housing costs are not covered by the COICOP or 'other expenditure items' categories. These additional costs are presented in this chapter to provide a comprehensive definition of Housing Expenditure. Such costs include: housing alterations and improvements; capital repayment of mortgages; purchase of a second dwelling; moving house; outright purchase of dwellings and deposits for that purpose. Table 2.1 details all the items that are included in the comprehensive definition.

COICOP

Since 2001–02, the COICOP system has been used to classify expenditure on the EFS. COICOP is the internationally agreed standard classification for reporting household consumption expenditure within National Accounts. COICOP is also used on Household Budget Surveys (HBS) across the EU. These surveys collect information on household consumption expenditure, which is then used to update the weights in the basket of goods and services used in consumer price indices.

Household consumption expenditure is broken into 12 COICOP headings, as shown in the tables presented in Appendix A. In line with national accounting definitions and conventions, additions to savings, investments or loans, repayments of loans and mortgage interest, cash grants or donations and other financial transactions, as well as house purchases and major renovations and alterations, are considered to be non-consumption expenditures. The COICOP system does not include expenditure related to housing such as mortgage interest payments, purchases or alterations of dwellings and mortgages. In order to look at total housing costs, this chapter includes housing expenditure as recorded under COICOP, together with additional items, as described in the Housing expenditure section above.

Table 2.1 Definition of total housing expenditure

Housing costs which are included in the COICOP classification:

- Actual rentals for housing
  - net rent (gross rent *less* housing benefit, rebates and allowances received)
  - second dwelling rent
- Maintenance and repair of dwelling
  - central heating maintenance and repair
  - house maintenance and repair
  - paint, wallpaper, timber
  - equipment hire, small materials

- Water supply and miscellaneous services relating to dwelling
  - water charges
  - other regular housing payments including service charge for rent
  - refuse collection, including skip hire.
- Household Insurances
  - structural insurance
  - contents insurance
  - insurance for household appliances.

Housing costs which are included as 'other expenditure items':

- Housing: mortgage interest payments etc
  - mortgage interest payments
  - mortgage protection premiums
  - council tax, domestic rates
  - council tax, mortgage, insurance (second dwelling).

Housing costs which are not treated as consumption expenditure but which are included here:

- Purchase or alteration of dwellings (contracted out), mortgages
  - outright purchase of houses, flats etc. including deposits
  - capital repayment of mortgage
  - central heating installation
  - DIY improvements: double glazing, kitchen units, sheds etc
  - home improvements (contracted out)
  - bathroom fittings
  - purchase of materials for capital improvements
  - purchase of second dwelling.

The household expenditure tables in Appendix A contain the category 'housing (net), fuel and power' under which all COICOP classified housing costs except insurance can be found. It is also worth noting that the tables use rent net of service charges and any benefit receipts associated with housing when calculating total expenditure, a convention continued within this chapter. This convention ensures that rebates, benefits and allowances are excluded from the total calculation of household expenditure on rent.

Income and Expenditure Balancing

The EFS is designed primarily as a survey of household expenditure on goods and services. It also gathers information about the income of household members and is an important and detailed source of income data. However, the survey is not designed to produce a balance sheet of income and expenditure either for individual households or groups of households[1].

Analysis

The first part of this chapter looks at variations in housing expenditure over time and by income, region and household characteristics (Tables 2.2 to 2.7). In this analysis, expenditure is averaged across all households including those reporting nil expenditure on a specific item. Therefore all households are deemed to pay a proportion of all housing costs. The impact of this is that all households are included when calculating both rent and mortgage interest, despite the fact that they are only actually likely to pay one or the other. In order to address this issue and explore housing costs further, an additional analysis was conducted that just looked at expenditure of renters and those paying mortgages. The results of this analysis are presented in the latter part of the chapter (Tables 2.8 to 2.11).

Results

Using the definition of housing expenditure given in Table 2.1, the average weekly expenditure on housing in 2006 was £143.30 (Table 2.2). This compared with £47.60 which was the total spent on housing under the narrower COICOP heading of 'housing, fuel and power' (see Table A1 in Appendix A).

Housing expenditure over time

Table 2.2 provides a comparison of housing costs over time, using data from the past three survey years (2004–05, 2005–06 and 2006). The table contains both average household consumption and non-consumption expenditure data. It also includes a total for all expenditure, both consumption and non-consumption expenditure, which is consequently greater than the expenditure total shown in the

tables in Appendix A. In 2006, the total for all recorded household spending was £658.00 per week, compared with £455.90 for expenditure under the COICOP definition plus other expenditure items (that are not considered to be consumption expenditure). The difference between total household spending and household consumption expenditure alone was similar in 2004–05 and 2005–06. In 2005–06, the corresponding amounts were £641.30 and £443.40. In 2004–05, total household spending was £619.70, compared with £434.40 for household expenditure under the COICOP definition plus other expenditure items.

Table 2.2 also shows that overall expenditure on housing rose from £127.40 in 2004–05 to £139.60 in 2005–06 to £143.30 in the current year. Expenditure on housing continued to grow as a proportion of all weekly recorded household spending, from 21 per cent in 2004–05 to 22 per cent in 2006. The largest component of housing spending for 2006 was mortgages (interest, protection and capital repayment), followed by charges (including council tax or domestic rates, water charges, refuse collection), household alterations and improvements and net rent. In the previous two years the results showed that household alterations and improvements data were greater than charges (including council tax or domestic rates, water charges, refuse collection). In 2006, households spent £52.00 per week on mortgages, £24.20 per week on charges, £23.10 per week on household alterations and improvements and £16.70 on net rent. As previously mentioned, these calculations average expenditure on all items, across all households in the sample and therefore every household is attributed a weekly expenditure on net rent and a mortgage.

Figure 2.1 and Table 2.2 show the amount spent by each household per week on mortgage, household alterations and improvements, charges, net rent, household maintenance and repair, secondary dwelling, household insurances and moving house, over the period 2004–05, 2005–06, 2006. The greatest increase was expenditure on mortgages where spending grew from £46.30 in 2004–05 to £48.60 in 2005–06 to £52.00 in the current year.

Expenditure by gross income

Table 2.3 shows expenditure on housing by gross income decile group. Overall, housing expenditure increased with income. The highest income group spent £316.40 per week on housing, more than double the average weekly expenditure for all UK households (£143.30) and nearly eight times that of the lowest income group who spent £40.90. This variation by income was mainly attributable to differences in mortgage and

Figure 2.1

Housing expenditure 2004-05 to 2006

£ per week

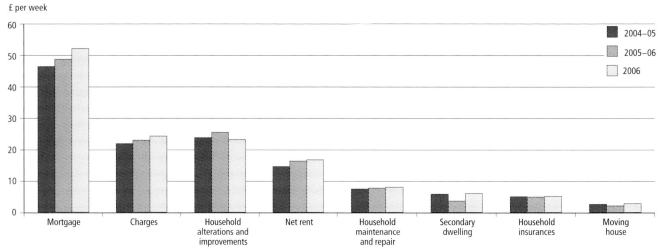

household alterations and improvements expenditure. Figure 2.2 shows, spending on mortgages increased sharply with income, from £6.50 and £6.90 per week among households in the first (lowest) and second income groups to £143.10 among those in the highest income group. The pattern was similar for expenditure on household alterations and improvements – households in the lowest income group spent £3.30 per week compared with £72.30 among those in the highest income group. The increase in expenditure by income was much less marked for household maintenance and repair and household insurance expenditure.

Most categories of expenditure progressively increased or decreased through the income decile groups. The main exception to this was net rent. Households in the ninth

Figure 2.2

Expenditure on selected items by gross income decile group, 2006

£ per week

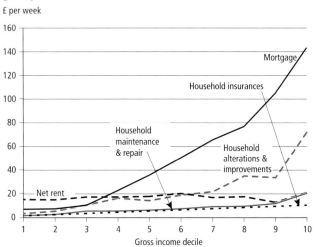

(£12.40) and second lowest income groups (£14.50) spent the least on net rent. Households in the sixth and tenth (highest) income deciles spent the most on net rent (£19.80 and £20.60 respectively).

Expenditure by age of the household reference person

Figure 2.3 shows weekly expenditure on the top five housing expenditures: mortgage; net rent; household alterations and improvements; charges and; household maintenance and repair, analysed by the age of the household reference person (HRP). Households containing a HRP between the age of 30 and 49 years spent the most on mortgages at £92.60, while those containing a HRP aged between 65 and 74 years or 75 years and over spent the least, £5.90 and £1.00 respectively. Households containing a HRP aged 30 years or less spent the most on net rent, £51.90, almost three times more than households with HRPs aged between 30 and 49 years (£19.40), and over nine times more than households with HRPs aged between 65 and 74 years (£5.50). Expenditure on net rent was particularly low among households containing a HRP aged 50 years or over, ranging from £5.50 to £9.20. Expenditure on household alterations and improvements was highest for households containing a HRP aged 30–49 (£29.00) and 50–64 (£28.80); three and a half times greater than where the HRP was aged less than 30 (£8.40).

Expenditure by region

Table 2.5 shows housing expenditure by UK country and Government Office Region. In Northern Ireland households pay rates rather than council tax which are not as high as council tax

Figure **2.3**

Expenditure on selected items by age of household reference person, 2006

£ per week

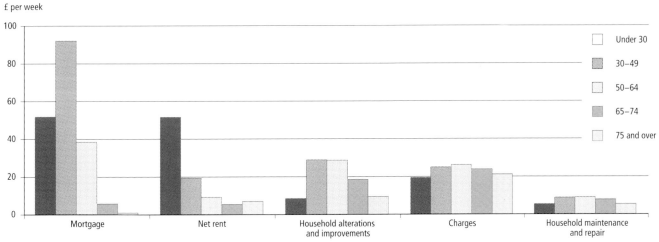

charges. As a result household expenditure on charges in Northern Ireland was much lower than the UK national average (£10.30 per week compared with £24.20 in the UK as a whole).

Figure 2.4 shows the percentage difference from the UK average net rent across regions within the UK. The average UK expenditure on net rent was £16.70, with only two regions spending more than the average: those renting in London spent more than double the UK average (£37.70); and those living in the South East spent 13 per cent more (£18.80). Among the other English regions, net rent ranged from £10.20 per week among those living in Yorkshire and The Humber (39 per cent less than the UK average) to £16.00 per week among those living in the East of England (4 per cent less than the UK average). Those living in Scotland paid the least net rent per

week at £8.70, which was 48 per cent less than the UK average. Expenditure on net rent in Wales was £14.00 per week, 16 per cent lower than the UK average, and in Northern Ireland net rent was £11.30 per week, 32 per cent lower than the UK average.

Figure 2.5 shows regional differences throughout the UK in terms of spending on mortgages. As with the expenditure on net rent, households living in London and the South East spent more than the UK average on their mortgages: those living in the South East (£69.20) spent 33 per cent more than the UK average (£52.00) whereas those in London (£64.80) spent 25 per cent more. Households in the East (£60.60) and the East Midlands (£53.40) also spent more on their mortgages than the UK average (3 and 17 per cent respectively).

Figure **2.4**

Percentage difference compared with UK average for net rent by UK Countries and Government Office Regions, 2006

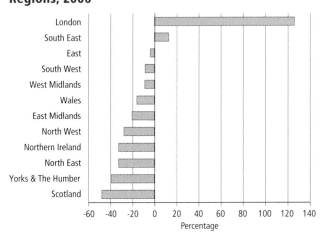

Figure **2.5**

Percentage difference compared with UK average for mortgage payments by UK countries and Government Office Regions, 2006

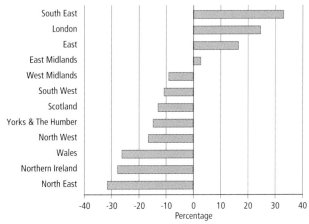

Figure **2.6**

Housing expenditure by socio-economic classification of household reference person, 2006

£ per week

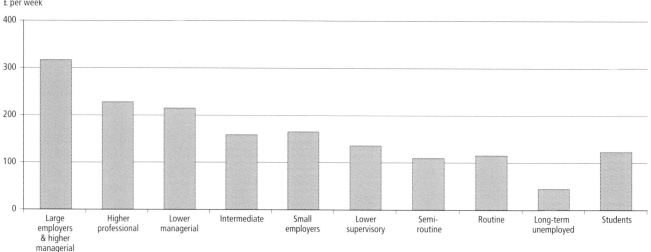

Households in all other regions spent less than the UK national average on mortgages. Households in the North East and Northern Ireland spent the least on their mortgages, £35.70 and £37.60, which was 31 and 28 per cent less than the UK average. Among the other regions, spending on mortgages ranged from £38.50 in Wales (26 per cent less than the UK average) to £47.30 in the West Midlands (9 per cent less than the UK average).

Expenditure by socio-economic classification

Table 2.6 and Figure 2.6 show average weekly housing expenditure data by the socio-economic classification of the household reference person (HRP). As Figure 2.6 shows, households containing HRPs in the 'large employers and higher managerial' occupational group spent £316.90 on average per week, which was almost three times higher than that spent by households containing a HRP in the 'routine' occupational group (£115.40).

Figure 2.7 shows housing expenditure on selected items by four different occupational groups. Overall, the variation by socio-economic classification was similar to that described above. This pattern was most marked for spending on mortgages and household alterations and improvements. For example, expenditure on household alterations and improvements fell from £83.40 per week among those classified as 'large employers and higher managerial' to £13.60 among those classified as 'routine'. This pattern was not found for expenditure on net rent: the group with the highest expenditure on net rent were students (£81.30 per week).

Figure **2.7**

Expenditure on selected items by socio-economic classification of household reference person, 2006

£ per week

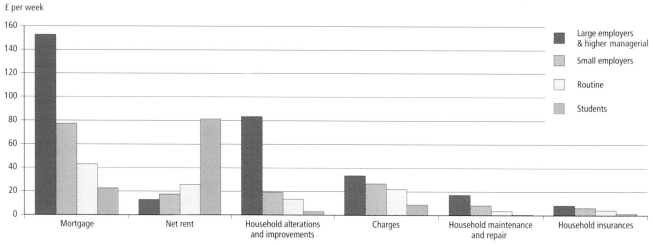

Expenditure by household composition

Table 2.7 shows expenditure on housing by household composition. One man, one woman non-retired households spent more on housing each week than their one adult counterparts. One man, one woman non-retired households spent £168.90 on average per week, compared with £105.10 in one adult non-retired households. A similar, but more pronounced, pattern was found among households with children. Households containing two adults and children spent over twice as much on housing as those containing one adult with children (£219.80 compared with £92.30). This pattern was not followed for retired households where one man, one woman retired households spent £66.40, whereas one adult retired households spent £74.40.

As Figure 2.8 shows, the difference between households comprising of two adults with children and one adult with children was most marked for mortgage expenditure: two adult households with children spent £111.10 on average per week on mortgages; this was almost three times that spent by one adult households with children, £39.90. On three other expenditure items (charges, household maintenance and repair, and household insurance), two adult households with children spent around twice as much as one adult households with children. The exceptions to this are net rent and household alterations and improvements; for net rent households with one adult and children spent £20.80, compared to £16.70 for households with two adults and children, whereas for household alterations and improvements, households with two adults and children spent over five times that spent by households with one adult and children (£38.90 compared to £7.00).

Analysis of rent and mortgage data by renters and mortgage holders alone

In order to explore further the housing costs for households which rent or are paying mortgages, an additional analysis was conducted. This analysis is the only occasion in the *Family Spending* publication where spending is averaged over only those households which spend money on the item concerned[2]. Therefore, figures for rent have been averaged across the 1,790 households that spent money on rent, and mortgage figures have been calculated based only on the 2,610 households that paid mortgages. The 2006 EFS sample comprised 6,650 households, of which 27 per cent paid rent, 39 per cent made mortgage payments and the remaining 34 per cent did not pay either rent or mortgage.

Tables 2.8 and 2.9 include data relating to expenditure on rent by households that spent money on rent and mortgages by households that paid mortgages alone. The effect of looking at expenditure based only on those who had such expenditure was an increase in the average amount spent. Therefore expenditure on net rent increased to £60.00 per week and the weekly expenditure on mortgages similarly rose to £131.50.

Table 2.10 shows the recalculated amounts spent on net rent and mortgages by gross income decile. Expenditure on mortgages generally increased across the deciles: households in the first decile spent £82.80 per week on mortgages, while those in the tenth (top) decile spent £218.70 per week. Expenditure on net rent increased steadily across the deciles from those in the lowest (first) decile who spent £22.60 per week on net rent to those in the tenth decile who spent £221.90.

Figure **2.8**

Expenditure on selected items among one adult and two adult households with children, 2006

£ per week

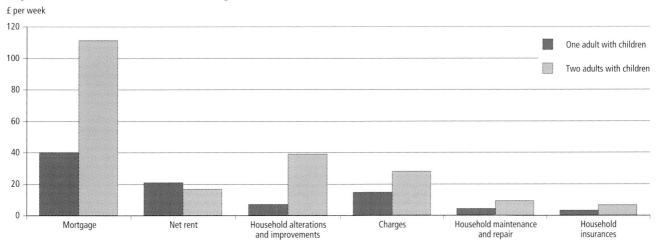

Figure 2.9

Expenditure on net rent[1] by UK Countries and Government Office Regions, 2006

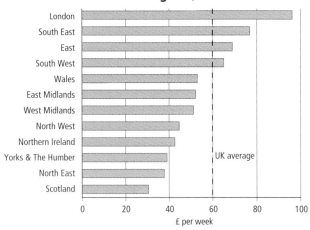

1 Averaged over those households spending on rent.

Figure 2.10

Expenditure on mortgages[1] by UK Countries and Government Office Regions, 2006

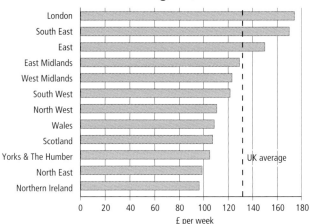

1 Averaged over those households spending on mortgages.

Table 2.11 and Figure 2.9 show expenditure on net rent among renters by UK Countries and Government Office Regions. The pattern among households that pay rent was very similar to the pattern for expenditure on rent among all households. The two most expensive regions for renters were London (£96.00) and the South East (£76.70). Households in Scotland paid the least, £30.30 a week. Among the other regions, rent was above the national UK average in the East and the South West but below the UK average in the remaining regions.

The analysis of expenditure on mortgages by those paying mortgages, revealed a similar pattern to that among all households (see Table 2.11, Figure 2.10). The UK national average in this analysis was £131.50 per week, a figure exceeded by three regions, the East (£149.90), the South East (£170.00) and London (£174.30). Northern Ireland had the lowest expenditure on mortgages at £96.10, followed closely by the North East at £98.50 per week. Among the other regions, mortgage expenditure remained less than the national average.

Notes

1   For further information on the balancing of income and expenditure figures, see 'Description and response rate of the survey', page 174.

2   All other findings shown in the *Family Spending* publication are shown as averages across all households irrespective of any expenditure on that item.

Table **2.2** Housing expenditure, 2004–05 to 2006

	2004–05			2005–06			2006		
	£ per week	% of total expend-iture	% of housing expend-iture	£ per week	% of total expend-iture	% of housing expend-iture	£ per week	% of total expend-iture	% of housing expend-iture
Weighted number of households (thousands)	24,430			24,800			24,790		
Total number of households in sample	6,800			6,790			6,650		
Total number of persons in sample	16,260			16,090			15,850		
Total number of adults in sample	12,260			12,170			12,000		
Weighted average number of persons per household	2.4			2.4			2.4		
Commodity or service	Average weekly household expenditure (£)								
Primary dwelling									
Rent	**24.70**	*4*	*19*	**27.50**	*4*	*20*	**27.80**	*4*	*19*
Gross rent	24.70	*4*	*19*	27.50	*4*	*20*	27.80	*4*	*19*
less housing benefit, rebates and allowances received	10.30	*2*	*8*	11.30	*2*	*8*	11.20	*2*	*8*
Net rent	14.50	*2*	*11*	16.30	*3*	*12*	16.70	*3*	*12*
Mortgage	**46.30**	*7*	*36*	**48.60**	*8*	*35*	**52.00**	*8*	*36*
Mortgage interest payments	28.90	*5*	*23*	30.20	*5*	*22*	32.60	*5*	*23*
Mortgage protection premiums	1.70	*0*	*1*	1.70	*0*	*1*	1.80	*0*	*1*
Capital repayment of mortgage	15.70	*3*	*12*	16.70	*3*	*12*	17.60	*3*	*12*
Outright purchase, including deposits	**0.50**	*0*	*0*	**8.00**	*1*	*6*	**[5.40]**	*1*	*4*
Secondary dwelling	**5.80**	*1*	*5*	**3.60**	*1*	*3*	**6.00**	*1*	*4*
Rent	[0.20]	*0*	*0*	[0.00]	*0*	*0*	[0.10]	*0*	*0*
Council tax, mortgage, insurance (secondary dwelling)	0.80	*0*	*1*	0.70	*0*	*0*	0.40	*0*	*0*
Purchase of second dwelling	4.80	*1*	*4*	2.90	*0*	*2*	5.50	*1*	*4*
Charges	**21.80**	*4*	*17*	**22.90**	*4*	*16*	**24.20**	*4*	*17*
Council tax, domestic rates	16.00	*3*	*13*	16.60	*3*	*12*	17.20	*3*	*12*
Water charges	5.00	*1*	*4*	5.30	*1*	*4*	5.70	*1*	*4*
Other regular housing payments including service charge for rent	0.80	*0*	*1*	0.90	*0*	*1*	1.20	*0*	*1*
Refuse collection, including skip hire	[0.10]	*0*	*0*	[0.10]	*0*	*0*	[0.10]	*0*	*0*
Moving house	**2.60**	*0*	*2*	**2.10**	*0*	*2*	**2.80**	*0*	*2*
Property transaction – purchase and sale	1.10	*0*	*1*	1.00	*0*	*1*	1.50	*0*	*1*
Property transaction – sale only	0.80	*0*	*1*	0.60	*0*	*0*	0.60	*0*	*0*
Property transaction – purchase only	0.50	*0*	*0*	0.50	*0*	*0*	0.60	*0*	*0*
Property transaction – other payments	0.10	*0*	*0*	0.10	*0*	*0*	0.20	*0*	*0*
Household maintenance and repair	**7.40**	*1*	*6*	**7.70**	*1*	*6*	**8.00**	*1*	*6*
Central heating repairs	1.10	*0*	*1*	1.10	*0*	*1*	1.20	*0*	*1*
House maintenance etc.	3.90	*1*	*3*	4.30	*1*	*3*	5.00	*1*	*3*
Paint, wallpaper, timber	1.30	*0*	*1*	1.20	*0*	*1*	1.00	*0*	*1*
Equipment hire, small materials	1.00	*0*	*1*	1.10	*0*	*1*	0.80	*0*	*1*
Household alterations and improvements	**23.70**	*4*	*19*	**25.40**	*4*	*18*	**23.10**	*4*	*16*
Central heating installation	1.10	*0*	*1*	0.90	*0*	*1*	1.00	*0*	*1*
DIY improvements: double glazing, kitchen units, sheds etc.	2.30	*0*	*2*	0.90	*0*	*1*	1.20	*0*	*1*
Home improvements – contracted out	17.70	*3*	*14*	21.80	*3*	*16*	19.70	*3*	*14*
Bathroom fittings	1.50	*0*	*1*	1.50	*0*	*1*	0.50	*0*	*0*
Purchase of materials for capital improvements	1.00	*0*	*1*	0.40	*0*	*0*	0.80	*0*	*1*
Household insurances	**5.00**	*1*	*4*	**4.90**	*1*	*4*	**5.10**	*1*	*4*
Structure	2.30	*0*	*2*	2.40	*0*	*2*	2.50	*0*	*2*
Contents	2.50	*0*	*2*	2.40	*0*	*2*	2.50	*0*	*2*
Household appliances	0.10	*0*	*0*	0.10	*0*	*0*	0.10	*0*	*0*
Housing expenditure	**127.40**	*21*	*100*	**139.60**	*22*	*100*	**143.30**	*22*	*100*
Total expenditure[1]	**619.70**			**641.30**			**658.00**		

1 This total includes all categories recorded in the EFS, including those outside the 'COICOP' total expenditure.

Table **2.3** Housing expenditure by gross income decile group, 2006

	Gross income decile group										
	1	2	3	4	5	6	7	8	9	10	All
Weighted number of households (thousands)	2,480	2,480	2,480	2,480	2,480	2,480	2,480	2,480	2,480	2,480	24,790
Total number of households in sample	680	680	700	690	690	680	660	630	640	590	6,650
Total number of persons in sample	930	1,200	1,350	1,500	1,650	1,800	1,790	1,880	1,930	1,840	15,850
Total number of adults in sample	760	920	1,110	1,130	1,250	1,320	1,340	1,380	1,400	1,380	12,000
Weighted average number of persons per household	1.4	1.7	1.9	2.1	2.3	2.6	2.7	2.9	3.0	3.0	2.4
Commodity or service						Average weekly household expenditure (£)					
Primary dwelling											
Rent	59.90	47.10	32.80	26.40	21.20	21.50	18.00	17.70	12.60	21.00	27.80
Gross rent	59.90	47.10	32.80	26.40	21.20	21.50	18.00	17.70	12.60	21.00	27.80
less housing benefit, rebates and allowances received	45.20	32.60	16.00	9.50	3.80	1.80	[1.70]	[0.60]	[0.10]	[0.40]	11.20
Net rent	14.70	14.50	16.80	16.90	17.30	19.80	16.40	17.10	12.40	20.60	16.70
Mortgage	**6.50**	**6.90**	**9.90**	**22.30**	**35.20**	**49.90**	**65.10**	**76.40**	**104.50**	**143.10**	**52.00**
Mortgage interest payments	4.80	4.40	6.80	14.50	22.80	32.30	41.10	47.60	66.00	85.50	32.60
Mortgage protection premiums	[0.10]	0.20	0.40	0.80	1.50	2.40	2.50	2.60	3.70	3.60	1.80
Capital repayment of mortgage	1.60	2.30	2.70	7.00	10.90	15.20	21.50	26.30	34.90	54.00	17.60
Outright purchase, including deposits	–	[22.30]	[29.20]	–	[0.10]	[2.10]	[0.10]	[0.20]	[0.10]	[0.10]	[5.40]
Secondary dwelling	[0.00]	[12.70]	[0.10]	[0.60]	[0.20]	[27.10]	[3.70]	[2.20]	[5.20]	8.20	6.00
Rent	–	–	–	–	–	–	–	[0.30]	–	[0.60]	[0.10]
Council tax, mortgage, insurance (secondary dwelling)	[0.00]	–	–	[0.20]	[0.00]	[0.20]	[0.30]	[0.70]	[0.90]	[1.50]	0.40
Purchase of second dwelling	–	[12.70]	[0.10]	[0.50]	[0.20]	[26.80]	[3.50]	[1.10]	[4.40]	[6.00]	5.50
Charges	**12.00**	**14.60**	**19.50**	**22.40**	**23.50**	**25.80**	**26.80**	**29.30**	**31.10**	**36.80**	**24.20**
Council tax, domestic rates	6.20	8.90	13.30	15.50	17.00	19.00	19.80	21.60	23.90	27.20	17.20
Water charges	4.70	4.80	5.30	5.40	5.40	5.70	5.90	6.20	6.20	7.00	5.70
Other regular housing payments including service charge for rent	1.10	0.90	0.90	1.30	1.00	1.00	0.90	1.40	0.90	2.40	1.20
Refuse collection, including skip hire	[0.00]	–	[0.10]	[0.20]	[0.00]	[0.10]	[0.20]	[0.10]	[0.20]	[0.30]	[0.10]
Moving house	[0.80]	[1.10]	[1.50]	2.40	2.30	3.00	3.30	3.00	4.90	5.90	2.80
Property transaction – purchase and sale	[0.50]	[0.70]	[1.10]	[0.90]	[1.30]	[1.80]	[1.20]	1.60	2.70	2.90	1.50
Property transaction – sale only	[0.20]	[0.20]	[0.30]	[0.90]	[0.40]	[0.60]	[0.30]	[0.60]	[0.90]	[1.80]	0.60
Property transaction – purchase only	[0.10]	[0.20]	[0.20]	[0.50]	0.50	[0.40]	1.50	0.70	0.90	0.80	0.60
Property transaction – other payments	[0.00]	[0.00]	[0.00]	[0.20]	[0.10]	[0.20]	[0.20]	[0.20]	[0.40]	0.50	0.20
Household maintenance and repair	**1.60**	**2.60**	**5.50**	**5.50**	**6.20**	**7.40**	**9.20**	**9.50**	**11.80**	**20.50**	**8.00**
Central heating repairs	0.30	0.50	1.30	1.10	1.00	1.30	1.40	1.40	1.50	2.20	1.20
House maintenance etc.	1.00	1.70	3.20	3.30	3.90	4.10	4.80	6.10	7.20	14.60	5.00
Paint, wallpaper, timber	0.30	0.30	0.60	0.70	0.70	1.10	1.40	1.20	1.60	2.10	1.00
Equipment hire, small materials	[0.00]	0.10	0.40	0.50	0.60	0.90	1.50	0.80	1.50	1.60	0.80
Household alterations and improvements	**3.30**	**5.30**	**10.50**	**16.30**	**14.20**	**18.90**	**21.80**	**35.00**	**33.60**	**72.30**	**23.10**
Central heating installation	[0.50]	[0.40]	[0.90]	[1.30]	[1.20]	[1.50]	[1.00]	[1.40]	[0.80]	[0.90]	1.00
DIY improvements: double glazing, kitchen units, sheds etc.	[0.10]	[0.60]	[0.40]	[0.60]	[0.40]	[0.80]	1.40	[0.60]	[3.60]	[3.80]	1.20
Home improvements – contracted out	2.60	4.10	8.90	12.90	12.30	15.50	18.30	29.80	26.10	66.10	19.70
Bathroom fittings	[0.00]	[0.10]	[0.20]	[1.30]	[0.10]	[0.50]	[0.50]	[0.70]	[0.20]	[1.20]	0.50
Purchase of materials for capital improvements	[0.10]	[0.10]	[0.10]	[0.20]	[0.30]	[0.60]	[0.60]	[2.40]	[3.00]	[0.30]	0.80
Household insurances	**1.90**	**2.80**	**3.60**	**4.00**	**4.90**	**5.40**	**6.10**	**6.10**	**7.50**	**8.90**	**5.10**
Structure	0.90	1.40	1.70	2.00	2.40	2.40	3.10	3.10	3.80	4.50	2.50
Contents	1.00	1.50	1.80	2.00	2.30	2.70	2.90	3.00	3.60	4.40	2.50
Household appliances	[0.00]	[0.00]	[0.10]	[0.00]	[0.20]	[0.30]	[0.10]	[0.10]	[0.10]	[0.10]	0.10
Housing expenditure	**40.90**	**82.90**	**96.70**	**90.50**	**104.00**	**159.30**	**152.40**	**178.70**	**211.20**	**316.40**	**143.30**
Total expenditure[1]	**165.80**	**250.60**	**340.20**	**402.00**	**478.50**	**612.90**	**707.10**	**861.50**	**1,089.70**	**1,671.30**	**658.00**

1 This total includes all categories recorded in the EFS, including those outside the 'COICOP' total expenditure.

Table 2.4 Housing expenditure by age of household reference person, 2006

	Under 30	30 to 49	50 to 64	65 to 74	75 or over	All
Weighted number of households (thousands)	2,450	9,610	6,430	3,190	3,100	24,790
Total number of households in sample	610	2,580	1,710	940	810	6,650
Total number of persons in sample	1,440	7,910	3,720	1,600	1,180	15,850
Total number of adults in sample	1,050	4,840	3,350	1,580	1,180	12,000
Weighted average number of persons per household	2.3	3.0	2.2	1.7	1.4	2.4
Commodity or service	Average weekly household expenditure (£)					
Primary dwelling						
Rent	69.00	29.20	19.20	16.10	20.90	27.80
Gross rent	69.00	29.20	19.20	16.10	20.90	27.80
less housing benefit, rebates and allowances received	17.00	9.80	10.00	10.60	13.80	11.20
Net rent	51.90	19.40	9.20	5.50	7.10	16.70
Mortgage	52.10	92.60	38.70	5.90	1.00	52.00
Mortgage interest payments	34.10	57.10	24.80	4.20	0.80	32.60
Mortgage protection premiums	2.10	3.20	1.20	[0.20]	[0.00]	1.80
Capital repayment of mortgage	16.00	32.30	12.80	1.50	[0.10]	17.60
Outright purchase, including deposits	[0.30]	[0.10]	[11.70]	–	[18.70]	[5.40]
Secondary dwelling	[0.40]	3.90	12.00	[10.20]	–	6.00
Rent	[0.00]	[0.10]	[0.20]	–	–	[0.10]
Council tax, mortgage, insurance (secondary dwelling)	[0.10]	[0.80]	[0.10]	[0.20]	–	0.40
Purchase of second dwelling	[0.30]	3.00	11.70	[10.00]	–	5.50
Charges	19.40	25.00	26.30	24.10	21.30	24.20
Council tax, domestic rates	12.90	18.20	19.00	17.40	14.00	17.20
Water charges	5.00	5.90	6.00	5.40	4.90	5.70
Other regular housing payments including service charge for rent	1.30	0.80	1.10	1.00	2.40	1.20
Refuse collection, including skip hire	[0.10]	[0.10]	[0.10]	[0.10]	[0.10]	[0.10]
Moving house	4.40	3.50	2.40	1.90	1.30	2.80
Property transaction – purchase and sale	1.30	1.90	1.10	[1.20]	[1.10]	1.50
Property transaction – sale only	[0.50]	0.70	0.90	[0.40]	[0.10]	0.60
Property transaction – purchase only	2.30	0.60	0.30	[0.10]	[0.10]	0.60
Property transaction – other payments	[0.20]	0.30	0.10	[0.20]	[0.00]	0.20
Household maintenance and repair	5.30	8.80	9.00	7.90	5.50	8.00
Central heating repairs	0.40	1.00	1.60	1.70	1.10	1.20
House maintenance etc.	3.80	5.40	5.50	4.50	4.00	5.00
Paint, wallpaper, timber	1.00	1.30	1.10	0.80	[0.10]	1.00
Equipment hire, small materials	0.20	1.10	0.80	0.90	0.20	0.80
Household alterations and improvements	8.40	29.00	28.80	18.70	9.50	23.10
Central heating installation	[0.40]	1.00	1.10	1.70	[0.60]	1.00
DIY improvements: double glazing, kitchen units, sheds etc.	[0.20]	0.80	1.90	[0.40]	[2.80]	1.20
Home improvements – contracted out	7.30	25.60	24.10	15.80	6.00	19.70
Bathroom fittings	[0.10]	0.70	0.60	[0.30]	[0.00]	0.50
Purchase of materials for capital improvements	[0.40]	0.90	[1.20]	[0.40]	–	0.80
Household insurances	2.90	5.60	5.80	5.10	4.00	5.10
Structure	1.30	2.80	2.90	2.50	2.00	2.50
Contents	1.60	2.80	2.80	2.50	2.00	2.50
Household appliances	[0.00]	0.10	0.10	[0.10]	[0.10]	0.10
Housing expenditure	**145.00**	**187.90**	**144.00**	**79.20**	**68.30**	**143.30**
Total expenditure[1]	**584.40**	**827.80**	**738.00**	**421.40**	**267.40**	**658.00**

1 This total includes all categories recorded in the EFS, including those outside the 'COICOP' total expenditure.

Table **2.5** Household expenditure by UK Countries and Government Office Region, 2006

	North East	North West	Yorkshire & The Humber	East Midlands	West Midlands	East	London
Weighted number of households (thousands)	1,100	2,810	2,110	1,720	2,180	2,260	2,950
Total number of households in sample	280	700	550	500	540	590	540
Total number of persons in sample	620	1,630	1,300	1,240	1,310	1,410	1,280
Total number of adults in sample	510	1,230	980	920	990	1,050	940
Weighted average number of persons per household	2.2	2.3	2.3	2.4	2.4	2.4	2.5
Commodity or service	Average weekly household expenditure (£)						
Primary dwelling							
Rent	21.70	23.70	19.70	21.70	25.30	24.40	60.20
Gross rent	21.70	23.70	19.70	21.70	25.30	24.40	60.20
less housing benefit, rebates and allowances received	10.50	11.60	9.50	8.40	10.10	8.30	22.50
Net rent	11.20	12.00	10.20	13.30	15.20	16.00	37.70
Mortgage	35.70	43.40	44.40	53.40	47.30	60.60	64.80
Mortgage interest payments	22.50	26.20	27.00	32.90	29.70	38.40	44.50
Mortgage protection premiums	1.20	1.70	1.60	2.00	1.70	2.30	1.80
Capital repayment of mortgage	11.90	15.50	15.70	18.50	15.90	20.00	18.50
Outright purchase, including deposits	[0.10]	[44.60]	–	[0.20]	–	[0.10]	[0.10]
Secondary dwelling	[30.00]	[0.40]	[1.20]	[6.20]	[3.40]	[2.40]	[2.30]
Rent	[0.40]	–	–	[0.60]	–	–	–
Council tax, mortgage, insurance (secondary dwelling)	[0.10]	[0.10]	[0.00]	[0.30]	[0.30]	[1.10]	[0.40]
Purchase of second dwelling	[29.50]	[0.30]	[1.20]	[5.30]	[3.10]	[1.30]	[1.90]
Charges	20.70	22.00	21.60	22.90	21.80	26.40	27.10
Council tax, domestic rates	14.90	15.40	15.20	16.80	15.40	18.90	17.70
Water charges	5.20	5.80	5.60	5.70	5.50	6.30	5.10
Other regular housing payments including service charge for rent	0.60	0.70	0.60	[0.30]	0.80	1.00	4.30
Refuse collection, including skip hire	–	[0.10]	[0.20]	[0.00]	[0.00]	0.30	–
Moving house	0.80	1.30	1.40	1.60	1.60	5.70	2.60
Property transaction – purchase and sale	[0.30]	[0.50]	[0.50]	[0.60]	[0.60]	3.60	[0.60]
Property transaction – sale only	–	[0.20]	[0.60]	[0.20]	[0.30]	[1.30]	[1.00
Property transaction – purchase only	[0.40]	0.40	[0.20]	[0.40]	[0.50]	0.60	[0.80]
Property transaction – other payments	[0.10]	[0.10]	[0.10]	[0.10]	[0.10]	[0.30]	[0.30]
Household maintenance and repair	5.70	7.30	7.60	5.60	4.80	12.10	8.50
Central heating repairs	1.10	1.00	1.20	1.20	1.00	1.50	1.30
House maintenance etc.	3.00	5.00	4.10	3.10	2.50	8.60	6.10
Paint, wallpaper, timber	1.00	0.90	1.20	0.90	0.90	1.00	0.60
Equipment hire, small materials	0.50	0.50	1.10	0.40	0.40	1.10	0.50
Household alterations and improvements	18.20	20.60	32.60	12.10	16.40	21.30	22.70
Central heating installation	[1.70]	[0.80]	[1.20]	[0.40]	[1.40]	[1.10]	[1.60]
DIY improvements: double glazing, kitchen units, sheds etc.	[1.10]	[0.50]	[0.60]	[0.60]	[0.30]	[1.50]	[0.10]
Home improvements – contracted out	15.40	18.40	27.50	9.90	14.30	18.30	20.40
Bathroom fittings	[0.00]	[0.60]	[0.20]	[0.10]	[0.20]	[0.40]	[0.30]
Purchase of materials for capital improvements	[0.00]	[0.30]	[3.00]	[1.00]	[0.20]	[0.10]	[0.30]
Household insurances	4.40	4.90	5.30	4.80	4.60	5.20	5.50
Structure	2.20	2.50	2.60	2.40	2.20	2.60	2.70
Contents	2.10	2.30	2.50	2.40	2.30	2.50	2.60
Household appliances	[0.20]	[0.10]	[0.10]	[0.00]	[0.20]	[0.10]	[0.20]
Housing expenditure	**126.80**	**156.60**	**124.20**	**120.10**	**115.10**	**150.00**	**171.10**
Total expenditure[1]	**527.30**	**622.80**	**595.70**	**614.10**	**588.90**	**679.90**	**786.10**

1 This total includes all categories recorded in the EFS, including those outside the 'COICOP' total expenditure.

Table 2.5 Household expenditure by UK Countries and Government Office Region, 2006 (cont.)

	South East	South West	England	Wales	Scotland	Northen Ireland	United Kingdom
Weighted number of households (thousands)	3,490	2,220	20,830	1,230	2,090	640	24,790
Total number of households in sample	890	580	5,170	310	580	590	6,650
Total number of persons in sample	2,120	1,300	12,220	720	1,370	1,540	15,850
Total number of adults in sample	1,610	1,040	9,280	560	1,040	1,130	12,000
Weighted average number of persons per household	2.3	2.2	2.4	2.4	2.4	2.7	2.4
Commodity or service	Average weekly household expenditure (£)						
Primary dwelling							
Rent	**28.10**	**23.20**	**29.10**	**24.10**	**19.50**	**20.00**	**27.80**
Gross rent	28.10	23.20	29.10	24.10	19.50	20.00	27.80
less housing benefit, rebates and allowances received	9.30	8.00	11.30	10.10	10.80	8.80	11.20
Net rent	18.80	15.20	17.80	14.00	8.70	11.30	16.70
Mortgage	**69.20**	**46.50**	**53.90**	**38.50**	**45.30**	**37.60**	**52.00**
Mortgage interest payments	41.90	29.80	34.00	24.30	26.40	23.60	32.60
Mortgage protection premiums	1.90	1.80	1.80	1.40	1.60	2.00	1.80
Capital repayment of mortgage	25.40	14.80	18.10	12.80	17.30	12.10	17.60
Outright purchase, including deposits	**[0.20]**	**[1.20]**	**[6.20]**	**[0.10]**	**[2.30]**	**[0.10]**	**[5.40]**
Secondary dwelling	**[2.60]**	**[2.10]**	**3.90**	**[2.20]**	**[30.70]**	**[1.90]**	**6.00**
Rent	[0.20]	[0.00]	[0.10]	–	–	–	[0.10]
Council tax, mortgage, insurance (secondary dwelling)	[0.30]	[1.10]	0.40	–	[0.10]	[0.20]	0.40
Purchase of second dwelling	[2.10]	[1.00]	3.30	[2.20]	[30.60]	[1.60]	5.50
Charges	**28.50**	**26.00**	**24.70**	**21.30**	**25.50**	**10.30**	**24.20**
Council tax, domestic rates	20.80	18.80	17.40	14.50	19.10	10.10	17.20
Water charges	5.80	6.60	5.80	6.40	5.80	–	5.70
Other regular housing payments including service charge for rent	1.50	0.50	1.30	[0.40]	0.70	0.20	1.20
Refuse collection, including skip hire	[0.30]	[0.10]	[0.10]	–	–	[0.00]	[0.10]
Moving house	**6.00**	**2.60**	**2.90**	**2.40**	**2.50**	**1.10**	**2.80**
Property transaction – purchase and sale	3.50	[1.70]	1.50	[0.60]	1.70	[0.70]	1.50
Property transaction – sale only	[1.40]	[0.30]	0.70	[0.60]	[0.20]	[0.10]	0.60
Property transaction – purchase only	0.70	[0.50]	0.50	[1.10]	[0.60]	[0.20]	0.60
Property transaction – other payments	[0.30]	[0.20]	0.20	[0.10]	[0.20]	[0.00]	0.20
Household maintenance and repair	**9.80**	**7.30**	**7.90**	**8.50**	**7.00**	**11.40**	**8.00**
Central heating repairs	1.40	1.50	1.20	0.80	1.20	0.60	1.20
House maintenance etc.	6.30	3.80	5.00	4.40	3.90	8.70	5.00
Paint, wallpaper, timber	1.10	0.90	0.90	1.60	1.20	1.50	1.00
Equipment hire, small materials	1.10	1.00	0.70	1.60	0.70	0.50	0.80
Household alterations and improvements	**[32.30]**	**[25.60]**	**23.40**	**[22.00]**	**[24.20]**	**[12.80]**	**23.10**
Central heating installation	[0.70]	[0.60]	1.00	[1.10]	[0.70]	[1.10]	1.00
DIY improvements: double glazing, kitchen units, sheds etc.	[0.70]	[7.30]	1.30	[0.70]	[0.70]	[0.50]	1.20
Home improvements – contracted out	27.80	17.20	19.70	20.10	21.70	10.10	19.70
Bathroom fittings	[1.50]	[0.20]	0.50	[0.00]	[0.70]	[0.10]	0.50
Purchase of materials for capital improvements	[1.70]	[0.20]	0.80	[0.00]	[0.50]	[1.00]	0.80
Household insurances	**5.90**	**4.90**	**5.20**	**4.90**	**5.30**	**4.30**	**5.10**
Structure	2.90	2.50	2.60	2.50	2.30	2.20	2.50
Contents	3.00	2.40	2.50	2.40	2.90	2.20	2.50
Household appliances	[0.00]	[0.00]	0.10	[0.00]	[0.10]	[0.10]	0.10
Housing expenditure	**173.30**	**131.30**	**145.80**	**113.80**	**151.50**	**90.80**	**143.30**
Total expenditure[1]	**766.80**	**638.90**	**665.90**	**557.70**	**659.40**	**586.40**	**658.00**

1 This total includes all categories recorded in the EFS, including those outside the 'COICOP' total expenditure.

Table 2.6 Housing expenditure by socio-economic classification of household reference person, 2006

	Large employers & higher managerial	Higher professional	Lower managerial & professional	Intermediate	Small employers	Lower supervisory
Weighted number of households (thousands)	1,200	1,820	4,520	1,460	1,560	1,580
Total number of households in sample	310	470	1,170	380	430	420
Total number of persons in sample	900	1,230	3,100	910	1,240	1,140
Total number of adults in sample	610	900	2,270	670	870	810
Weighted average number of persons per household	2.8	2.5	2.6	2.5	2.8	2.7
Commodity or service	Average weekly household expenditure (£)					
Primary dwelling						
Rent	13.10	20.40	16.40	25.30	20.50	23.20
Gross rent	13.10	20.40	16.40	25.30	20.50	23.20
less housing benefit, rebates and allowances received	[0.10]	[0.10]	0.70	2.50	2.80	2.20
Net rent	13.00	20.30	15.60	22.80	17.70	20.90
Mortgage	152.80	106.50	94.30	64.00	77.50	56.90
Mortgage interest payments	90.00	67.70	58.20	41.80	49.10	35.40
Mortgage protection premiums	3.80	2.60	3.30	2.20	3.00	2.40
Capital repayment of mortgage	59.00	36.20	32.80	19.90	25.40	19.10
Outright purchase, including deposits	[0.10]	[0.10]	[0.10]	[3.30]	[0.10]	[0.10]
Secondary dwelling	[3.40]	5.30	[18.70]	[2.30]	[7.00]	[0.50]
Rent	[0.60]	[0.20]	[0.00]	[0.30]	–	[0.40]
Council tax, mortgage, insurance (secondary dwelling)	[1.90]	[1.60]	[0.50]	[0.80]	[0.40]	[0.10]
Purchase of second dwelling	[0.80]	[3.60]	18.20	[1.20]	[6.60]	–
Charges	33.50	32.30	29.20	25.20	26.80	24.10
Council tax, domestic rates	25.10	23.30	21.50	18.50	20.50	17.90
Water charges	6.60	6.20	6.00	5.70	5.70	5.90
Other regular housing payments including service charge for rent	1.50	2.50	1.40	1.10	0.60	0.30
Refuse collection, including skip hire	[0.30]	[0.30]	[0.20]	–	–	–
Moving house	5.00	5.40	4.40	4.80	2.40	2.50
Property transaction – purchase and sale	[2.70]	[1.80]	2.30	[3.40]	[0.80]	[1.20]
Property transaction – sale only	[1.10]	[1.50]	0.90	[0.40]	[0.70]	[0.50]
Property transaction – purchase only	[0.70]	1.80	1.00	[0.80]	[0.70]	[0.60]
Property transaction – other payments	[0.60]	[0.30]	0.30	[0.20]	[0.20]	[0.20]
Household maintenance and repair	17.20	10.40	12.90	7.50	8.30	5.90
Central heating repairs	2.10	1.30	1.70	0.80	0.80	0.90
House maintenance etc.	12.20	5.90	8.30	5.60	5.00	2.70
Paint, wallpaper, timber	2.30	1.30	1.40	0.80	1.30	1.50
Equipment hire, small materials	0.60	1.90	1.50	0.30	1.30	0.80
Household alterations and improvements	83.40	40.00	33.10	23.70	19.40	19.90
Central heating installation	[1.00]	[1.40]	0.80	[1.80]	[1.70]	[0.40]
DIY improvements: double glazing, kitchen units, sheds etc.	[0.30]	[4.10]	0.90	[0.70]	[0.80]	[5.30]
Home improvements – contracted out	80.80	30.00	29.70	20.90	12.80	13.10
Bathroom fittings	[1.40]	[1.60]	1.00	[0.20]	[0.10]	[0.10]
Purchase of materials for capital improvements	[0.00]	[2.80]	[0.70]	[0.00]	[4.00]	[1.00]
Household insurances	8.30	7.50	6.60	5.40	6.20	5.30
Structure	4.10	3.70	3.30	2.60	3.10	2.60
Contents	4.20	3.50	3.20	2.80	3.00	2.70
Household appliances	[0.00]	[0.30]	0.10	[0.00]	[0.10]	[0.10]
Housing expenditure	**316.90**	**227.80**	**214.80**	**159.00**	**165.50**	**136.10**
Total expenditure[1]	**1,438.30**	**1,122.80**	**981.20**	**690.10**	**698.80**	**643.20**

1 This total includes all categories recorded in the EFS, including those outside the 'COICOP' total expenditure.

Table **2.6** Housing expenditure by socio-economic classification of household reference person, 2006 (cont.)

	Semi-routine	Routine	Long-term unemployed	Students	Occupation not stated & not classifiable	All groups
Weighted number of households (thousands)	1,810	1,570	480	310	8,460	24,790
Total number of households in sample	490	430	130	70	2,360	6,650
Total number of persons in sample	1,290	1,190	380	180	4,300	15,850
Total number of adults in sample	900	840	210	150	3,770	12,000
Weighted average number of persons per household	2.6	2.8	2.8	2.7	1.8	2.4
Commodity or service			Average weekly household expenditure (£)			
Primary dwelling						
Rent	36.20	31.90	78.10	92.80	32.50	27.80
Gross rent	36.20	31.90	78.10	92.80	32.50	27.80
less housing benefit, rebates and allowances received	9.70	6.00	59.30	[11.50]	23.90	11.20
Net rent	26.50	25.90	18.80	81.30	8.60	16.70
Mortgage	37.30	43.10	6.80	22.90	4.10	52.00
Mortgage interest payments	24.10	28.00	[4.40]	[16.30]	2.90	32.60
Mortgage protection premiums	1.50	2.40	[0.20]	[1.30]	0.10	1.80
Capital repayment of mortgage	11.70	12.70	[2.20]	[5.20]	1.10	17.60
Outright purchase, including deposits	[0.20]	–	–	[0.80]	[15.10]	[5.40]
Secondary dwelling	[0.40]	[0.80]	–	[3.30]	[3.80]	6.00
Rent	–	–	–	–	–	[0.10]
Council tax, mortgage, insurance (secondary dwelling)	–	–	–	–	[0.00]	0.40
Purchase of second dwelling	[0.40]	[0.80]	–	[3.30]	[3.80]	5.50
Charges	22.60	22.30	12.20	8.90	19.70	24.20
Council tax, domestic rates	16.20	16.20	6.00	3.50	13.20	17.20
Water charges	5.70	5.60	5.10	4.70	5.20	5.70
Other regular housing payments including service charge for rent	0.70	0.50	[0.80]	[0.80]	1.30	1.20
Refuse collection, including skip hire	[0.00]	–	[0.30]	–	[0.10]	[0.10]
Moving house	1.90	1.80	[0.50]	[0.60]	1.50	2.80
Property transaction – purchase and sale	[1.10]	[0.80]	–	–	0.90	1.50
Property transaction – sale only	[0.50]	[0.40]	[0.50]	–	[0.30]	0.60
Property transaction – purchase only	[0.30]	[0.40]	–	[0.50]	[0.10]	0.60
Property transaction – other payments	[0.10]	[0.20]	–	[0.10]	[0.10]	0.20
Household maintenance and repair	3.70	3.70	3.50	[0.40]	6.20	8.00
Central heating repairs	0.70	0.70	[1.50]	[0.10]	1.20	1.20
House maintenance etc.	1.60	1.80	[1.10]	[0.30]	4.00	5.00
Paint, wallpaper, timber	1.00	0.80	[0.40]	–	0.60	1.00
Equipment hire, small materials	0.40	0.40	[0.50]	–	0.40	0.80
Household alterations and improvements	12.90	13.60	[1.30]	[3.30]	12.70	23.10
Central heating installation	[0.70]	[0.60]	–	–	1.10	1.00
DIY improvements: double glazing, kitchen units, sheds etc.	[0.80]	[0.80]	[0.10]	[0.10]	0.60	1.20
Home improvements – contracted out	11.30	11.50	[1.10]	[3.20]	10.70	19.70
Bathroom fittings	[0.10]	[0.10]	[0.00]	–	0.20	0.50
Purchase of materials for capital improvements	[0.10]	[0.60]	[0.00]	–	[0.20]	0.80
Household insurances	4.00	4.30	1.80	1.40	3.90	5.10
Structure	1.90	2.00	0.90	[0.50]	1.90	2.50
Contents	2.20	1.90	0.90	0.90	1.90	2.50
Household appliances	[0.00]	[0.30]	–	–	0.10	0.10
Housing expenditure	**109.50**	**115.40**	**44.80**	**122.90**	**75.60**	**143.30**
Total expenditure[1]	**523.20**	**547.20**	**279.90**	**471.00**	**341.90**	**658.00**

1 This total includes all categories recorded in the EFS, including those outside the 'COICOP' total expenditure.

Table 2.7 Housing expenditure by household composition, 2006

	Retired households		Non-retired		Retired and non-retired households			
	One person	One man and one woman	One person	One man and one woman	One adult with children	Two adults with children	Three or more adults without children	with children
Weighted number of households (thousands)	3,180	2,580	3,760	5,050	1,460	4,810	2,380	990
Total number of households in sample	850	760	960	1,320	460	1,390	490	260
Total number of persons in sample	850	1,530	960	2,640	1,240	5,430	1,620	1,280
Total number of adults in sample	850	1,530	960	2,640	460	2,790	1,620	870
Weighted average number of persons per household	1.0	2.0	1.0	2.0	2.7	3.9	3.3	4.9
Commodity or service	Average weekly household expenditure (£)							
Primary dwelling								
Rent	27.30	11.50	33.30	19.20	66.80	23.70	35.60	29.00
Gross rent	27.30	11.50	33.30	19.20	66.80	23.70	35.60	29.00
less housing benefit, rebates & allowances received	20.40	5.70	14.30	2.80	45.90	7.00	3.50	14.60
Net rent	7.00	5.80	19.00	16.40	20.80	16.70	32.10	14.40
Mortgage	1.40	2.70	44.70	65.30	39.90	111.10	39.00	74.00
Mortgage interest payments	1.00	1.90	29.70	41.30	25.30	67.20	23.70	49.10
Mortgage protection premiums	[0.00]	[0.10]	1.30	2.30	1.20	3.80	1.40	3.30
Capital repayment of mortgage	[0.40]	0.70	13.70	21.70	13.30	40.10	13.90	21.70
Outright purchase, including deposits	[17.40]	[1.00]	[1.30]	[0.20]	–	[0.10]	[29.40]	[0.20]
Secondary dwelling	[9.80]	[0.20]	[1.00]	3.90	[0.20]	5.40	[2.20]	[62.60]
Rent	–	–	–	[0.20]	–	[0.10]	[0.30]	–
Council tax, mortgage, insurance (secondary dwelling)	[0.00]	[0.00]	[0.10]	0.80	–	[0.90]	–	–
Purchase of second dwelling	[9.80]	[0.20]	[0.80]	[2.90]	[0.20]	4.30	[1.80]	[62.60]
Charges	17.60	26.90	19.30	28.40	14.60	27.90	26.60	26.90
Council tax, domestic rates	10.90	19.70	12.20	21.20	8.70	20.90	19.80	19.80
Water charges	4.50	5.80	4.60	5.90	5.70	6.50	6.30	6.60
Other regular housing payments including service charge for rent	2.10	1.20	2.50	1.20	0.20	0.40	0.50	[0.40]
Refuse collection, including skip hire	[0.00]	[0.20]	–	[0.20]	–	[0.20]	–	[0.10]
Moving house	2.30	[0.90]	2.50	4.30	2.40	4.00	1.10	[2.50]
Property transaction – purchase and sale	[1.50]	[0.70]	0.60	2.20	[0.30]	2.40	[0.70]	[2.00]
Property transaction – sale only	[0.40]	[0.10]	[0.60]	0.90	[1.50]	0.80	[0.30]	–
Property transaction – purchase only	[0.20]	[0.10]	1.20	0.90	[0.50]	0.60	[0.10]	[0.50]
Property transaction – other payments	[0.10]	[0.10]	[0.20]	0.20	[0.10]	0.30	[0.10]	–
Household maintenance and repair	4.50	8.10	4.60	11.60	4.20	9.20	7.00	17.20
Central heating repairs	1.00	2.10	0.70	1.70	0.50	1.00	1.40	0.90
House maintenance etc.	3.30	4.70	3.00	7.10	1.90	5.50	3.80	13.80
Paint, wallpaper, timber	0.20	0.50	0.60	1.60	0.50	1.40	1.20	1.60
Equipment hire, small materials	[0.10]	0.80	0.20	1.20	[1.30]	1.20	0.60	1.00
Household alterations and improvements	10.80	15.80	8.90	32.70	7.00	38.90	27.70	25.20
Central heating installation	[1.20]	[1.10]	[0.80]	1.30	[0.10]	1.00	[0.80]	[0.80]
DIY improvements: double glazing, kitchen units, sheds etc.	[0.60]	[1.10]	[0.40]	2.10	[0.70]	0.90	[3.40]	[0.30]
Home improvements – contracted out	8.80	12.80	7.00	27.30	6.20	34.20	23.00	24.00
Bathroom fittings	[0.10]	[0.30]	[0.50]	0.60	[0.10]	1.00	[0.20]	[0.00]
Purchase of materials for capital improvements	[0.10]	[0.40]	[0.20]	1.40	–	[1.90]	[0.20]	[0.10]
Household insurances	3.60	5.00	3.80	6.10	3.10	6.50	5.60	6.40
Structure	1.70	2.50	1.90	3.00	1.50	3.10	2.80	3.20
Contents	1.90	2.40	1.90	3.00	1.60	3.20	2.70	3.10
Household appliances	[0.00]	[0.10]	[0.00]	[0.20]	[0.00]	0.10	[0.10]	[0.10]
Housing expenditure	74.40	66.40	105.10	168.90	92.30	219.80	170.70	229.40
Total expenditure[1]	236.30	402.50	440.80	836.00	385.30	947.40	918.20	1,004.10

1 This total includes all categories recorded in the EFS, including those outside the 'COICOP' total expenditure.

Table **2.8** Expenditure on rent[1] by renters, 2004–05 to 2006

	2004–05		2005–06		2006	
	£[2]	% of total expenditure	£[2]	% of total expenditure	£[2]	% of total expenditure
Weighted number of households (thousands)	6,990		7,160		6,890	
Total number of households in sample	1,930		1,930		1,790	
Total number of persons in sample	4,300		4,260		4,040	
Total number of adults in sample	3,030		3,050		2,870	
Weighted average number of persons per household	2.2		2.2		2.3	
Total expenditure for renters	367.40		359.60		374.30	
Rent	86.30	23.5	95.40	26.5	100.10	26.8
Gross rent	86.30	23.5	95.40	26.5	100.10	26.8
less housing benefit, rebates and allowances received	35.90	9.8	39.00	10.8	40.20	10.7
Net rent	50.50	13.7	56.40	15.7	60.00	16.0

1 Primary dwelling.
2 Average weekly household expenditure (£).

Table **2.9** Expenditure on mortgages[1] by mortgage holders, 2004–05 to 2006

	2004–05		2005–06		2006	
	£[2]	% of total expenditure	£[2]	% of total expenditure	£[2]	% of total expenditure
Weighted number of households (thousands)	9,890		9,460		9,760	
Total number of households in sample	2,730		2,560		2,610	
Total number of persons in sample	7,870		7,320		7,430	
Total number of adults in sample	5,470		5,040		5,090	
Weighted average number of persons per household	2.9		2.8		2.8	
Total expenditure for mortgage payers	907.30		943.80		938.70	
Mortgage	114.00	12.6	127.30	13.5	131.50	14.0
Mortgage interest payments	71.10	7.8	79.10	8.4	82.40	8.8
Mortgage protection premiums	4.20	0.5	4.60	0.5	4.50	0.5
Capital repayment of mortgage	38.70	4.3	43.60	4.6	44.70	4.8

1   Primary dwelling.
2   Average weekly household expenditure (£).

Table **2.10** Expenditure on rent and mortgages[1] by renters and mortgage holders by gross income decile group, 2006

	Gross income decile group										
	1	2	3	4	5	6	7	8	9	10	All
Weighted number of households (thousands)	1,610	1,240	890	770	580	560	420	360	230	230	6,890
Total number of households in sample	440	340	240	220	150	140	100	80	50	40	1,790
Total number of persons in sample	620	680	540	590	410	410	280	250	150	120	4,040
Total number of adults in sample	480	460	380	360	290	280	210	180	130	110	2,870
Weighted average number of persons per household	1.4	2.0	2.2	2.6	2.6	2.9	2.9	3.0	2.9	3.2	2.3
Commodity or service	Average weekly household expenditure (£)										
Rent by renters	92.20	94.00	92.00	84.70	90.20	95.90	106.50	121.40	138.10	226.40	100.10
Gross rent	92.20	94.00	92.00	84.70	90.20	95.90	106.50	121.40	138.10	226.40	100.10
less housing benefit, rebates and allowances received	69.50	65.00	44.80	30.50	16.30	7.90	[9.80]	[4.10]	[1.50]	[4.40]	40.20
Net rent	22.60	28.90	47.20	54.20	73.90	88.00	96.60	117.30	136.60	221.90	60.00
Weighted number of households (thousands)	200	210	330	640	920	1,220	1,400	1,490	1,730	1,620	9,760
Total number of households in sample	50	60	100	170	260	340	390	390	450	400	2,610
Total number of persons in sample	90	130	210	370	680	950	1,110	1,210	1,400	1,300	7,430
Total number of adults in sample	70	80	150	250	440	630	760	830	960	910	5,090
Weighted average number of persons per household	1.6	2.1	2.1	2.1	2.6	2.7	2.8	3.0	3.1	3.1	2.8
Commodity or service	Average weekly household expenditure (£)										
Mortgage by mortgage holders	82.80	82.30	74.10	85.60	94.00	100.10	114.10	126.70	149.30	218.70	131.50
Mortgage interest payments	61.00	52.40	50.30	55.50	60.80	64.80	72.00	78.90	94.20	130.80	82.40
Mortgage protection premiums	[1.20]	2.70	3.10	3.10	4.00	4.80	4.40	4.30	5.20	5.40	4.50
Capital repayment of mortgage	20.60	27.20	20.70	27.10	29.30	30.50	37.70	43.60	49.90	82.50	44.70

1 Primary dwelling.

Table 2.11 **Expenditure on rent and mortgages[1] by renters and mortgage holders by UK Countries and Government Office Region, 2006**

	North East	North West	Yorkshire & The Humber	East Midlands	West Midlands	East	London
Weighted number of households (thousands)	330	760	550	440	650	530	1,150
Total number of households in sample	90	180	140	130	160	130	210
Total number of persons in sample	170	440	300	300	360	310	490
Total number of adults in sample	130	300	220	210	260	210	340
Weighted average number of persons per household	1.9	2.3	2.1	2.3	2.3	2.3	2.5
Commodity or service	Average weekly household expenditure (£)						
Rent by renters	72.60	87.40	75.20	85.00	85.20	104.60	153.40
Gross rent	72.60	87.40	75.20	85.00	85.20	104.60	153.40
less housing benefit, rebates and allowances received	35.00	42.90	36.30	33.10	34.10	35.80	57.40
Net rent	37.60	44.40	38.90	52.00	51.10	68.80	96.00
Weighted number of households (thousands)	400	1,100	890	710	840	910	1,090
Total number of households in sample	100	270	230	210	210	230	200
Total number of persons in sample	250	750	640	610	600	710	530
Total number of adults in sample	190	520	440	410	410	470	370
Weighted average number of persons per household	2.6	2.7	2.7	2.9	2.8	3.0	2.8
Commodity or service	Average weekly household expenditure (£)						
Mortgage by mortgage holders	98.50	110.60	104.80	129.20	123.10	149.90	174.30
Mortgage interest payments	62.20	66.80	63.90	79.60	77.30	94.80	119.70
Mortgage protection premiums	3.40	4.30	3.80	4.90	4.40	5.70	4.90
Capital repayment of mortgage	32.90	39.50	37.10	44.70	41.40	49.40	49.80

	South East	South West	England	Wales	Scotland	Northern Ireland	United Kingdom
Weighted number of households (thousands)	860	520	5,790	330	600	170	6,890
Total number of households in sample	210	130	1,380	80	170	160	1,790
Total number of persons in sample	490	290	3,150	170	360	370	4,040
Total number of adults in sample	350	210	2,230	120	260	260	2,870
Weighted average number of persons per household	2.3	2.2	2.3	2.0	2.1	2.4	2.3
Commodity or service	Average weekly household expenditure (£)						
Rent by renters	114.40	98.80	104.70	90.90	67.90	75.70	100.10
Gross rent	114.40	98.80	104.70	90.90	67.90	75.70	100.10
less housing benefit, rebates and allowances received	37.70	33.90	40.80	38.20	37.60	33.20	40.20
Net rent	76.70	64.80	63.90	52.70	30.30	42.50	60.00
Weighted number of households (thousands)	1,410	850	8,190	430	880	250	9,760
Total number of households in sample	370	220	2,030	110	240	220	2,610
Total number of persons in sample	1,030	590	5,720	320	670	710	7,430
Total number of adults in sample	710	430	3,940	220	470	470	5,090
Weighted average number of persons per household	2.7	2.6	2.8	2.9	2.8	3.2	2.8
Commodity or service	Average weekly household expenditure (£)						
Mortgage by mortgage holders	170.00	121.50	136.40	108.50	107.10	96.10	131.50
Mortgage interest payments	102.80	78.00	85.90	68.50	62.40	60.20	82.40
Mortgage protection premiums	4.60	4.60	4.60	4.00	3.70	5.00	4.50
Capital repayment of mortgage	62.70	38.80	46.00	36.00	41.00	30.90	44.70

1 Primary dwelling.

Equivalised income

Chapter 3

Background

This chapter presents results using equivalised income. It describes the methodology used and its impact on EFS data. Equivalisation was incorporated into the 2004 edition of *Family Spending* in response to requests from users of the data. Equivalisation is a standard methodology that adjusts the total annual income of a household to account for differing demands on resources by considering the household size and composition. This is the only chapter of the current edition of *Family Spending* that presents equivalised income data; all other tables and figures in the publication use non-equivalised income data. This chapter presents a selection of tables and charts using equivalised income data; other tables included within Family Spending are available on an equivalised income basis on request from ONS (see page xviii Introduction).

Equivalisation Methodology

An adjustment often made when seeking to compare household incomes, particularly as a measure of economic well-being or standard of living, is to equivalise them by adjusting for household size and composition. The McClements (1977) and the Modified OECD scales are typically used for such equivalisation.

The process reflects the common sense notion that a household of five will need a higher income than a single person living alone to enjoy a comparable standard of living. It takes into account both the greater income needs of larger households and the economies of scale achieved when people live together because household resources, especially housing, can be shared. By adjusting income in this way it is possible to make sensible income comparisons between households of different sizes and compositions.

There are several equivalisation scales, the most widely used being the McClements and the Modified OECD. Following consultation with a group of the main EFS users, it was decided to use the McClements (Before Housing Costs) Scale for this report as this is currently the most commonly used by ONS. Tables using the Modified OECD scale are also available on request.

The process of equivalisation utilises a scale which weights each household member and compares the total income of that household against that of a childless cohabiting/married couple. The scale takes childless couple households as standard (that is, they are weighted by one) and scales up the income of households with fewer people and scales down the income of households with more people. The weight applied to each additional adult has a decreasing value, childrens' weights are also applied on a sliding scale according to age. The logic

behind this is that the additional cost of adding another adult to the household decreases and that children have lower costs than adults dependent upon their age.

McClements Equivalence Scale (Before Housing Costs)	
Position of household member	**Equivalence value**
Cohabiting head of household	0.61
Partner/Spouse	0.39
1st additional adult	0.42
Subsequent adults	0.36
Single head of household	0.61
1st additional adult	0.46
2nd additional adult	0.42
Subsequent adults	0.36
Child aged: 16–18	0.36
13–15	0.27
11–12	0.25
8–10	0.23
5–7	0.21
2–4	0.18
Under 2	0.09

Equivalised income is calculated by firstly assigning an equivalence value from the McClements Equivalence Scale to each household member. These individual values are then summed to give a total equivalence number for the household. The household disposable income is then divided by this total equivalence number to produce the equivalised disposable income.

Equivalisation reduces relatively the incomes of households with three or more persons (since their incomes are divided by values greater than one) and increases the incomes of single person households (since their incomes are divided by values less than one).

For example, if a household consisting of a married couple and two children (aged 12 and 16) has an income of £30,000, their equivalised household size is 0.61 + 0.39 + 0.36 + 0.25 = 1.61. This implies they need 61 per cent more income than a couple with no children to have the same standard of living. Their equivalised income would therefore be £30,000/1.61 = £18,634.

A household consisting of one-person with an income of £30,000 has an equivalised household size of 0.61 and an equivalised income of £30,000/0.61=£49,180. Single person households generally need less money than couples, hence when their income is equivalised it increases in relation to a couple with the same income.

Results

Equivalised household incomes were calculated for each EFS household in 2006 using the McClements Equivalence Scale. Household equivalised incomes were then ranked in ascending order and divided into deciles, with households having the lowest equivalised income in the first decile. All individuals in the household were then allocated to the equivalised income decile to which their household had been allocated. For the purposes of analysis, some tables (3.2E, 3.3E and 3.2, 3.3) show ten income groups (deciles) and some (3.4E to 3.11E and 3.4 to 3.11) show five income groups (quintiles); all have a comparable number of households in each group.

In 2006 the income deciles shown in Tables 3.2E and 3.2 (household expenditure by gross equivalised income and gross income decile group in £ per week) were as follows:

Income decile	Gross weekly equivalised income	Gross weekly income
1	Up to £183	Up to £142
2	£184 to £239	£143 to £214
3	£240 to £310	£215 to £292
4	£311 to £386	£293 to £383
5	£387 to £475	£384 to £496
6	£476 to £576	£497 to £623
7	£577 to £689	£624 to £762
8	£690 to £840	£763 to £938
9	£841 to £1,126	£939 to £1,273
10	£1,127 and over	£1,274 and over

Household composition by income groups

To assess the impact that the scale has on the composition of households in the lowest and highest income groups, Table 3.1 shows the household composition in each income decile group by equivalised and gross (recorded, that is, non-equivalised) income. Equivalisation changed the distribution of income from that depicted by gross incomes among some household types.

Equivalisation of income had a large impact on one-person retired households. As Table 3.1 shows, this group accounted for around two-fifths of all households in the lowest income decile (43 per cent). When their income was equivalised the proportion of such households in the lowest income decile fell to 9 per cent. It can be seen that these households moved up the income distribution by the process of equivalisation; one-person retired households were 22 per cent of the third gross income decile but 27 per cent of the third decile after income was equivalised and they accounted for 21 per cent of equivalised income in the fourth decile, compared with 11 per cent of gross income. This trend continued in the remaining deciles. There were almost four times as many one-person retired households in the sixth and seventh equivalised income deciles combined, compared with the gross income deciles: 8 per cent in the sixth equivalised income decile, compared with 2 per cent in the gross income decile; and 6 per cent in the seventh equivalised income decile, compared with 1 per cent in the gross income decile. There were 1 per cent or less of one-person retired households in each of the seventh, eighth, ninth and highest gross income deciles, but after equivalisation these households accounted for 6, 4, 3 and 2 per cent respectively.

Figure 3.1

Percentage of households with children in each gross income decile group, 2006

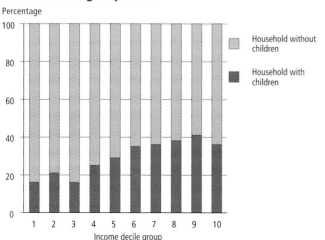

Figure 3.2

Percentage of households with children in each gross equivalised income decile group, 2006

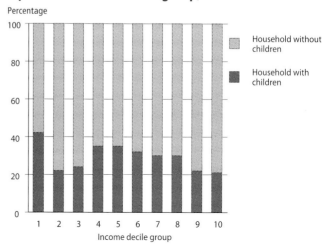

As with one person non-retired households is made up of a larger proportion of deciles in the bottom half of the gross income distribution (that is, in the five lowest deciles) than after equivalisation. At the other end of the distribution, one-person non-retired households increased as a proportion of each decile after equivalisation. For example, the percentage of one-person non-retired households fell from being 32 per cent of the lowest gross income decile to 24 per cent of the lowest equivalised income decile, while in the top decile increased from 4 per cent to 23 per cent after equivalisation.

The effect of equivalisation on households with two adults and one or more child was the reverse: the proportion of such households in the lower deciles increased with equivalisation while the proportion in the higher deciles fell.

As discussed above, equivalisation tends to increase relatively the incomes of single person households and to reduce incomes of households with three or more persons and so these changes were expected.

Figures 3.1 and 3.2 show the distribution of households before and after income equivalisation by whether or not they have children. It can be seen that as gross income increased, the proportion of households with children increased: the proportion increased from 16 per cent of households in the bottom gross income decile to 36 per cent of those in the top gross income decile (Figure 3.1). The pattern was somewhat different after equivalisation: the decile with the highest proportion of households with children was the first (42 per cent), the proportion fell to 22 per cent in the second decile, and then slowly increased to 35 per cent in the fourth and fifth deciles. After the fifth decile (as equivalised income increased) the proportion of each decile made up of households with

children fell (Figure 3.2). One characteristic of low income families (who are likely to be found in the lowest equivalised income decile) is lone parents. This is evident in the equivalised income data where households consisting of one adult and two or more children, make up 3 per cent of the first decile when considering gross income and yet account for 12 per cent of the first equivalised income decile.

The average number of persons per household is also shown in Table 3.1 for each income group. As gross income increased, the average number of people in each household also increased: the highest income group had more than twice the average household size of the lowest income group (three people compared with 1.4 people). After income was equivalised the average number of people in each household was very similar over the income deciles (ranging from two in the second decile to 2.6 in the fifth decile group – reflecting the effect of equivalisation).

Household expenditure by income

Tables 3.2E, 3.2, 3.3E and 3.3 show household expenditure on commodities and services. The figures include information from the expenditure diaries kept by adults and by children aged seven to 15. Differences in spending may be the result of other factors as well as income (for example, household size) and so the tables show both gross income deciles and equivalised income deciles.

Generally, although expenditure on different commodities and services increased as income increased using both the measures of income, the effect was slightly less marked when equivalised income was used. In the lowest gross income decile, households spent £155.60 on average per week, rising to

Figure **3.3**

Expenditure on food and non-alcoholic drinks by gross and equivalised income decile group, 2006

£ per week

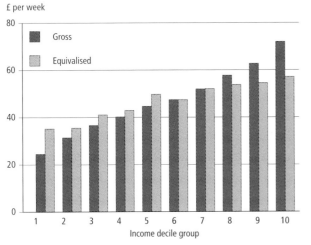

Figure **3.4**

Expenditure on clothing and footwear by gross and equivalised income decile group, 2006

£ per week

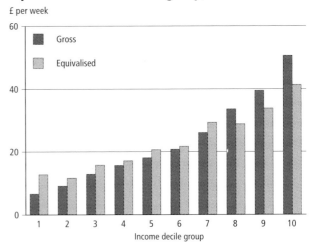

£964.40 in the highest decile (Table 3.2). In comparison, households in the lowest equivalised income decile spent £228.50 on average per week, rising to £882.90 in the highest equivalised income decile (Table 3.2E).

This pattern is particularly evident for spending on food and non-alcoholic drinks, and clothing and footwear (see Figures 3.3 and 3.4). In the lowest gross income decile, households spent £24.50 on average per week on food and non-alcoholic drinks, rising to £71.90 in the highest decile. In comparison, households in the lowest equivalised income decile spent £35.10 on average per week, rising to £57.10 in the highest decile. In terms of spending on clothing and footwear, households in the lowest gross income decile spent £6.60 on average per week, increasing to £50.50 in the highest decile. The corresponding results for the lowest and highest equivalised income deciles were £12.70 and £41.20. The pattern is less evident when expenditure on other individual items is considered.

There were also some notable differences in the expenditure patterns of households with different levels of equivalised income. Generally, total household expenditure increased as equivalised income increased. However, expenditure in the lowest equivalised income decile was higher than that in the second decile: households in the lowest income decile spent, on average, £228.50 a week, compared with an average spend of £225.90 in the second decile and £303.80 in the third decile.

This difference may be explained by the large proportion of households with children found in the lowest equivalised income decile: after equivalisation the proportions of households with children in the lowest decile was almost

double that of the corresponding proportion in decile two (42 per cent compared with 22 per cent) (Table 3.1). Alternatively, this could be related to the tendency (as seen in gross income) for the lowest income decile to contain several households with a temporarily low income, where the household reference person has recently left work, either through redundancy or other reasons but are maintaining a higher level of expenditure.

Table 3.3E shows the percentage of total expenditure spent on different commodities and services by equivalised income decile group. As a proportion of total expenditure, households in the lowest equivalised income decile group spent over twice as much on food and non-alcoholic drinks as households in the highest income decile group (15 per cent compared with 6 per cent). Households in the lowest equivalised income decile group also spent a considerably higher proportion of their total expenditure on housing, fuel and power than households in the highest income decile group (18 per cent compared with 8 per cent). Conversely, households with the highest equivalised incomes spent a greater proportion of their income on transport than those with lower equivalised incomes: 16 per cent of the expenditure of the highest decile of equivalised income distribution was on transport, compared with 11 per cent of the expenditure of those households in the first decile group (see Figure 3.5).

Household expenditure by household composition and income

This section looks at the effect that equivalisation has on the expenditure of different household types. Tables 3.4E to 3.11E and 3.4 to 3.11 show the expenditure of different household composition groups by equivalised income and gross income. The analysis focuses on one and two adult households, with and without children. It is worth noting that the following groups contain a small number of households and should therefore be treated with caution: one-person retired households mainly dependent on the state pension (190 households); and one man one woman retired households mainly dependent on the state pension (150 households). The number of households within each income group is also low for some of the other household composition groups.

As discussed earlier, equivalisation increases relatively the incomes of single person households and reduces the incomes of households with three or more persons. We would therefore expect equivalisation to have the greatest effect on the expenditure of these types of households.

Figure **3.5**

Percentage of total expenditure on selected items by equivalised income decile group, 2006

Percentage

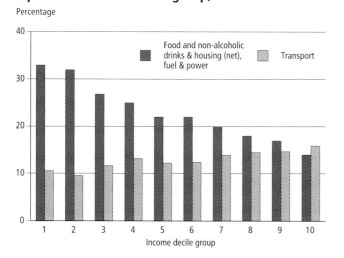

As anticipated, equivalisation had a large affect among one-person non-retired and retired (not mainly dependent on the state pension) households, and two adult households with children. For example, the average amount spent each week on all expenditure items by one-person non-retired households in the top fifth of the gross income distribution was £605.70 compared with an average £464.50 in the top fifth of the equivalised income distribution (see Tables 3.4 and 3.4E). Among one-person retired households not mainly dependent on the state pension, the average amount spent each week on all expenditure items was £886.40 in the top fifth gross income group, compared with £519.90 in the top equivalised income group (see Tables 3.5 and 3.5E). Equivalisation increased spending among two adult households with children: the average amount spent each week on all expenditure items was £912.40 in the top fifth of the gross income distribution compared with £968.80 in the top fifth of the equivalised income distribution (see Tables 3.6 and 3.6E).

In contrast, the expenditure patterns of the following households composition groups were not markedly different when using the two income measures: one man one woman non-retired households (Tables 3.8 and 3.8E); one-person retired households mainly dependant on state pensions (Tables 3.9 and 3.9E); one man one woman retired households mainly dependent on the state pension (Tables 3.10 and 3.10E); one man one woman retired households not mainly dependent on the state pension (Tables 3.11 and 3.11E).

Sources of income

Households receive income from a variety of sources, the main ones being earnings and self-employment, Social Security Benefits/Tax Credits, interest on investments and occupational pensions.

Tables 3.12E and 3.12 and Figures 3.6 and 3.7 show the distribution of gross income sources for each income quintile, by gross household income and equivalised household income. The various sources of income are shown as a percentage of the total gross income of the quintile.

Social security benefits were the principal source of income (77 per cent) of the lowest gross income quintile, this did not change markedly when income was equivalised (70 per cent). However, the proportion of income made up from wages and salaries was smaller in the lowest gross income quintile than for the lowest equivalised income quintile: 6 per cent compared with 15 per cent. The reverse was true for annuities and pensions, the proportion almost halved when income was equivalised: among households in the lowest gross income quintile, 9 per cent of income consisted of annuities and pensions, compared with 5 per cent for households in the lowest gross equivalised income quintile. These differences largely reflect the fact that after equivalising income, the lowest quintile group contained fewer pensioner households.

Figure **3.6**

Sources of income by gross income quintile group, 2006

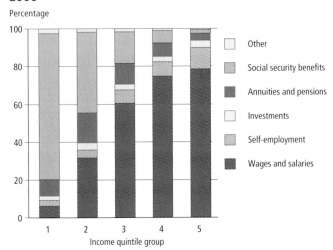

Figure **3.7**

Sources of income by gross equivalised income quintile group, 2006

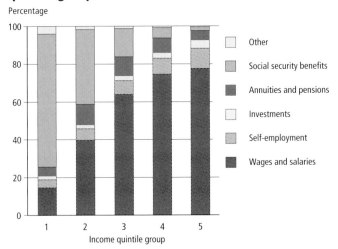

Table 3.1 Percentage of households by composition in each gross, and equivalised income decile group, 2006

Percentages

	Income decile group									
	Lowest ten per cent		Second		Third		Fourth		Fifth	
	Gross	Equivalised	Gross	Equivalised	Gross	Equivalised	Gross	Equivalised	Gross	Equivalised
Lower boundary of group (£ per week)			143	184	215	240	293	311	384	387
Average size of household	1.4	2.4	1.7	2.0	1.9	2.2	2.1	2.5	2.3	2.6
One adult retired mainly dependent on state pensions¹	15	5	9	11	[2]	6	[0]	3	[0]	[1]
One adult, other retired	28	4	33	26	19	20	11	17	5	11
One adult, non-retired	32	24	12	9	16	8	25	8	20	10
One adult, one child	10	11	4	4	4	3	4	4	2	2
One adult, two or more children	3	12	9	4	4	4	4	3	3	[2]
One man one woman, retired mainly dependent on state pensions¹	[2]	5	8	9	8	5	[2]	[1]	[0]	[0]
One man and one woman, other retired	[0]	[2]	6	12	20	16	20	16	15	13
One man and one woman, non-retired	5	10	7	6	12	10	11	10	21	15
One man and one woman, one child	[1]	4	[3]	3	3	[2]	4	7	8	7
One man and one woman, two children	[1]	4	[2]	3	[2]	6	5	9	7	13
One man and one woman, three children	[0]	[2]	[0]	[1]	[1]	2	[2]	4	[2]	4
Two adults, four or more children	[1]	3	[0]	[1]	[0]	[1]	[2]	[1]	[1]	[1]
Three adults	[1]	5	[2]	[3]	[3]	4	[3]	5	7	8
Three adults, one or more children	[0]	3	[1]	[3]	[1]	4	[2]	4	3	4
All other households without children	[1]	[3]	[2]	[3]	[3]	5	3	3	[3]	6
All other households with children	[0]	[2]	[1]	[2]	[0]	[2]	[1]	3	[2]	[2]

	Income decile group									
	Sixth		Seventh		Eighth		Ninth		Highest ten per cent	
	Gross	Equivalised	Gross	Equivalised	Gross	Equivalised	Gross	Equivalised	Gross	Equivalised
Lower boundary of group (£ per week)	497	476	624	577	763	690	939	841	1,274	1,127
Average size of household	2.6	2.5	2.7	2.5	2.9	2.3	3.0	2.2	3.0	2.4
One adult retired mainly dependent on state pensions¹	–	–	–	–	–	[0]	–	–	–	–
One adult, other retired	[2]	8	[1]	6	[1]	4	[0]	[3]	[0]	[2]
One adult, non-retired	16	17	12	14	8	17	7	21	4	23
One adult, one child	[2]	[2]	[2]	[2]	[1]	[2]	[1]	[1]	[0]	[1]
One adult, two or more children	3	[2]	[1]	[0]	[1]	[0]	[1]	[1]	[1]	[0]
One man one woman, retired mainly dependent on state pensions¹	[0]	[0]	–	[0]	–	–	–	–	–	–
One man and one woman, other retired	8	8	7	6	3	4	[2]	3	[2]	3
One man and one woman, non-retired	25	19	31	26	30	30	29	34	32	43
One man and one woman, one child	8	8	11	9	11	11	13	9	10	9
One man and one woman, two children	12	12	13	11	13	11	17	8	13	7
One man and one woman, three children	4	4	3	3	4	[2]	4	[1]	4	[2]
Two adults, four or more children	[1]	[0]	[1]	[0]	[1]	[0]	[1]	[0]	[1]	–
Three adults	7	8	7	12	14	7	12	12	13	5
Three adults, one or more children	3	3	4	[3]	5	[2]	4	[1]	5	[2]
All other households without children	6	7	6	7	6	8	8	5	12	[3]
All other households with children	[2]	[1]	[2]	[1]	3	[2]	[1]	[0]	[3]	[0]

1 Mainly dependent on state pension and not economically active – see Appendix B.

Table 3.2E Household expenditure by gross equivalised income decile group, 2006

based on weighted data and including children's expenditure

	Lowest ten per cent	Second decile group	Third decile group	Fourth decile group	Fifth decile group	Sixth decile group
Lower boundary of group (£ per week)		184	240	311	387	476
Weighted number of households (thousands)	2,480	2,480	2,480	2,480	2,480	2,480
Total number of households in sample	690	680	710	690	690	660
Total number of persons in sample	1,670	1,410	1,580	1,720	1,840	1,660
Total number of adults in sample	1,050	1,060	1,230	1,260	1,360	1,250
Weighted average number of persons per household	2.4	2.0	2.2	2.5	2.6	2.5
Commodity or service	Average weekly household expenditure (£)					
1 Food & non-alcoholic drinks	35.10	35.40	41.00	42.90	49.60	47.30
2 Alcoholic drinks, tobacco & narcotics	7.90	6.80	9.40	10.50	11.50	12.00
3 Clothing & footwear	12.70	11.60	15.80	17.10	20.60	21.70
4 Housing (net)[1], fuel & power	40.80	37.80	42.10	43.30	42.50	47.60
5 Household goods & services	12.80	16.40	22.20	23.10	26.60	27.30
6 Health	2.10	2.60	2.80	4.60	6.20	6.50
7 Transport	24.10	21.60	35.50	45.50	51.30	54.50
8 Communication	8.20	7.50	9.20	10.50	12.70	12.60
9 Recreation & culture	25.60	27.40	40.00	42.60	61.70	59.10
10 Education	4.00	2.70	1.90	2.90	2.30	3.30
11 Restaurants & hotels	17.60	16.10	20.50	24.60	33.50	36.10
12 Miscellaneous goods & services	14.40	16.30	24.70	27.10	33.40	34.50
1–12 All expenditure groups	205.20	202.10	265.00	294.80	351.70	362.50
13 Other expenditure items	22.40	23.80	38.70	49.70	67.30	76.30
Total expenditure	**227.60**	**225.90**	**303.80**	**344.60**	**419.00**	**438.70**
Average weekly expenditure per person (£) **Total expenditure**	**94.60**	**111.80**	**138.10**	**139.00**	**160.00**	**177.30**

Note: The commodity and service categories are not comparable to those in publications before 2001–02.

1 Excluding mortgage interest payments, council tax and Northern Ireland Rates.

Table 3.2E Household expenditure by gross equivalised income decile group, 2006 (cont.)
based on weighted data and including children's expenditure

	Seventh decile group	Eighth decile group	Ninth decile group	Highest ten per cent	All house-holds
Lower boundary of group (£ per week)	577	690	841	1,127	
Weighted number of households (thousands)	2,480	2,480	2,480	2,480	24,790
Total number of households in sample	650	650	620	610	6,650
Total number of persons in sample	1,630	1,590	1,420	1,330	15,850
Total number of adults in sample	1,280	1,250	1,170	1,110	12,000
Weighted average number of persons per household	2.5	2.5	2.3	2.2	2.4
Commodity or service	Average weekly household expenditure (£)				
1 Food & non-alcoholic drinks	52.10	53.80	54.50	57.10	46.90
2 Alcoholic drinks, tobacco & narcotics	12.60	14.00	12.70	13.70	11.10
3 Clothing & footwear	29.30	28.80	33.70	41.20	23.30
4 Housing (net)[1], fuel & power	52.90	48.60	52.20	67.80	47.60
5 Household goods & services	33.10	34.80	42.00	64.20	30.30
6 Health	6.10	6.10	11.50	10.10	5.90
7 Transport	72.60	82.70	91.70	140.60	62.00
8 Communication	13.30	13.60	14.40	15.40	11.70
9 Recreation & culture	68.20	76.40	78.80	104.90	58.50
10 Education	6.10	7.80	11.70	29.70	7.20
11 Restaurants & hotels	48.00	49.10	52.80	80.50	37.90
12 Miscellaneous goods & services	40.80	46.40	53.00	69.50	36.00
1–12 All expenditure groups	435.30	462.20	508.90	694.80	378.30
13 Other expenditure items	87.00	108.10	114.30	188.10	77.60
Total expenditure	**522.30**	**570.30**	**623.20**	**882.90**	**455.90**
Average weekly expenditure per person (£)					
Total expenditure	**206.80**	**230.80**	**272.40**	**409.20**	**192.80**

Note: The commodity and service categories are not comparable to those in publications before 2001–02.
1 Excluding mortgage interest payments, council tax and Northern Ireland Rates.

Table 3.2 Household expenditure by gross income decile group, 2006

based on weighted data and including children's expenditure

		Lowest ten per cent	Second decile group	Third decile group	Fourth decile group	Fifth decile group	Sixth decile group
Lower boundary of group (£ per week)			143	215	293	384	497
Weighted number of households (thousands)		2,480	2,480	2,480	2,480	2,480	2,480
Total number of households in sample		680	680	700	690	690	680
Total number of persons in sample		930	1,200	1,350	1,500	1,650	1,800
Total number of adults in sample		760	920	1,110	1,130	1,250	1,320
Weighted average number of persons per household		1.4	1.7	1.9	2.1	2.3	2.6
Commodity or service		Average weekly household expenditure (£)					
1	Food & non-alcoholic drinks	24.50	31.40	36.60	40.10	44.60	47.40
2	Alcoholic drinks, tobacco & narcotics	5.30	6.00	8.30	9.20	11.60	11.70
3	Clothing & footwear	6.60	9.10	12.80	15.70	18.10	20.70
4	Housing (net)[1], fuel & power	32.30	35.20	42.50	43.30	45.40	49.90
5	Household goods & services	11.20	14.70	17.60	24.80	23.90	29.50
6	Health	1.80	2.80	4.40	4.40	5.60	5.50
7	Transport	13.90	16.90	33.20	40.50	46.60	55.40
8	Communication	5.70	6.80	8.50	9.40	12.10	12.00
9	Recreation & culture	17.10	25.20	34.70	39.40	51.50	58.20
10	Education	[1.70]	1.50	2.70	2.10	2.40	2.80
11	Restaurants & hotels	10.10	13.60	17.50	23.40	29.00	36.30
12	Miscellaneous goods & services	9.80	14.30	22.20	26.00	28.80	35.80
1–12	All expenditure groups	140.00	177.40	240.90	278.40	319.60	365.20
13	Other expenditure items	15.60	22.40	30.50	54.60	60.60	72.90
Total expenditure		**155.60**	**199.80**	**271.40**	**333.00**	**380.20**	**438.10**
Average weekly expenditure per person (£) **Total expenditure**		**114.60**	**114.80**	**142.40**	**157.00**	**163.70**	**166.90**

Note: The commodity and service categories are not comparable to those in publications before 2001–02.

1 Excluding mortgage interest payments, council tax and Northern Ireland rates.

Table 3.2 Household expenditure by gross income decile group, 2006 (cont.)

based on weighted data and including children's expenditure

		Seventh decile group	Eighth decile group	Ninth decile group	Highest ten per cent	All house-holds
Lower boundary of group (£ per week)		624	763	939	1,274	
Weighted number of households (thousands)		2,480	2,480	2,480	2,480	24,790
Total number of households in sample		660	630	640	590	6,650
Total number of persons in sample		1,790	1,880	1,930	1,840	15,850
Total number of adults in sample		1,340	1,380	1,400	1,380	12,000
Weighted average number of persons per household		2.7	2.9	3.0	3.0	2.4
Commodity or service		Average weekly household expenditure (£)				
1	Food & non-alcoholic drinks	51.90	57.80	62.70	71.90	46.90
2	Alcoholic drinks, tobacco & narcotics	13.60	14.90	15.30	15.20	11.10
3	Clothing & footwear	26.00	33.50	39.40	50.50	23.20
4	Housing(net)[1], fuel & power	48.90	52.60	51.10	74.30	47.60
5	Household goods & services	33.60	36.90	46.10	64.40	30.30
6	Health	5.00	6.90	6.40	15.90	5.90
7	Transport	65.40	84.70	107.50	156.20	62.00
8	Communication	13.80	14.80	16.70	17.80	11.70
9	Recreation & culture	67.40	83.70	92.10	115.40	58.50
10	Education	3.30	8.20	15.00	32.60	7.20
11	Restaurants & hotels	44.80	53.30	66.00	84.80	37.90
12	Miscellaneous goods & services	44.10	48.00	57.40	73.80	36.00
1–12	All expenditure groups	417.90	495.10	575.80	772.80	378.30
13	Other expenditure items	89.00	99.00	139.70	191.60	77.60
Total expenditure		**506.90**	**594.10**	**715.50**	**964.40**	**455.90**
Average weekly expenditure per person (£) **Total expenditure**		**190.40**	**205.40**	**240.40**	**317.10**	**192.80**

Note: The commodity and service categories are not comparable to those in publications before 2001–02.
1 Excluding mortgage interest payments, council tax and Northern Ireland rates.

Table 3.3E Household expenditure as a percentage of total expenditure by gross equivalised income decile group, 2006

based on weighted data and including children's expenditure

	Lowest ten per cent	Second decile group	Third decile group	Fourth decile group	Fifth decile group	Sixth decile group
Lower boundary of group (£ per week)		184	240	311	387	476
Weighted number of households (thousands)	2,480	2,480	2,480	2,480	2,480	2,480
Total number of households in sample	690	680	710	690	690	660
Total number of persons in sample	1,670	1,410	1,580	1,720	1,840	1,660
Total number of adults in sample	1,050	1,060	1,230	1,260	1,360	1,250
Weighted average number of persons per household	2.4	2.0	2.2	2.5	2.6	2.5
Commodity or service	Percentage of total expenditure					
1 Food & non-alcoholic drinks	15	16	13	12	12	11
2 Alcoholic drinks, tobacco & narcotics	3	3	3	3	3	3
3 Clothing & footwear	6	5	5	5	5	5
4 Housing (net)[1], fuel & power	18	17	14	13	10	11
5 Household goods & services	6	7	7	7	6	6
6 Health	1	1	1	1	1	1
7 Transport	11	10	12	13	12	12
8 Communication	4	3	3	3	3	3
9 Recreation & culture	11	12	13	12	15	13
10 Education	2	1	1	1	1	1
11 Restaurants & hotels	8	7	7	7	8	8
12 Miscellaneous goods & services	6	7	8	8	8	8
1–12 All expenditure groups	90	89	87	86	84	83
13 Other expenditure items	10	11	13	14	16	17
Total expenditure	100	100	100	100	100	100

Note: The commodity and service categories are not comparable to those in publications before 2001–02.
1 Excluding mortgage interest payments, council tax and Northern Ireland rates.

Table **3.3E** **Household expenditure as a percentage of total expenditure by gross equivalised income decile group, 2006 (cont.)**
based on weighted data and including children's expenditure

	Seventh decile group	Eighth decile group	Ninth decile group	Highest ten per cent	All house-holds
Lower boundary of group (£ per week)	577	690	841	1,127	
Weighted number of households (thousands)	2,480	2,480	2,480	2,480	24,790
Total number of households in sample	650	650	620	610	6,650
Total number of persons in sample	1,630	1,590	1,420	1,330	15,850
Total number of adults in sample	1,280	1,250	1,170	1,110	12,000
Weighted average number of persons per household	2.5	2.5	2.3	2.2	2.4
Commodity or service	Percentage of total expenditure				
1 Food & non-alcoholic drinks	10	9	9	6	10
2 Alcoholic drinks, tobacco & narcotics	2	2	2	2	2
3 Clothing & footwear	6	5	5	5	5
4 Housing (net)[1], fuel & power	10	9	8	8	10
5 Household goods & services	6	6	7	7	7
6 Health	1	1	2	1	1
7 Transport	14	15	15	16	14
8 Communication	3	2	2	2	3
9 Recreation & culture	13	13	13	12	13
10 Education	1	1	2	3	2
11 Restaurants & hotels	9	9	8	9	8
12 Miscellaneous goods & services	8	8	8	8	8
1–12 All expenditure groups	83	81	82	79	83
13 Other expenditure items	17	19	18	21	17
Total expenditure	100	100	100	100	100

Note: The commodity and service categories are not comparable to those in publications before 2001–02.
1 Excluding mortgage interest payments, council tax and Northern Ireland rates.

Table 3.3 Household expenditure as a percentage of total expenditure by gross income decile group, 2006

based on weighted data and including children's expenditure

	Lowest ten per cent	Second decile group	Third decile group	Fourth decile group	Fifth decile group	Sixth decile group
Lower boundary of group (£ per week)		143	215	293	384	497
Weighted number of households (thousands)	2,480	2,480	2,480	2,480	2,480	2,480
Total number of households in sample	680	680	700	690	690	680
Total number of persons in sample	930	1,200	1,350	1,500	1,650	1,800
Total number of adults in sample	760	920	1,110	1,130	1,250	1,320
Weighted average number of persons per household	1.4	1.7	1.9	2.1	2.3	2.6
Commodity or service	Percentage of total expenditure					
1 Food & non-alcoholic drinks	16	16	13	12	12	11
2 Alcoholic drinks, tobacco & narcotics	3	3	3	3	3	3
3 Clothing & footwear	4	5	5	5	5	5
4 Housing (net)[1], fuel & power	21	18	16	13	12	11
5 Household goods & services	7	7	6	7	6	7
6 Health	1	1	2	1	1	1
7 Transport	9	8	12	12	12	13
8 Communication	4	3	3	3	3	3
9 Recreation & culture	11	13	13	12	14	13
10 Education	[1]	1	1	1	1	1
11 Restaurants & hotels	6	7	6	7	8	8
12 Miscellaneous goods & services	6	7	8	8	8	8
1–12 All expenditure groups	90	89	89	84	84	83
13 Other expenditure items	10	11	11	16	16	17
Total expenditure	100	100	100	100	100	100

Note: The commodity and service categories are not comparable to those in publications before 2001–02.
1 Excluding mortgage interest payments, council tax and Northern Ireland rates.

Table 3.3 **Household expenditure as a percentage of total expenditure by gross income decile group, 2006 (cont.)**

based on weighted data and including children's expenditure

	Seventh decile group	Eighth decile group	Ninth decile group	Highest ten per cent	All house-holds
Lower boundary of group (£ per week)	624	763	939	1,274	
Weighted number of households (thousands)	2,480	2,480	2,480	2,480	24,790
Total number of households in sample	660	630	640	590	6,650
Total number of persons in sample	1,790	1,880	1,930	1,840	15,850
Total number of adults in sample	1,340	1,380	1,400	1,380	12,000
Weighted average number of persons per household	2.7	2.9	3.0	3.0	2.4
Commodity or service	Percentage of total expenditure				
1 Food & non-alcoholic drinks	10	10	9	7	10
2 Alcoholic drinks, tobacco & narcotics	3	3	2	2	2
3 Clothing & footwear	5	6	6	5	5
4 Housing (net)[1], fuel & power	10	9	7	8	10
5 Household goods & services	7	6	6	7	7
6 Health	1	1	1	2	1
7 Transport	13	15	15	16	14
8 Communication	3	2	2	2	3
9 Recreation & culture	13	14	13	12	13
10 Education	1	1	2	3	2
11 Restaurants & hotels	9	9	9	9	8
12 Miscellaneous goods & services	9	8	8	8	8
1–12 All expenditure groups	82	83	80	80	83
13 Other expenditure items	18	17	20	20	17
Total expenditure	**100**	**100**	**100**	**100**	**100**

Note: The commodity and service categories are not comparable to those in publications before 2001–02.
1 Excluding mortgage interest payments, council tax and Northern Ireland rates.

Table **3.4E** Expenditure of one person non-retired households by gross equivalised income quintile group, 2006

based on weighted data

	Lowest twenty per cent	Second quintile group	Third quintile group	Fourth quintile group	Highest twenty per cent	All house- holds
Lower boundary of group (£ per week)		240	387	577	841	
Weighted number of households (thousands)	820	410	670	760	1100	3,760
Total number of households in sample	220	110	170	200	270	960
Total number of persons in sample	220	110	170	200	270	960
Total number of adults in sample	220	110	170	200	270	960
Weighted average number of persons per household	1.0	1.0	1.0	1.0	1.0	1.0
Commodity or service	Average weekly household expenditure (£)					
1 Food & non-alcoholic drinks	18.40	21.30	21.40	25.00	30.40	24.10
2 Alcoholic drinks, tobacco & narcotics	7.40	6.70	7.80	8.20	8.40	7.80
3 Clothing & footwear	5.00	8.00	11.80	9.00	19.10	11.40
4 Housing (net)[1], fuel & power	29.20	42.40	46.10	42.90	46.90	41.60
5 Household goods & services	12.40	10.90	16.10	17.90	29.80	19.10
6 Health	0.80	3.20	2.70	3.70	4.40	3.00
7 Transport	19.00	31.20	27.20	37.70	60.10	37.50
8 Communication	5.70	8.50	9.50	8.90	10.80	8.80
9 Recreation & culture	15.00	26.30	27.70	33.20	54.30	33.60
10 Education	[0.30]	[0.90]	[1.60]	[0.80]	[4.70]	2.00
11 Restaurants & hotels	11.90	12.10	17.20	25.40	43.10	24.70
12 Miscellaneous goods & services	7.10	13.60	16.40	21.70	37.10	21.20
1–12 All expenditure groups	132.30	185.20	205.50	234.20	349.00	234.80
13 Other expenditure items	16.70	31.30	46.90	65.30	115.60	62.30
Total expenditure	**148.90**	**216.50**	**252.40**	**299.60**	**464.50**	**297.10**
Average weekly expenditure per person (£) **Total expenditure**	**148.90**	**216.50**	**252.40**	**299.60**	**464.50**	**297.10**

Note: The commodity and service categories are not comparable to those in publications before 2001–02.

1 Excluding mortgage interest payments, council tax and Northern Ireland rates.

Table 3.4 Expenditure of one person non-retired households by gross income quintile group, 2006

based on weighted data

	Lowest twenty per cent	Second quintile group	Third quintile group	Fourth quintile group	Highest twenty per cent	All house-holds
Lower boundary of group (£ per week)		215	384	624	939	
Weighted number of households (thousands)	1,110	1,000	890	490	270	3,760
Total number of households in sample	290	260	230	120	60	960
Total number of persons in sample	290	260	230	120	60	960
Total number of adults in sample	290	260	230	120	60	960
Weighted average number of persons per household	1.0	1.0	1.0	1.0	1.0	1.0
Commodity or service		Average weekly household expenditure (£)				
1 Food & non-alcoholic drinks	19.20	21.60	27.00	31.60	29.70	24.10
2 Alcoholic drinks, tobacco & narcotics	7.00	8.00	7.10	10.30	8.60	7.80
3 Clothing & footwear	5.40	11.80	10.90	19.10	22.80	11.40
4 Housing (net)[1], fuel & power	32.10	46.50	39.00	43.50	66.90	41.60
5 Household goods & services	11.60	17.00	15.80	35.00	38.80	19.10
6 Health	1.60	3.40	3.20	3.10	7.00	3.00
7 Transport	18.60	35.10	41.60	60.80	68.40	37.50
8 Communication	6.40	9.20	8.70	11.10	13.40	8.80
9 Recreation & culture	18.50	26.90	38.20	61.00	55.50	33.60
10 Education	[0.50]	[1.20]	[0.70]	[3.90]	[11.80]	2.00
11 Restaurants & hotels	12.00	17.80	29.50	40.40	57.90	24.70
12 Miscellaneous goods & services	8.30	18.20	21.50	46.60	37.70	21.20
1–12 All expenditure groups	141.30	216.80	243.30	366.50	418.50	234.80
13 Other expenditure items	21.20	46.30	71.50	102.40	187.20	62.30
Total expenditure	**162.50**	**263.10**	**314.80**	**468.90**	**605.70**	**297.10**
Average weekly expenditure per person (£)						
Total expenditure	**162.50**	**263.10**	**314.80**	**468.90**	**605.70**	**297.10**

Note: The commodity and service categories are not comparable to those in publications before 2001–02.

1 Excluding mortgage interest payments, council tax and Northern Ireland rates.

Table **3.5E** **Expenditure of one person retired households not mainly dependent on state pensions[1]**
by gross equivalised income quintile group, 2006
based on weighted data

	Lowest twenty per cent	Second quintile group	Third quintile group	Fourth quintile group	Highest twenty per cent	All house-holds
Lower boundary of group (£ per week)		240	387	577	841	
Weighted number of households (thousands)	740	940	470	240	120	2,500
Total number of households in sample	190	250	130	70	30	670
Total number of persons in sample	190	250	130	70	30	670
Total number of adults in sample	190	250	130	70	30	670
Weighted average number of persons per household	1.0	1.0	1.0	1.0	1.0	1.0
Commodity or service	Average weekly household expenditure (£)					
1 Food & non-alcoholic drinks	22.40	24.60	27.00	32.30	29.10	25.40
2 Alcoholic drinks, tobacco & narcotics	3.80	4.20	4.90	6.80	[7.70]	4.60
3 Clothing & footwear	4.80	6.20	6.30	11.90	[12.80]	6.70
4 Housing (net)[2], fuel & power	29.10	28.90	29.70	40.60	45.90	31.00
5 Household goods & services	9.80	15.30	22.40	20.30	46.20	17.00
6 Health	2.80	2.50	9.50	6.50	[3.60]	4.30
7 Transport	5.90	12.40	22.20	36.70	75.50	17.70
8 Communication	4.80	5.00	5.80	7.20	7.30	5.40
9 Recreation & culture	15.70	17.30	22.40	46.80	90.00	24.10
10 Education	[0.00]	–	[1.00]	[0.30]	[20.10]	[1.20]
11 Restaurants & hotels	5.70	7.40	12.60	21.00	29.80	10.30
12 Miscellaneous goods & services	9.00	14.40	17.00	39.90	77.70	18.80
1–12 All expenditure groups	113.80	138.20	180.90	270.30	445.60	166.40
13 Other expenditure items	9.20	17.90	29.30	52.60	74.30	23.50
Total expenditure	**123.00**	**156.10**	**210.20**	**322.90**	**519.90**	**190.00**
Average weekly expenditure per person (£) **Total expenditure**	**123.00**	**156.10**	**210.20**	**322.90**	**519.90**	**190.00**

Note: The commodity and service categories are not comparable to those in publications before 2001–02.
1 Mainly dependent on state pension and not economically active – see Appendix B.
2 Excluding mortgage interest payments, council tax and Northern Ireland Rates.

Table **3.5** **Expenditure of one person retired households not mainly dependent on state pensions[1]**
by gross income quintile group, 2006
based on weighted data

	Lowest twenty per cent	Second quintile group	Third quintile group	Fourth quintile group	Highest twenty per cent	All house-holds
Lower boundary of group (£ per week)		215	384	624	939	
Weighted number of households (thousands)	1,490	750	190	60	10	2,500
Total number of households in sample	400	200	50	20	–	670
Total number of persons in sample	400	200	50	20	–	670
Total number of adults in sample	400	200	50	20	–	670
Weighted average number of persons per household	1.0	1.0	1.0	1.0	1.0	1.0
Commodity or service	Average weekly household expenditure (£)					
1 Food & non-alcoholic drinks	23.20	27.30	32.40	[32.00]	[24.50]	25.40
2 Alcoholic drinks, tobacco & narcotics	3.80	5.50	7.20	[6.50]	[8.70]	4.60
3 Clothing & footwear	5.50	7.00	11.90	[13.90]	[10.90]	6.70
4 Housing (net)[2], fuel & power	28.50	31.60	44.30	[43.10]	[41.30]	31.00
5 Household goods & services	12.90	20.50	29.60	[33.40]	[18.30]	17.00
6 Health	2.70	6.90	7.50	[2.00]	[0.30]	4.30
7 Transport	7.20	23.30	51.80	[86.70]	[79.50]	17.70
8 Communication	4.90	5.70	8.00	[7.30]	[5.90]	5.40
9 Recreation & culture	15.90	24.30	55.00	[40.20]	[458.80]	24.10
10 Education	[0.00]	[0.60]	[0.40]	[39.50]	–	[1.20]
11 Restaurants & hotels	6.50	12.20	22.90	[35.30]	[31.80]	10.30
12 Miscellaneous goods & services	10.50	21.90	59.10	[53.90]	[19.40]	18.80
1–12 All expenditure groups	121.60	186.70	330.10	[393.90]	[699.40]	166.40
13 Other expenditure items	13.10	29.80	60.50	[52.10]	[187.00]	23.50
Total expenditure	**134.70**	**216.50**	**390.60**	**[446.00]**	**[886.40]**	**190.00**
Average weekly expenditure per person (£) **Total expenditure**	**134.70**	**216.50**	**390.60**	**[446.00]**	**[886.40]**	**190.00**

Note: The commodity and service categories are not comparable to those in publications before 2001–02.
1 Mainly dependent on state pension and not economically active – see appendix B.
2 Excluding mortgage interest payments, council tax and Northern Ireland rates.

Table 3.6E Expenditure of two adult households with children by gross equivalised income quintile group, 2006

based on weighted data and including children's expenditure

	Lowest twenty per cent	Second quintile group	Third quintile group	Fourth quintile group	Highest twenty per cent	All house-holds
Lower boundary of group (£ per week)		240	387	577	841	
Weighted number of households (thousands)	610	870	1,240	1,180	900	4,810
Total number of households in sample	180	260	360	340	260	1,390
Total number of persons in sample	780	1,050	1,390	1,280	930	5,430
Total number of adults in sample	360	510	710	690	510	2,790
Weighted average number of persons per household	4.2	4.1	3.9	3.7	3.6	3.9
Commodity or service	Average weekly household expenditure (£)					
1 Food & non-alcoholic drinks	56.00	54.10	61.50	67.50	77.90	64.00
2 Alcoholic drinks, tobacco & narcotics	12.40	13.80	13.20	13.60	14.80	13.60
3 Clothing & footwear	24.40	30.10	28.50	37.50	53.10	35.10
4 Housing (net)[1], fuel & power	50.30	56.10	43.20	50.40	66.50	52.60
5 Household goods & services	18.90	35.50	36.00	43.40	65.90	41.20
6 Health	1.50	2.50	3.80	6.40	9.00	4.90
7 Transport	43.90	64.80	66.50	99.10	144.90	86.10
8 Communication	11.60	15.80	13.30	16.00	16.50	14.80
9 Recreation & culture	41.80	53.10	75.50	89.30	111.60	77.30
10 Education	7.90	4.40	5.20	18.60	61.40	19.20
11 Restaurants & hotels	30.70	33.40	40.70	54.60	74.20	47.80
12 Miscellaneous goods & services	25.50	35.50	43.60	63.40	86.80	52.80
1–12 All expenditure groups	324.90	399.00	430.90	559.70	782.70	509.40
13 Other expenditure items	46.70	69.40	106.60	149.80	204.10	121.20
Total expenditure	**371.60**	**468.40**	**537.50**	**709.50**	**986.80**	**630.60**
Average weekly expenditure per person (£) **Total expenditure**	**87.50**	**115.60**	**138.90**	**191.90**	**274.80**	**163.50**

Note: The commodity and service categories are not comparable to those in publications before 2001–02.

1 Excluding mortgage interest payments, council tax and Northern Ireland rates.

Table **3.6** **Expenditure of two adult households with children by gross income quintile group, 2006**
based on weighted data and including children's expenditure

	Lowest twenty per cent	Second quintile group	Third quintile group	Fourth quintile group	Highest twenty per cent	All house-holds
Lower boundary of group (£ per week)		215	384	624	939	
Weighted number of households (thousands)	210	530	1,110	1,430	1,530	4,810
Total number of households in sample	60	160	330	420	440	1,390
Total number of persons in sample	220	640	1,280	1,600	1,690	5,430
Total number of adults in sample	120	320	650	830	870	2,790
Weighted average number of persons per household	3.8	4.0	3.9	3.8	3.8	3.9
Commodity or service	Average weekly household expenditure (£)					
1 Food & non-alcoholic drinks	49.40	53.80	54.60	63.40	77.00	64.00
2 Alcoholic drinks, tobacco & narcotics	10.50	12.50	14.50	12.60	14.70	13.60
3 Clothing & footwear	17.10	29.70	24.10	32.50	49.90	35.10
4 Housing (net)[1] fuel & power	43.70	56.60	51.00	47.50	58.30	52.60
5 Household goods & services	9.70	26.70	36.90	36.20	58.20	41.20
6 Health	0.70	1.90	3.50	4.20	8.20	4.90
7 Transport	27.70	56.00	59.70	75.50	133.70	86.10
8 Communication	9.10	13.60	14.10	14.40	16.90	14.80
9 Recreation & culture	26.60	44.50	54.80	82.50	107.30	77.30
10 Education	[15.40]	4.70	3.00	7.10	48.00	19.20
11 Restaurants & hotels	29.70	29.20	33.70	43.30	71.30	47.80
12 Miscellaneous goods & services	15.10	33.20	36.70	53.40	76.00	52.80
1–12 All expenditure groups	254.90	362.40	386.70	472.60	719.40	509.40
13 Other expenditure items	31.40	56.20	82.00	112.30	193.00	121.20
Total expenditure	**286.40**	**418.60**	**468.60**	**584.90**	**912.40**	**630.60**
Average weekly expenditure per person (£)						
Total expenditure	**76.00**	**103.70**	**121.40**	**152.70**	**238.60**	**163.50**

Note: The commodity and service categories are not comparable to those in publications before 2001–02.
1 Excluding mortgage interest payments, council tax and Northern Ireland rates.

Table 3.7E Expenditure of one adult households with children by gross equivalised income quintile group, 2006

based on weighted data and including children's expenditure

	Lowest twenty per cent	Second quintile group	Third quintile group	Fourth quintile group	Highest twenty per cent	All house-holds
Lower boundary of group (£ per week)		240	387	577	841	
Weighted number of households (thousands)	740	330	200	120	80	1460
Total number of households in sample	240	100	70	30	20	460
Total number of persons in sample	670	270	170	70	60	1240
Total number of adults in sample	240	100	70	30	20	460
Weighted average number of persons per household	2.8	2.6	2.6	2.2	2.6	2.7
Commodity or service			Average weekly household expenditure (£)			
1 Food & non-alcoholic drinks	35.20	38.80	44.00	41.70	44.50	38.20
2 Alcoholic drinks, tobacco & narcotics	6.50	9.50	7.60	9.70	[7.70]	7.70
3 Clothing & footwear	13.80	18.60	27.00	30.40	[40.40]	19.30
4 Housing (net)[1], fuel & power	40.40	53.00	39.20	36.00	66.00	44.10
5 Household goods & services	15.80	18.00	20.60	27.30	49.60	19.60
6 Health	1.40	1.10	2.30	[2.40]	[11.60]	2.10
7 Transport	14.60	30.50	43.50	52.40	76.10	28.20
8 Communication	8.40	11.00	14.20	13.80	15.70	10.60
9 Recreation & culture	27.00	35.40	56.00	73.90	152.20	43.00
10 Education	1.80	[1.60]	[6.60]	[1.50]	[105.60]	7.70
11 Restaurants & hotels	14.60	21.20	25.00	27.70	43.30	20.00
12 Miscellaneous goods & services	13.70	26.40	45.80	35.10	87.10	26.40
1–12 All expenditure groups	193.20	265.20	331.90	352.00	699.70	266.70
13 Other expenditure items	15.60	54.40	89.90	90.60	210.20	50.30
Total expenditure	**208.80**	**319.50**	**421.80**	**442.60**	**909.80**	**317.00**
Average weekly expenditure per person (£) **Total expenditure**	**74.40**	**120.80**	**159.40**	**204.30**	**351.60**	**118.00**

Note: The commodity and service categories are not comparable to those in publications before 2001–02.

1 Excluding mortgage interest payments, council tax and Northern Ireland rates.

Table **3.7** **Expenditure of one adult households with children by gross income quintile group, 2006**
based on weighted data and including children's expenditure

	Lowest twenty per cent	Second quintile group	Third quintile group	Fourth quintile group	Highest twenty per cent	All house-holds
Lower boundary of group (£ per week)		215	384	624	939	
Weighted number of households (thousands)	660	390	260	100	50	1,460
Total number of households in sample	210	130	90	30	10	460
Total number of persons in sample	530	360	240	70	40	1,240
Total number of adults in sample	210	130	90	30	10	460
Weighted average number of persons per household	2.6	2.8	2.8	2.4	2.8	2.7
Commodity or service	Average weekly household expenditure (£)					
1 Food & non-alcoholic drinks	33.00	39.40	46.40	42.10	[45.40]	38.20
2 Alcoholic drinks, tobacco & narcotics	6.90	7.70	9.60	[9.10]	[4.00]	7.70
3 Clothing & footwear	13.20	16.00	30.90	38.70	[27.00]	19.30
4 Housing (net)[1], fuel & power	39.30	53.10	39.90	51.20	[44.70]	44.10
5 Household goods & services	15.90	13.80	28.60	33.40	[39.20]	19.60
6 Health	1.50	1.30	2.20	[2.30]	[15.30]	2.10
7 Transport	14.30	30.60	38.30	60.40	[77.20]	28.20
8 Communication	7.20	12.20	14.00	15.10	[15.20]	10.60
9 Recreation & culture	25.00	38.20	51.20	123.30	[116.30]	43.00
10 Education	1.90	[1.70]	[5.50]	[6.90]	[150.70]	7.70
11 Restaurants & hotels	13.30	20.70	26.40	31.90	[46.20]	20.00
12 Miscellaneous goods & services	12.90	24.90	41.80	36.80	[115.60]	26.40
1–12 All expenditure groups	184.40	259.50	334.70	451.20	[696.80]	266.70
13 Other expenditure items	12.80	55.40	76.40	113.40	[247.60]	50.30
Total expenditure	**197.20**	**314.90**	**411.20**	**564.60**	**[944.40]**	**317.00**
Average weekly expenditure per person (£)						
Total expenditure	**76.60**	**111.70**	**144.40**	**231.70**	**[333.20]**	**118.00**

Note: The commodity and service categories are not comparable to those in publications before 2001–02.
1 Excluding mortgage interest payments, council tax and Northern Ireland rates.

Table **3.8E** **Expenditure of one man one woman non-retired households by gross equivalised income quintile group, 2006**

based on weighted data

	Lowest twenty per cent	Second quintile group	Third quintile group	Fourth quintile group	Highest twenty per cent	All house-holds
Lower boundary of group (£ per week)		240	387	577	841	
Weighted number of households (thousands)	400	510	860	1,370	1,900	5,050
Total number of households in sample	110	140	240	360	470	1,320
Total number of persons in sample	230	290	470	720	940	2,640
Total number of adults in sample	230	290	470	720	940	2,640
Weighted average number of persons per household	2.0	2.0	2.0	2.0	2.0	2.0
Commodity or service			Average weekly household expenditure (£)			
1 Food & non-alcoholic drinks	42.00	45.10	45.60	47.60	53.00	48.60
2 Alcoholic drinks, tobacco & narcotics	9.80	13.00	12.60	14.00	15.40	13.80
3 Clothing & footwear	11.20	13.40	20.00	22.10	37.40	25.80
4 Housing (net)[1], fuel & power	38.70	43.90	50.00	50.00	58.60	51.70
5 Household goods & services	18.90	33.80	24.90	35.90	62.10	42.40
6 Health	5.20	5.00	7.60	8.00	9.20	7.90
7 Transport	36.70	51.60	47.00	65.30	115.40	77.40
8 Communication	7.50	9.20	11.40	12.60	14.50	12.30
9 Recreation & culture	35.90	52.10	67.90	70.80	89.10	72.50
10 Education	[2.90]	[0.20]	[0.20]	4.30	8.50	4.60
11 Restaurants & hotels	23.00	23.70	35.80	43.60	74.30	50.20
12 Miscellaneous goods & services	21.50	34.20	28.90	36.50	56.30	41.20
1–12 All expenditure groups	253.20	325.30	352.00	410.70	593.80	448.50
13 Other expenditure items	33.40	76.00	61.00	83.60	164.60	105.50
Total expenditure	**286.60**	**401.30**	**413.00**	**494.20**	**758.40**	**554.00**
Average weekly expenditure per person (£) **Total expenditure**	**143.30**	**200.70**	**206.50**	**247.10**	**379.20**	**277.00**

Note: The commodity and service categories are not comparable to those in publications before 2001–02.

1 Excluding mortgage interest payments, council tax and Northern Ireland rates.

Table **3.8** **Expenditure of one man one woman non-retired households by gross income quintile group, 2006**
based on weighted data

	Lowest twenty per cent	Second quintile group	Third quintile group	Fourth quintile group	Highest twenty per cent	All house-holds
Lower boundary of group (£ per week)		215	384	624	939	
Weighted number of households (thousands)	300	590	1,130	1,500	1,530	5,050
Total number of households in sample	90	170	300	390	380	1,320
Total number of persons in sample	170	330	610	770	760	2,640
Total number of adults in sample	170	330	610	770	760	2,640
Weighted average number of persons per household	2.0	2.0	2.0	2.0	2.0	2.0
Commodity or service	Average weekly household expenditure (£)					
1 Food & non-alcoholic drinks	40.00	45.50	45.60	47.70	54.50	48.60
2 Alcoholic drinks, tobacco & narcotics	9.50	12.60	12.80	14.50	15.30	13.80
3 Clothing & footwear	8.90	14.30	18.30	24.00	40.90	25.80
4 Housing (net)[1], fuel & power	38.20	43.20	49.70	48.90	61.90	51.70
5 Household goods & services	14.20	33.60	27.40	37.60	67.00	42.40
6 Health	4.30	5.50	7.60	7.70	9.90	7.90
7 Transport	33.40	51.00	47.70	70.80	124.90	77.40
8 Communication	7.70	8.80	11.60	12.80	14.80	12.30
9 Recreation & culture	35.90	49.90	65.20	71.20	95.20	72.50
10 Education	[0.00]	[2.20]	[1.40]	3.20	10.40	4.60
11 Restaurants & hotels	18.10	26.30	35.90	44.80	81.70	50.20
12 Miscellaneous goods & services	17.70	34.40	28.80	39.30	59.50	41.20
1–12 All expenditure groups	228.00	327.40	352.00	422.40	636.10	448.50
13 Other expenditure items	30.00	71.40	61.70	89.80	181.50	105.50
Total expenditure	**258.00**	**398.80**	**413.70**	**512.20**	**817.60**	**554.00**
Average weekly expenditure per person (£)						
Total expenditure	**129.00**	**199.40**	**206.90**	**256.10**	**408.80**	**277.00**

Note: The commodity and service categories are not comparable to those in publications before 2001–02.
1 Excluding mortgage interest payments, council tax and Northern Ireland rates.

Table 3.9E Expenditure of one person retired households mainly dependent on state pensions[1] by gross equivalised income quintile group, 2006

based on weighted data

	Lowest twenty per cent	Second quintile group	Third quintile group	Fourth quintile group	Highest twenty per cent	All house- holds
Lower boundary of group (£ per week)		240	387	577	841	
Weighted number of households (thousands)	400	230	40	..	..	680
Total number of households in sample	110	60	..	..	..	190
Total number of persons in sample	110	60	..	..	..	190
Total number of adults in sample	110	60	..	..	..	190
Weighted average number of persons per household	1.0	1.0	1.0	1.0	0.0	1.0
Commodity or service	Average weekly household expenditure (£)					
1 Food & non-alcoholic drinks	22.00	21.70	[20.60]	[32.00]	–	21.90
2 Alcoholic drinks, tobacco & narcotics	1.70	3.00	[1.00]	[4.70]	–	2.20
3 Clothing & footwear	5.30	4.90	[8.80]	–	–	5.20
4 Housing (net)[2], fuel & power	28.60	28.70	[30.60]	[12.90]	–	28.50
5 Household goods & services	10.90	12.60	[17.20]	[4.10]	–	11.70
6 Health	1.70	1.30	[17.60]	[4.20]	–	2.40
7 Transport	8.00	6.60	[10.20]	[6.10]	–	7.60
8 Communication	4.30	4.50	[4.20]	[3.40]	–	4.40
9 Recreation & culture	12.70	21.90	[17.70]	[4.20]	–	16.00
10 Education	–	–	–	–	–	–
11 Restaurants & hotels	5.70	8.40	[7.70]	–	–	6.70
12 Miscellaneous goods & services	12.00	13.50	[10.40]	[13.30]	–	12.40
1–12 All expenditure groups	112.90	127.00	[146.10]	[84.90]	–	119.10
13 Other expenditure items	15.60	21.00	[48.00]	[1.50]	–	19.00
Total expenditure	**128.50**	**148.00**	**[194.00]**	**[86.30]**	**–**	**138.10**
Average weekly expenditure per person (£) **Total expenditure**	**128.50**	**148.00**	**[194.00]**	**[86.30]**	**–**	**138.10**

Note: The commodity and service categories are not comparable to those in publications before 2001–02.

1 Mainly dependent on state pensions and not economically active – see Appendix B.

2 Excluding mortgage interest payments, council tax and Northern Ireland rates.

Table **3.9** **Expenditure of one person retired households mainly dependent on state pensions[1]
by gross income quintile group, 2006**
based on weighted data

	Lowest twenty per cent	Second quintile group	Third quintile group	Fourth quintile group	Highest twenty per cent	All house- holds
Lower boundary of group (£ per week)		215	384	624	939	
Weighted number of households (thousands)	610	60	..	0	0	680
Total number of households in sample	170	20	..	0	0	190
Total number of persons in sample	170	20	..	0	0	190
Total number of adults in sample	170	20	..	0	0	190
Weighted average number of persons per household	1.0	1.0	1.0	0	0	1.0
Commodity or service	Average weekly household expenditure (£)					
1 Food & non-alcoholic drinks	21.60	[23.60]	[32.00]	–	–	21.90
2 Alcoholic drinks, tobacco & narcotics	2.10	[2.50]	[4.70]	–	–	2.20
3 Clothing & footwear	5.30	[5.80]	–	–	–	5.20
4 Housing (net)[2], fuel & power	29.10	[24.90]	[12.90]	–	–	28.50
5 Household goods & services	11.50	[14.00]	[4.10]	–	–	11.70
6 Health	1.50	[10.90]	[4.20]	–	–	2.40
7 Transport	7.40	[10.10]	[6.10]	–	–	7.60
8 Communication	4.30	[4.90]	[3.40]	–	–	4.40
9 Recreation & culture	15.80	[19.10]	[4.20]	–	–	16.00
10 Education	–	–	–	–	–	–
11 Restaurants & hotels	6.90	[5.30]	–	–	–	6.70
12 Miscellaneous goods & services	12.30	[13.60]	[13.30]	–	–	12.40
1–12 All expenditure groups	117.90	[134.90]	[84.90]	–	–	119.10
13 Other expenditure items	18.10	[29.90]	[1.50]	–	–	19.00
Total expenditure	**136.00**	**[164.80]**	**[86.30]**	**–**	**–**	**138.10**
Average weekly expenditure per person (£) **Total expenditure**	**136.00**	**[164.80]**	**[86.30]**	**–**	**–**	**138.10**

Note: The commodity and service categories are not comparable to those in publications before 2001–02.

1 Mainly dependent on state pensions and not economically active – see Appendix B.

2 Excluding mortgage interest payments, council tax and Northern Ireland rates.

Table **3.10E** **Expenditure of one man one woman retired households mainly dependent on state pensions[1]**
by gross equivalised income quintile group, 2006

based on weighted data

	Lowest twenty per cent	Second quintile group	Third quintile group	Fourth quintile group	Highest twenty per cent	All house-holds
Lower boundary of group (£ per week)		240	387	577	841	
Weighted number of households (thousands)	330	160	..	..	0	500
Total number of households in sample	100	50	..	..	0	150
Total number of persons in sample	190	100	..	..	0	290
Total number of adults in sample	190	100	..	..	0	290
Weighted average number of persons per household	2.0	2.0	2.0	2.0	0.0	2.0
Commodity or service			Average weekly household expenditure (£)			
1 Food & non-alcoholic drinks	41.60	41.60	[52.50]	[26.60]	–	41.70
2 Alcoholic drinks, tobacco & narcotics	6.00	10.50	[19.70]	–	–	7.60
3 Clothing & footwear	7.50	12.40	[10.50]	[14.00]	–	9.10
4 Housing (net)[2], fuel & power	37.30	33.90	[17.00]	[31.50]	–	35.90
5 Household goods & services	15.60	18.10	[1.40]	[4.10]	–	16.10
6 Health	3.10	3.40	–	[56.50]	–	3.50
7 Transport	25.10	40.20	[13.20]	[108.50]	–	30.20
8 Communication	6.20	5.90	[4.20]	[4.10]	–	6.10
9 Recreation & culture	32.60	42.80	[13.80]	[7.90]	–	35.40
10 Education	–	–	–	–	–	–
11 Restaurants & hotels	11.10	19.30	[11.50]	[35.00]	–	13.80
12 Miscellaneous goods & services	17.10	21.20	[6.80]	[38.40]	–	18.40
1–12 All expenditure groups	203.30	249.20	[150.50]	[326.60]	–	217.80
13 Other expenditure items	22.00	28.70	[9.90]	[23.50]	–	23.90
Total expenditure	**225.20**	**278.00**	**[160.40]**	**[350.10]**	**–**	**241.70**
Average weekly expenditure per person (£)						
Total expenditure	**112.60**	**139.00**	**[80.20]**	**[175.10]**	**–**	**120.90**

Note: The commodity and service categories are not comparable to those in publications before 2001–02.

1 Mainly dependent on state pensions and not economically active – see Appendix B.

2 Excluding mortgage interest payments, council tax and Northern Ireland rates.

Table **3.10** **Expenditure of one man one woman retired households mainly dependent on state pensions[1]**
by gross income quintile group, 2006
based on weighted data

	Lowest twenty per cent	Second quintile group	Third quintile group	Fourth quintile group	Highest twenty per cent	All house-holds
Lower boundary of group (£ per week)		215	384	624	939	
Weighted number of households (thousands)	230	250	10	0	0	500
Total number of households in sample	70	80	..	0	0	150
Total number of persons in sample	140	150	..	0	0	290
Total number of adults in sample	140	150	..	0	0	290
Weighted average number of persons per household	2.0	2.0	2.0	0	0	2.0
Commodity or service			Average weekly household expenditure (£)			
1 Food & non-alcoholic drinks	41.60	41.80	[42.10]	–	–	41.70
2 Alcoholic drinks, tobacco & narcotics	6.10	8.50	[16.90]	–	–	7.60
3 Clothing & footwear	8.50	9.70	[9.50]	–	–	9.10
4 Housing (net)[2], fuel & power	37.50	34.60	[32.30]	–	–	35.90
5 Household goods & services	12.40	20.30	[2.70]	–	–	16.10
6 Health	2.70	3.60	[15.50]	–	–	3.50
7 Transport	28.10	31.90	[34.90]	–	–	30.20
8 Communication	6.00	6.10	[6.40]	–	–	6.10
9 Recreation & culture	34.10	37.50	[18.60]	–	–	35.40
10 Education	–	–	–	–	–	–
11 Restaurants & hotels	11.30	16.10	[13.90]	–	–	13.80
12 Miscellaneous goods & services	17.90	18.90	[15.90]	–	–	18.40
1–12 All expenditure groups	206.10	228.90	[208.60]	–	–	217.80
13 Other expenditure items	22.20	25.90	[17.20]	–	–	23.90
Total expenditure	**228.30**	**254.80**	**[225.80]**	**–**	**–**	**241.70**
Average weekly expenditure per person (£)						
Total expenditure	**114.20**	**127.40**	**[112.90]**	**–**	**–**	**120.90**

Note: The commodity and service categories are not comparable to those in publications before 2001–02.
1 Mainly dependent on state pensions and not economically active – see Appendix B.
2 Excluding mortgage interest payments, council tax and Northern Ireland rates.

Table **3.11E** Expenditure of one man one woman retired households not mainly dependent on state pensions[1] by gross equivalised income quintile group, 2006

based on weighted data

	Lowest twenty per cent	Second quintile group	Third quintile group	Fourth quintile group	Highest twenty per cent	All house- holds
Lower boundary of group (£ per week)		240	387	577	841	
Weighted number of households (thousands)	360	800	510	260	150	2,080
Total number of households in sample	100	240	160	80	40	620
Total number of persons in sample	190	490	310	160	80	1,230
Total number of adults in sample	190	490	310	160	80	1,230
Weighted average number of persons per household	2.0	2.0	2.0	2.0	2.0	2.0
Commodity or service	Average weekly household expenditure (£)					
1 Food & non-alcoholic drinks	42.50	48.20	49.50	58.80	65.70	50.10
2 Alcoholic drinks, tobacco & narcotics	6.80	7.80	9.80	13.20	15.10	9.30
3 Clothing & footwear	7.60	12.50	16.20	27.80	29.10	15.70
4 Housing (net)[2], fuel & power	36.00	32.20	40.60	46.80	50.80	38.10
5 Household goods & services	19.30	22.80	24.00	47.60	31.00	26.20
6 Health	5.20	6.40	11.60	10.90	22.40	9.10
7 Transport	22.10	37.20	47.10	66.60	132.90	47.50
8 Communication	6.40	6.80	11.50	10.10	9.80	8.50
9 Recreation & culture	25.80	49.10	61.90	81.80	123.20	57.60
10 Education	–	[0.40]	–	[2.40]	[6.40]	[0.90]
11 Restaurants & hotels	10.70	20.70	26.10	60.70	45.50	27.10
12 Miscellaneous goods & services	17.90	23.80	29.00	35.80	84.30	29.80
1–12 All expenditure groups	200.40	267.80	327.30	462.40	616.20	319.90
13 Other expenditure items	28.00	31.20	48.60	63.20	84.40	42.70
Total expenditure	**228.40**	**299.10**	**375.90**	**525.50**	**700.60**	**362.60**
Average weekly expenditure per person (£) **Total expenditure**	**114.20**	**149.50**	**187.90**	**262.80**	**350.30**	**181.30**

Note: The commodity and service categories are not comparable to those in publications before 2001–02.

1 Mainly dependent on state pension and not economically active – see Appendix B.

2 Excluding mortgage interest payments, council tax and Northern Ireland Rates.

Table **3.11** **Expenditure of one man one woman retired households not mainly dependent on state pensions[1] by gross income quintile group, 2006**
based on weighted data

Commodity or service	Lowest twenty per cent	Second quintile group	Third quintile group	Fourth quintile group	Highest twenty per cent	All house-holds
Lower boundary of group (£ per week)		215	384	624	939	
Weighted number of households (thousands)	160	990	570	250	110	2,080
Total number of households in sample	40	290	180	70	30	620
Total number of persons in sample	90	590	350	150	60	1,230
Total number of adults in sample	90	590	350	150	60	1,230
Weighted average number of persons per household	2.0	2.0	2.0	2.0	2.0	2.0
Commodity or service			Average weekly household expenditure (£)			
1 Food & non-alcoholic drinks	40.50	47.40	49.70	60.00	68.90	50.10
2 Alcoholic drinks, tobacco & narcotics	6.70	7.70	9.30	14.80	15.60	9.30
3 Clothing & footwear	6.00	11.90	16.20	28.80	[31.00]	15.70
4 Housing (net)[2], fuel & power	30.10	33.70	42.10	44.30	53.90	38.10
5 Household goods & services	23.30	21.30	28.50	36.90	38.60	26.20
6 Health	8.30	5.60	10.70	15.70	19.60	9.10
7 Transport	14.80	35.60	46.30	76.70	144.50	47.50
8 Communication	7.20	6.60	11.20	10.40	9.60	8.50
9 Recreation & culture	26.60	44.50	60.60	82.00	151.50	57.60
10 Education	–	[0.30]	–	[5.50]	[1.60]	[0.90]
11 Restaurants & hotels	8.30	19.00	28.40	60.00	45.40	27.10
12 Miscellaneous goods & services	19.00	22.50	28.30	44.50	88.10	29.80
1–12 All expenditure groups	191.00	256.10	331.20	479.70	668.20	319.90
13 Other expenditure items	33.70	29.80	47.20	72.60	81.90	42.70
Total expenditure	**224.60**	**285.90**	**378.40**	**552.20**	**750.00**	**362.60**
Average weekly expenditure per person (£) **Total expenditure**	**112.30**	**143.00**	**189.20**	**276.10**	**375.00**	**181.30**

Note: The commodity and service categories are not comparable to those in publications before 2001–02.
1 Mainly dependent on state pension and not economically active – see appendix B.
2 Excluding mortgage interest payments, council tax and Northern Ireland rates.

Table **3.12E** Income and source of income
by gross equivalised income quintile group, 2006
based on weighted data

Gross equivalised income quintile group	Weighted number of house-holds	Number of house-holds in the sample	Weekly household income		Source of income					
			Dispo-sable	Gross	Wages and salaries	Self employ-ment	Invest-ments	Annuities and pensions[1]	Social security benefits[2]	Other sources
	(000s)	Number	£	£	Percentage of gross weekly household income					
Lowest twenty per cent	4,960	1,370	164	169	15	4	2	5	70	4
Second quintile group	4,960	1,400	302	330	40	6	2	11	40	2
Third quintile group	4,960	1,360	456	538	64	7	3	10	15	1
Fourth quintile group	4,950	1,290	630	783	75	8	3	8	5	1
Highest twenty per cent	4,960	1,230	1,052	1,389	78	11	4	5	2	0

1 Other than social security benefits.
2 Excluding housing benefit and council tax benefit (rates rebate in Northern Ireland) – see Appendix B.

Table **3.12** Income and source of income
by gross income quintile group, 2006
based on weighted data

Gross income quintile group	Weighted number of house-holds	Number of house-holds in the sample	Weekly household income		Source of income					
			Dispo-sable	Gross	Wages and salaries	Self employ-ment	Invest-ments	Annuities and pensions[1]	Social security benefits[2]	Other sources
	(000s)	Number	£	£	Percentage of gross weekly household income					
Lowest twenty per cent	4,950	1,360	138	140	6	3	2	9	77	2
Second quintile group	4,960	1,390	270	295	32	4	4	16	43	2
Third quintile group	4,960	1,370	427	501	61	7	3	11	17	2
Fourth quintile group	4,960	1,300	624	770	75	8	3	7	7	1
Highest twenty per cent	4,950	1,230	1,147	1,503	79	11	4	4	2	1

1 Other than social security benefits.
2 Excluding housing benefit and council tax benefit (rates rebate in Northern Ireland) – see Appendix B.

Trends in household expenditure over time

Chapter 4

Trends in household expenditure over time

This chapter presents household expenditure data over time using both the Family Expenditure Survey (FES) and the Classification Of Individual COnsumption by Purpose (COICOP) classifications. COICOP is the internationally agreed standard classification for reporting household consumption expenditure.

Prior to the introduction of the EFS in 2001–02, expenditure data were collected via the Family Expenditure Survey (FES) and were classified using the FES classification. Time series data based on the FES classification are presented in Tables 4.1 and 4.2. These data have been retained and published alongside the COICOP time series, as they illustrate family spending patterns since 1986, whereas COICOP data are only available from 2001–02. The COICOP data are presented in Tables 4.3 and 4.4.

It should be noted that time series data based on the FES classification from 2001–02 (Tables 4.1 and 4.2) have been constructed by mapping EFS COICOP data onto the FES classification. This has been done to preserve a time series from 1986 to 2006. These data are presented solely for the purpose of historical comparisons. In addition, from 2001–02, the 'all expenditure groups' totals in Table 4.1 may not equal the sum of the component commodities or services, as the mapping process is not exact. It should also be stressed that it is not possible to directly compare the FES time series data with the COICOP data presented in this chapter and the other chapters and appendices in the publication. This is due to the differences in the definitions of the classification headings (for example, 'Motoring' in the FES classification includes vehicle insurance, whereas the 'Transport' heading under COICOP excludes this expenditure item).

COICOP time series data in this publication are not directly comparable with UK National Accounts household expenditure data, which are published in *Consumer Trends* (www.statistics. gov.uk/statbase/Product.asp?vlnk=242). The *Family Spending* time series tables present average weekly household expenditure at 2006 prices. In contrast, *Consumer Trends* tables present total household final consumption expenditure at current prices and also as chained volume measures. National Accounts figures draw on a number of sources in addition to the EFS (please refer to Appendix B of *Consumer Trends* for details) and may be more appropriate for deriving long term trends on expenditure.

Table 4.1 Household expenditure based on the FES classification, 1986 to 2006 at 2006 prices[1]

	1986	1988	1990	1992	1994 –95	1995[2] –96	1995[3] –96	1996 –97	1997 –98
Weighted number of households (thousands)							24,130	24,310	24,560
Total number of households in sample	7,180	7,270	7,050	7,420	6,850	6,800	6,800	6,420	6,410
Total number of persons	18,330	18,280	17,440	18,170	16,620	16,590	16,590	15,730	15,430
Average number of persons per household	2.6	2.5	2.5	2.5	2.4	2.4	2.4	2.5	2.4
Commodity or service	Average weekly household expenditure (£)								
1 Housing (Net)	60.60	66.40	69.80	67.70	63.30	63.70	64.20	63.10	64.20
2 Fuel and power	21.10	19.40	17.50	18.60	17.70	17.10	16.90	17.10	15.70
3 Food and non-alcoholic drinks	70.80	70.90	70.40	68.20	68.70	69.80	71.40	72.30	71.20
4 Alcoholic drink	16.60	17.00	15.70	15.80	16.80	15.10	16.20	16.90	17.70
5 Tobacco	9.20	8.20	7.60	7.70	7.60	7.70	7.80	8.00	7.90
6 Clothing and footwear	27.30	26.90	25.20	23.40	23.30	22.60	23.50	24.10	25.30
7 Household goods	27.70	27.80	31.40	31.30	30.90	31.00	31.50	34.30	33.60
8 Household services	17.20	18.20	19.30	19.20	20.60	20.00	20.00	20.90	22.10
9 Personal goods and services	13.10	15.10	14.90	14.60	14.70	15.20	15.50	15.20	15.80
10 Motoring	43.00	46.90	53.20	51.00	49.30	48.80	50.40	54.30	59.00
11 Fares and other travel costs	8.50	9.00	9.70	10.30	9.10	8.10	8.80	9.90	10.70
12 Leisure goods	17.30	17.90	17.70	19.10	18.90	18.10	19.10	20.40	21.70
13 Leisure services	26.70	33.60	33.80	39.40	42.50	42.30	43.20	45.10	49.30
14 Miscellaneous	1.50	1.40	2.20	2.50	3.10	3.10	1.60	1.30	1.30
1–14 All expenditure groups	360.70	378.80	388.30	388.90	386.50	382.60	390.10	403.00	415.40
Average weekly expenditure per person (£) **All expenditure groups**	**138.70**	**151.50**	**155.30**	**155.50**	**161.10**	**159.40**	**163.00**	**161.20**	**173.10**
	Average weekly household income (£)[5]								
Gross income (£)	448	497	498	491	503	503	514	521	536
Disposable income (£)	364	403	405	401	407	405	413	425	436

Note: The commodity and service categories are not comparable to the COICOP categories used in Tables 4.3 and 4.4.

    Figures are based on FES data between 1984 and 2000–01 and EFS data thereafter.

1 Figures have been deflated to 2006 prices using the RPI all items index.

2 From 1984 to this version of 1995–96, figures shown are based on unweighted, adult only data.

3 From this version of 1995–96, figures are shown based on weighted data, including children's expenditure. Weighting is based on the population figures from the 1991 and 2001 Censuses.

4 From 2001–02 onwards, commodities and services are based on COICOP codes broadly mapped to FES.

5 Does not include imputed income from owner-occupied and rent-free households.

Table **4.1** Household expenditure based on the FES classification, 1986 to 2006 at 2006 prices[1] (cont.)

	1998 −99	1999 −2000	2000 −01	2001[4] −02	2002 −03	2003 −04	2004 −05	2005 −06	2006
Weighted number of households (thousands)	24,660	25,330	25,030	24,450	24,350	24,670	24,430	24,800	24,790
Total number of households in sample	6,630	7,100	6,640	7,470	6,930	7,050	6,800	6,790	6,650
Total number of persons	16,220	16,790	15,930	18,120	16,590	16,970	16,260	16,090	15,850
Weighted average number of persons per household	2.4	2.3	2.4	2.4	2.4	2.4	2.4	2.4	2.4
Commodity or service	Average weekly household expenditure (£)								
1 Housing (Net)	69.20	67.90	73.90	75.10	74.50	75.90	80.80	83.00	85.40
2 Fuel and power	14.10	13.50	13.70	13.40	13.10	13.00	13.20	14.20	15.90
3 Food and non-alcoholic drinks	71.30	71.00	71.60	70.50	71.80	70.50	70.90	69.70	70.40
4 Alcoholic drink	16.90	18.20	17.40	16.30	16.50	16.00	15.60	15.20	14.90
5 Tobacco	7.00	7.10	7.00	6.20	6.10	5.90	5.20	4.70	4.60
6 Clothing and footwear	26.30	25.00	25.40	25.50	24.50	24.30	24.70	23.00	22.90
7 Household goods	35.90	36.60	37.70	37.60	37.80	38.10	37.50	34.40	34.50
8 Household services	22.90	22.50	25.40	26.90	26.10	27.00	27.70	27.80	26.60
9 Personal goods and services	16.10	16.50	17.00	17.00	17.00	17.50	16.90	17.40	17.60
10 Motoring	62.60	62.60	63.70	66.00	68.80	67.70	65.90	65.50	62.40
11 Fares and other travel costs	10.00	10.90	10.90	10.60	10.80	10.50	10.00	11.40	11.10
12 Leisure goods	21.60	22.10	22.80	22.40	22.90	23.30	22.60	19.90	19.60
13 Leisure services	50.70	52.30	58.50	59.10	59.80	59.70	62.70	64.60	66.300
14 Miscellaneous	1.50	1.70	0.80	2.10	2.20	2.10	2.10	2.20	2.10
1–14 All expenditure groups	426.20	428.10	446.10	448.80	451.80	451.50	455.90	452.90	454.30
Average weekly expenditure per person (£) **All expenditure groups**	**177.60**	**186.10**	**189.50**	**189.70**	**189.70**	**191.60**	**191.00**	**191.00**	**190.50**
	Average weekly household income (£)[5]								
Gross income (£)	553	572	581	616	616	619	633	632	642
Disposable income (£)	449	466	473	504	506	504	515	513	521

Note: The commodity and service categories are not comparable to the COICOP categories used in Tables 4.3 and 4.4.
    Figures are based on FES data between 1984 and 2000–01 and EFS data thereafter.
1 Figures have been deflated to 2006 prices using the RPI all items index.
2 From 1984 to this version of 1995–96, figures shown are based on unweighted, adult only data.
3 From this version of 1995–96, figures are shown based on weighted data, including children's expenditure. Weighting is based on the population figures from the 1991 and 2001 Censuses.
4 From 2001–02 onwards, commodities and services are based on COICOP codes broadly mapped to FES.
5 Does not include imputed income from owner-occupied and rent-free households.

Table 4.2 Household expenditure as a percentage of total expenditure, 1984 to 2006 based on the FES classification at 2006 prices[1]

	1986	1988	1990	1992	1994 -95	1995[2] -96	1995[3] -96	1996 -97	1997 -98
Weighted number of households (thousands)							24,130	24,310	24,560
Total number of households in sample	7,180	7,270	7,050	7,420	6,850	6,800	6,800	6,420	6,410
Total number of persons	18,330	18,280	17,440	18,170	16,620	16,590	16,590	15,730	15,430
Average number of persons per household	2.6	2.5	2.5	2.5	2.4	2.4	2.4	2.5	2.4
Commodity or service	Percentage of total expenditure								
1 Housing (Net)	17	18	18	17	16	17	16	16	15
2 Fuel and power	6	5	4	5	5	4	4	4	4
3 Food and non-alcoholic drinks	20	19	18	18	18	18	18	18	17
4 Alcoholic drink	5	4	4	4	4	4	4	4	4
5 Tobacco	3	2	2	2	2	2	2	2	2
6 Clothing and footwear	8	7	6	6	6	6	6	6	6
7 Household goods	8	7	8	8	8	8	8	9	8
8 Household services	5	5	5	5	5	5	5	5	5
9 Personal goods and services	4	4	4	4	4	4	4	4	4
10 Motoring	12	12	14	13	13	13	13	13	14
11 Fares and other travel costs	2	2	3	3	2	2	2	2	3
12 Leisure goods	5	5	5	5	5	5	5	5	5
13 Leisure services	7	9	9	10	11	11	11	11	12
14 Miscellaneous	0	0	1	1	1	1	0	0	0
1–14 All expenditure groups	100	100	100	100	100	100	100	100	100

Note: The commodity and service categories are not comparable to the COICOP categories used in Tables 4.3 and 4.4.

   Figures are based on FES data between 1984 and 2000–01 and EFS data thereafter

1 Figures have been deflated to 2006 prices using the RPI all items index.

2 From 1984 to this version of 1995–96, figures shown are based on unweighted, adult only data.

3 From this version of 1995–96, figures are shown based on weighted data, including children's expenditure. Weighting is based on the population figures from the 1991 and 2001 Censuses.

Table 4.2 **Household expenditure as a percentage of total expenditure, 1984 to 2006 based on the FES classification at 2006 prices[1] (cont.)**

		1998 –1999	1999 –2000	2000 –01	2001[4] –02	2002 –03	2003 –04	2004 –05	2005 –06	2006
Weighted number of households (thousands)		24,660	25,330	25,030	24,450	24,350	24,670	24,430	24,800	24,790
Total number of households in sample		6,630	7,100	6,640	7,470	6,930	7,050	6,800	6,790	6,650
Total number of persons		16,220	16,790	15,930	18,120	16,590	16,970	16,260	16,090	15,850
Average number of persons per household		2.4	2.3	2.4	2.4	2.4	2.4	2.4	2.4	2.4
Commodity or service		Percentage of total expenditure								
1	Housing (Net)	16	16	17	17	16	17	18	18	19
2	Fuel and power	3	3	3	3	3	3	3	3	3
3	Food and non-alcoholic drinks	17	17	16	16	16	16	16	15	15
4	Alcoholic drink	4	4	4	4	4	4	3	3	3
5	Tobacco	2	2	2	1	1	1	1	1	1
6	Clothing and footwear	6	6	6	6	5	5	5	5	5
7	Household goods	8	9	8	8	8	8	8	8	8
8	Household services	5	5	6	6	6	6	6	6	6
9	Personal goods and services	4	4	4	4	4	4	4	4	4
10	Motoring	15	15	14	15	15	15	14	14	14
11	Fares and other travel costs	2	3	2	2	2	2	2	3	2
12	Leisure goods	5	5	5	5	5	5	5	4	4
13	Leisure services	12	12	13	13	13	13	14	14	15
14	Miscellaneous	0	0	0	0	0	0	0	0	0
1–14	All expenditure groups	100	100	100	100	100	100	100	100	100

Note: The commodity and service categories are not comparable to the COICOP categories used in Tables 4.3 and 4.4.
     Figures are based on FES data between 1984 and 2000–01 and EFS data thereafter.
1 Figures have been deflated to 2006 prices using the RPI all items index.
2 From 1984 to this version of 1995–96, figures shown are based on unweighted, adult only data.
3 From this version of 1995–96, figures are shown based on weighted data, including children's expenditure. Weighting is based on the population figures from the 1991 and 2001 Censuses.
4 From 2001–02 onwards, commodities and services are based on COICOP codes broadly mapped to FES.

Table 4.3 Household expenditure based on COICOP classification, 2001–02 to 2006 at 2006 prices[1]
based on weighted data and including children's expenditure

	2001–02	2002–03	2003–04	2004–05	2005–06	2006
Weighted number of households (thousands)	24,450	24,350	24,670	24,430	24,800	24,790
Total number of households in sample	7,470	6,930	7,050	6,800	6,790	6,650
Total number of persons in sample	18,120	16,590	16,970	16,260	16,090	15,850
Total number of adults in sample	13,450	12,450	12,620	12,260	12,170	12,000
Weighted average number of persons per household	2.4	2.4	2.4	2.4	2.4	2.4
Commodity or service	Average weekly household expenditure (£)					
1 Food & non-alcoholic drinks	47.50	47.70	47.30	47.10	46.50	46.90
2 Alcoholic drinks, tobacco & narcotics	12.80	12.70	12.70	11.90	11.10	11.10
3 Clothing & footwear	25.90	24.90	24.70	25.10	23.30	23.20
4 Housing (net)[2], fuel & power	40.60	41.20	42.30	42.60	45.30	47.60
5 Household goods & services	34.60	33.70	33.90	33.20	30.80	30.30
6 Health	5.20	5.40	5.50	5.20	5.60	5.90
7 Transport	65.20	66.10	65.90	62.70	63.40	62.00
8 Communication	11.70	11.80	12.20	12.30	12.20	11.70
9 Recreation & culture	61.10	62.90	62.20	62.10	59.00	58.50
10 Education	6.30	5.80	5.70	6.90	6.70	7.20
11 Restaurants & hotels	37.40	39.60	37.90	38.00	37.70	37.90
12 Miscellaneous goods & services	34.80	36.90	36.50	36.70	35.50	36.00
1–12 All expenditure groups	383.10	388.70	386.90	384.00	377.10	378.30
13 Other expenditure items	66.70	64.60	67.20	73.40	77.70	77.60
Total expenditure	**449.80**	**453.40**	**454.00**	**457.50**	**454.90**	**455.90**
Average weekly expenditure per person (£) **Total expenditure**	**189.30**	**190.30**	**192.60**	**191.70**	**192.90**	**192.80**
	Average weekly household income (£)					
Gross income (£)	616	616	619	633	632	642
Disposable income (£)	504	506	504	515	513	521

Note: The commodity and service categories are not comparable to the FES categories used in Tables 4.1 and 4.2.

1 Figures have been deflated to 2006 prices using the RPI all items index.

2 Excluding mortgage interest payments, council tax and Northern Ireland rates.

Table 4.4 Household expenditure as a percentage of total expenditure based on COICOP classification, 2001–02 to 2006 at 2006 prices[1]

based on weighted data and including children's expenditure

		2001–02	2002–03	2003–04	2004–05	2005–06	2006
Weighted number of households (thousands)		24,450	24,350	24,670	24,430	24,800	24,790
Total number of households in sample		7,470	6,930	7,050	6,800	6,790	6,650
Total number of persons in sample		18,120	16,590	16,970	16,260	16,090	15,850
Total number of adults in sample		13,450	12,450	12,620	12,260	12,170	12,000
Weighted average number of persons per household		2.4	2.4	2.4	2.4	2.4	2.4
Commodity or service		Percentage of total expenditure					
1	Food & non-alcoholic drinks	11	11	10	10	10	10
2	Alcoholic drinks, tobacco & narcotics	3	3	3	3	2	2
3	Clothing & footwear	6	5	5	5	5	5
4	Housing(net)[2], fuel & power	9	9	9	9	10	10
5	Household goods & services	8	7	7	7	7	7
6	Health	1	1	1	1	1	1
7	Transport	14	15	15	14	14	14
8	Communication	3	3	3	3	3	3
9	Recreation & culture	14	14	14	14	13	13
10	Education	1	1	1	1	1	2
11	Restaurants & hotels	8	9	8	8	8	8
12	Miscellaneous goods & services	8	8	8	8	8	8
1–12	All expenditure groups	85	86	85	84	83	83
13	Other expenditure items	15	14	15	16	17	17
Total expenditure		100	100	100	100	100	100

Note: The commodity and service categories are not comparable to the FES categories used in Tables 4.1 and 4.2.

1. Figures have been deflated to 2006 prices using the RPI all items index.

2. Excluding mortgage interest payments, council tax and Northern Ireland rates.

Appendix A

Table **A1** Components of household expenditure, 2006

based on weighted data and including children's expenditure

Commodity or service			Average weekly expenditure all house-holds (£)	Total weekly expenditure (£ million)	Recording house-holds in sample	Percentage standard error (full method)
Total number of households					6,650	
Commodity or service						
1	Food & non-alcoholic drinks		46.90	1,162	6,600	*0.8*
	1.1	Food	42.80	1,061	6,600	*0.8*
	1.1.1	Bread, rice and cereals	4.30	105	6,470	*0.9*
		1.1.1.1 Rice	0.30	6	1,450	*5.2*
		1.1.1.2 Bread	2.30	56	6,290	*0.9*
		1.1.1.3 Other breads and cereals	1.70	43	5,300	*1.4*
	1.1.2	Pasta products	0.30	8	2,650	*2.6*
	1.1.3	Buns, cakes, biscuits etc.	2.90	72	5,880	*1.3*
		1.1.3.1 Buns, crispbread and biscuits	1.60	39	5,350	*1.4*
		1.1.3.2 Cakes and puddings	1.30	33	4,380	*1.9*
	1.1.4	Pastry (savoury)	0.70	16	2,360	*2.2*
	1.1.5	Beef (fresh, chilled or frozen)	1.60	40	3,240	*2.5*
	1.1.6	Pork (fresh, chilled or frozen)	0.60	14	1,740	*3.3*
	1.1.7	Lamb (fresh, chilled or frozen)	0.70	16	1,300	*3.7*
	1.1.8	Poultry (fresh, chilled or frozen)	1.70	42	3,410	*2.0*
	1.1.9	Bacon and ham	0.90	21	3,080	*2.1*
	1.1.10	Other meats and meat preparations	4.90	122	5,930	*1.3*
		1.1.10.1 Sausages	0.60	15	2,900	*2.2*
		1.1.10.2 Offal, pate etc.	0.10	2	930	*4.0*
		1.1.10.3 Other preserved or processed meat and meat preparations	4.20	104	5,720	*1.4*
		1.1.10.4 Other fresh, chilled or frozen edible meat	0.00	0	30	*26.0*
	1.1.11	Fish and fish products	2.20	55	4,330	*2.0*
		1.1.11.1 Fish (fresh, chilled or frozen)	0.80	19	1,740	*3.7*
		1.1.11.2 Seafood, dried, smoked or salted fish	0.50	12	1,400	*3.9*
		1.1.11.3 Other preserved or processed fish and seafood	0.90	23	3,400	*2.0*
	1.1.12	Milk	2.30	56	6,180	*1.2*
		1.1.12.1 Whole milk	0.60	16	2,190	*3.1*
		1.1.12.2 Low fat milk	1.50	37	5,020	*1.5*
		1.1.12.3 Preserved milk	0.20	4	560	*6.6*
	1.1.13	Cheese and curd	1.50	38	4,750	*1.8*
	1.1.14	Eggs	0.40	11	3,750	*1.7*
	1.1.15	Other milk products	1.70	41	5,010	*1.5*
		1.1.15.1 Other milk products	0.70	18	3,630	*2.0*
		1.1.15.2 Yoghurt	0.90	23	3,690	*1.8*
	1.1.16	Butter	0.30	7	2,080	*2.5*
	1.1.17	Margarine, other vegetable fats and peanut butter	0.40	11	3,230	*2.0*
	1.1.18	Cooking oils and fats	0.20	6	1,510	*4.6*
		1.1.18.1 Olive oil	0.10	3	520	*6.9*
		1.1.18.2 Edible oils and other edible animal fats	0.10	3	1,080	*4.8*
	1.1.19	Fresh fruit	2.90	72	5,650	*1.6*
		1.1.19.1 Citrus fruits (fresh)	0.40	11	2,940	*2.3*
		1.1.19.2 Bananas (fresh)	0.50	12	4,290	*1.6*
		1.1.19.3 Apples (fresh)	0.50	13	3,500	*1.9*
		1.1.19.4 Pears (fresh)	0.20	4	1,470	*3.2*
		1.1.19.5 Stone fruits (fresh)	0.40	11	1,890	*3.6*
		1.1.19.6 Berries (fresh)	0.90	21	3,150	*2.4*
	1.1.20	Other fresh, chilled or frozen fruits	0.30	8	1,770	*4.0*
	1.1.21	Dried fruit and nuts	0.50	12	2,230	*3.1*
	1.1.22	Preserved fruit and fruit based products	0.10	4	1,440	*3.5*
	1.1.23	Fresh vegetables	3.60	88	5,990	*1.3*
		1.1.23.1 Leaf and stem vegetables (fresh or chilled)	0.80	19	4,050	*2.0*
		1.1.23.2 Cabbages (fresh or chilled)	0.40	10	3,350	*2.0*
		1.1.23.3 Vegetables grown for their fruit (fresh, chilled or frozen)	1.30	31	4,930	*1.5*
		1.1.23.4 Root crops, non-starchy bulbs and mushrooms (fresh, chilled or frozen)	1.20	29	5,330	*1.6*

Note: The commodity and service categories are not comparable with those in publications before 2001–02.
The numbering is sequential, it does not use actual COICOP codes.

Table **A1** Components of household expenditure, 2006 (cont.)

based on weighted data and including children's expenditure

			Average weekly expenditure all house-holds (£)	Total weekly expenditure (£ million)	Recording house-holds in sample	Percentage standard error (full method)
Commodity or service						
1	Food & non-alcoholic drinks (continued)					
	1.1.24	Dried vegetables and other preserved or processed vegetables	1.10	27	4,950	1.7
	1.1.25	Potatoes	0.70	17	4,290	1.5
	1.1.26	Other tubers and products of tuber vegetables	1.20	29	4,490	1.4
	1.1.27	Sugar and sugar products	0.30	7	2,480	2.4
		1.1.27.1 Sugar	0.20	5	2,180	2.4
		1.1.27.2 Other sugar products	0.10	2	540	5.5
	1.1.28	Jams, marmalades	0.20	6	1,920	2.8
	1.1.29	Chocolate	1.40	34	3,900	3.0
	1.1.30	Confectionery products	0.50	13	3,130	2.3
	1.1.31	Edible ices and ice cream	0.50	12	2,230	2.4
	1.1.32	Other food products	2.00	50	5,410	2.1
		1.1.32.1 Sauces, condiments	1.00	25	4,260	1.7
		1.1.32.2 Baker's yeast, dessert preparations, soups	0.80	19	3,700	3.9
		1.1.32.3 Salt, spices, culinary herbs and other food products	0.20	06	1,640	8.2
	1.2	Non-alcoholic drinks	4.10	101	6,090	1.1
	1.2.1	Coffee	0.50	12	2,000	2.6
	1.2.2	Tea	0.40	11	2,470	2.2
	1.2.3	Cocoa and powdered chocolate	0.10	2	670	1.1
	1.2.4	Fruit and vegetable juices (inc. fruit squash)	1.20	29	4,120	21.3
	1.2.5	Mineral or spring waters	0.30	7	1,580	0.9
	1.2.6	Soft drinks (inc. fizzy and ready to drink fruit drinks)	1.60	39	4,430	10.4
2	Alcoholic drink, tobacco & narcotics		11.10	276	4,210	1.9
	2.1	Alcoholic drinks	6.50	160	3,490	2.4
	2.1.1	Spirits and liqueurs (brought home)	1.30	31	900	4.5
	2.1.2	Wines, fortified wines (brought home)	3.30	82	2,380	3.3
		2.1.2.1 Wine from grape or other fruit (brought home)	2.90	71	2,190	3.3
		2.1.2.2 Fortified wine (brought home)	0.20	4	250	8.4
		2.1.2.3 Champagne and sparkling wines (brought home)	0.30	7	240	13.7
	2.1.3	Beer, lager, ciders and perry (brought home)	1.80	45	1,780	3.4
		2.1.3.1 Beer and lager (brought home)	1.60	40	1,570	3.7
		2.1.3.2 Ciders and perry (brought home)	0.20	5	390	6.5
	2.1.4	Alcopops (brought home)	0.10	2	170	10.6
	2.2	Tobacco and narcotics	4.60	115	1,630	3.2
	2.2.1	Cigarettes	4.20	103	1,500	3.3
	2.2.2	Cigars, other tobacco products and narcotics	0.50	12	380	7.6
		2.2.2.1 Cigars	0.10	2	60	20.7
		2.2.2.2 Other tobacco	0.40	10	320	7.0
		2.2.2.3 Narcotics	[0.00]	[1]	–	69.2
3	Clothing & footwear		23.20	576	4,610	2.4
	3.1	Clothing	18.90	468	4,370	2.5
	3.1.1	Men's outer garments	4.60	113	1,440	4.4
	3.1.2	Men's under garments	0.40	10	560	6.5
	3.1.3	Women's outer garments	8.50	210	2,560	3.4
	3.1.4	Women's under garments	1.40	34	1,370	4.9
	3.1.5	Boys' outer garments (5–15)	0.80	19	510	6.5
	3.1.6	Girls' outer garments (5–15)	1.00	26	610	5.8
	3.1.7	Infants' outer garments (under 5)	0.70	16	540	6.1
	3.1.8	Children's under garments (under 16)	0.40	10	640	5.7

Note: The commodity and service categories are not comparable with those in publications before 2001–02.

The numbering is sequential, it does not use actual COICOP codes.

Table **A1** Components of household expenditure, 2006 (cont.)

based on weighted data and including children's expenditure

Commodity or service			Average weekly expenditure all house-holds (£)	Total weekly expenditure (£ million)	Recording house-holds in sample	Percentage standard error (full method)
3	Clothing & footwear (continued)					
	3.1.9	Accessories	0.70	18	1,010	6.8
		3.1.9.1 Men's accessories	0.20	6	350	8.1
		3.1.9.2 Women's accessories	0.40	9	480	10.2
		3.1.9.3 Children's accessories	0.10	2	290	9.0
		3.1.9.4 Protective head gear (crash helmets)	0.00	1	20	30.1
	3.1.10	Haberdashery, clothing materials and clothing hire	0.20	6	330	11.1
	3.1.11	Dry cleaners, laundry and dyeing	0.30	7	260	9.0
		3.1.11.1 Dry cleaners and dyeing	0.20	6	200	10.3
		3.1.11.2 Laundry, launderettes	0.10	1	70	16.9
3.2	Footwear		4.30	108	1,870	3.5
	3.2.1	Footwear for men	1.30	33	530	6.1
	3.2.2	Footwear for women	2.20	55	1,110	4.4
	3.2.3	Footwear for children (5 to 15 years) and infants (under 5)	0.70	18	530	5.8
	3.2.4	Repair and hire of footwear	0.10	2	80	18.3
4	Housing (net)[1], fuel & power		47.60	1,179	6,620	1.8
4.1	Actual rentals for housing		27.90	692	1,790	2.8
	4.1.1	Gross rent	27.80	690	1,780	2.8
	4.1.2	*less* housing benefit, rebates and allowances received	11.20	277	1,210	3.5
	4.1.3	Net rent	16.70	413	1,310	4.0
	4.1.4	Second dwelling – rent	[0.10]	[2]	–	48.3
4.2	Maintenance and repair of dwelling		8.00	198	2,990	5.2
	4.2.1	Central heating repairs	1.20	30	1,760	5.6
	4.2.2	House maintenance etc.	5.00	123	1,330	7.7
	4.2.3	Paint, wallpaper, timber	1.00	25	570	7.1
	4.2.4	Equipment hire, small materials	0.80	19	510	12.6
4.3	Water supply and miscellaneous services relating to the dwelling		6.90	172	5,630	2.3
	4.3.1	Water charges	5.70	140	5,420	0.7
	4.3.2	Other regular housing payments including service charge for rent	1.20	29	770	12.6
	4.3.3	Refuse collection, including skip hire	[0.10]	[3]	20	27.0
4.4	Electricity, gas and other fuels		15.90	394	6,260	0.9
	4.4.1	Electricity	7.50	187	6,070	1.0
	4.4.2	Gas	7.20	177	4,910	1.2
	4.4.3	Other fuels	1.20	29	620	7.3
		4.4.3.1 Coal and coke	0.20	5	140	20.0
		4.4.3.2 Oil for central heating	0.90	23	460	7.1
		4.4.3.3 Paraffin, wood, peat, hot water etc.	0.00	1	70	22.7
5	Household goods & services		30.30	750	6,130	2.8
5.1	Furniture and furnishings, carpets and other floor coverings		16.50	410	2,580	4.1
	5.1.1	Furniture and furnishings	12.50	309	2,150	4.6
		5.1.1.1 Furniture	11.30	280	1,480	4.9
		5.1.1.2 Fancy, decorative goods	0.90	22	900	10.0
		5.1.1.3 Garden furniture	0.30	7	70	22.5
	5.1.2	Floor coverings	4.10	101	920	6.0
		5.1.2.1 Soft floor coverings	3.60	90	880	6.2
		5.1.2.2 Hard floor coverings	0.40	11	60	23.3
5.2	Household textiles		1.90	47	1,170	7.2
	5.2.1	Bedroom textiles, including duvets and pillows	0.80	19	430	8.3
	5.2.2	Other household textiles, including cushions, towels, curtains	1.10	28	880	9.8

Note: The commodity and service categories are not comparable with those in publications before 2001–02.

The numbering is sequential, it does not use actual COICOP codes.

1 Excluding mortgage interest payments, council tax and NI rates.

Table A1 Components of household expenditure, 2006 (cont.)
based on weighted data and including children's expenditure

Commodity or service			Average weekly expenditure all house-holds (£)	Total weekly expenditure (£ million)	Recording house-holds in sample	Percentage standard error (full method)
5	Household goods & services (continued)					
5.3	Household appliances		3.00	75	610	9.1
	5.3.1	Gas cookers	[0.10]	[2]	–	73.6
	5.3.2	Electric cookers, combined gas/electric cookers	0.30	6	40	32.9
	5.3.3	Clothes washing machines and drying machines	0.40	10	80	19.7
	5.3.4	Refrigerators, freezers and fridge-freezers	0.60	14	60	25.8
	5.3.5	Other major electrical appliances, dishwashers, micro-waves vacuum cleaners, heaters etc.	1.00	24	170	16.2
	5.3.6	Fire extinguisher, water softener, safes etc	[0.00]	[0]	–	74.9
	5.3.7	Small electric household appliances, excluding hairdryers	0.40	11	250	9.6
	5.3.8	Repairs to gas and electrical appliances and spare parts	0.30	7	80	17.5
	5.3.9	Rental/hire of major household appliances	[0.00]	[0]	–	49.3
5.4	Glassware, tableware and household utensils		1.60	39	1,960	4.9
	5.4.1	Glassware, china, pottery, cutlery and silverware	0.50	14	860	6.8
	5.4.2	Kitchen and domestic utensils	0.60	15	1,030	7.9
	5.4.3	Repair of glassware, tableware and household utensils	[0.00]	[0]	–	62.6
	5.4.4	Storage and other durable household articles	0.40	10	710	5.8
5.5	Tools and equipment for house and garden		2.10	51	2,200	4.2
	5.5.1	Electrical tools	0.20	5	80	18.6
	5.5.2	Garden tools, equipment and accessories e.g. lawn mowers etc.	0.30	8	330	9.7
	5.5.3	Small tools	0.30	8	450	8.3
	5.5.4	Door, electrical and other fittings	0.60	14	500	8.8
	5.5.5	Electrical consumables	0.60	15	1,480	5.0
5.6	Goods and services for routine household maintenance		5.20	129	5,650	2.9
	5.6.1	Cleaning materials	2.30	57	4,820	2.1
		5.6.1.1 Detergents, washing-up liquid, washing powder	1.10	27	3,400	1.9
		5.6.1.2 Disinfectants, polishes, other cleaning materials etc.	1.20	30	3,990	3.3
	5.6.2	Household goods and hardware	1.20	29	4,100	2.6
		5.6.2.1 Kitchen disposables	0.70	16	3,340	2.9
		5.6.2.2 Household hardware and appliances, matches	0.30	6	920	7.6
		5.6.2.3 Kitchen gloves, cloths etc.	0.10	3	1,210	4.0
		5.6.2.4 Pins, needles, tape measures, nails, nuts and bolts etc.	0.10	3	460	7.3
	5.6.3	Domestic services, carpet cleaning	1.70	43	1,090	7.7
		5.6.3.1 Domestic services, including cleaners, gardeners, au pairs	1.20	29	390	9.1
		5.6.3.2 Carpet cleaning, ironing service, window cleaner	0.50	13	810	8.9
		5.6.3.3 Hire/repair of household furniture and furnishings	[0.00]	[1]	–	58.6
6	Health		5.90	145	3,480	8.4
6.1	Medical products, appliances and equipment		3.10	77	3,280	5.8
	6.1.1	Medicines, prescriptions and healthcare products	1.70	42	3,110	6.8
		6.1.1.1 NHS prescription charges and payments	0.30	6	280	9.6
		6.1.1.2 Medicines and medical goods (not NHS)	1.20	30	2,870	3.2
		6.1.1.3 Other medical products (e.g. plasters, condoms, hot water bottle etc.)	0.10	2	360	9.1
		6.1.1.4 Non-optical appliances and equipment (e.g. wheelchairs, batteries for hearing aids, shoe build-up)	0.10	4	30	74.2
	6.1.2	Spectacles, lenses, accessories and repairs	1.40	35	380	9.7
		6.1.2.1 Purchase of spectacles, lenses, prescription sunglasses	1.40	34	310	10.0
		6.1.2.2 Accessories/repairs to spectacles/lenses	0.10	1	70	19.0
6.2	Hospital services		2.70	68	520	16.8
	6.2.1	Out patient services	2.70	66	510	17.2
		6.2.1.1 NHS medical, optical, dental and medical auxiliary services	0.90	22	250	10.1
		6.2.1.2 Private medical, optical, dental and medical auxiliary services	1.80	43	280	25.3
		6.2.1.3 Other services	[0.00]	[0]	–	66.9
	6.2.2	In-patient hospital services	[0.10]	[2]	–	88.2

Note: The commodity and service categories are not comparable with those in publications before 2001–02.
   The numbering is sequential, it does not use actual COICOP codes.

Table A1 Components of household expenditure, 2006 (cont.)

based on weighted data and including children's expenditure

Commodity or service			Average weekly expenditure all house-holds (£)	Total weekly expenditure (£ million)	Recording house-holds in sample	Percentage standard error (full method)
7	Transport		62.00	1,538	5,710	2.2
7.1	Purchase of vehicles		23.40	581	1,720	4.6
	7.1.1	Purchase of new cars and vans	8.30	206	440	9.2
		7.1.1.1 Outright purchases	4.90	122	150	10.5
		7.1.1.2 Loan/Hire Purchase of new car/van	3.40	84	310	13.0
	7.1.2	Purchase of second hand cars or vans	14.50	360	1,290	5.1
		7.1.2.1 Outright purchases	10.20	252	800	6.3
		7.1.2.2 Loan/Hire Purchase of second hand car/van	4.30	107	590	8.2
	7.1.3	Purchase of motorcycles	0.60	15	90	14.9
		7.1.3.1 Outright purchases of new or second hand motorcycles	0.20	4	30	26.9
		7.1.3.2 Loan/Hire Purchase of new or second hand motorcycles	0.10	3	20	29.8
		7.1.3.3 Purchase of bicycles and other vehicles	0.30	8	40	21.2
7.2	Operation of personal transport		28.60	709	4,880	1.5
	7.2.1	Spares and accessories	2.10	51	540	7.4
		7.2.1.1 Car/van accessories and fittings	0.30	9	150	23.1
		7.2.1.2 Car/van spare parts	1.50	37	320	8.5
		7.2.1.3 Motorcycle accessories and spare parts	0.10	2	20	30.9
		7.2.1.4 Bicycle accessories, repairs and other costs	0.20	4	100	26.5
	7.2.2	Petrol, diesel and other motor oils	18.20	452	4,340	1.5
		7.2.2.1 Petrol	14.50	360	3,790	1.7
		7.2.2.2 Diesel oil	3.70	91	1,000	4.0
		7.2.2.3 Other motor oils	0.10	1	80	15.0
	7.2.3	Repairs and servicing	5.90	147	2,080	3.4
		7.2.3.1 Car or van repairs, servicing and other work	5.80	145	2,060	3.4
		7.2.3.2 Motorcycle repairs and servicing	0.10	2	30	27.9
	7.2.4	Other motoring costs	2.40	59	2,560	4.1
		7.2.4.1 Motoring organisation subscription (e.g. AA and RAC)	0.50	11	1,080	6.7
		7.2.4.2 Garage rent, other costs (excluding fines), car washing etc.	0.70	16	410	9.8
		7.2.4.3 Parking fees, tolls, and permits (excluding motoring fines)	0.80	20	1,500	4.8
		7.2.4.4 Driving lessons	0.40	9	90	12.5
		7.2.4.5 Anti-freeze, battery water, cleaning materials	0.10	3	300	12.5
7.3	Transport services		10.00	247	2,670	4.7
	7.3.1	Rail and tube fares	2.20	54	740	6.5
		7.3.1.1 Season tickets	0.80	19	150	12.6
		7.3.1.2 Other than season tickets	1.40	35	650	6.3
	7.3.2	Bus and coach fares	1.30	33	1,250	4.8
		7.3.2.1 Season tickets	0.40	10	210	8.4
		7.3.2.2 Other than season tickets	0.90	23	1,150	4.9
	7.3.3	Combined fares	1.00	25	220	10.8
		7.3.3.1 Combined fares other than season tickets	0.20	5	110	13.4
		7.3.3.2 Combined fares season tickets	0.80	19	140	12.4
	7.3.4	Other travel and transport	5.50	136	1,500	7.6
		7.3.4.1 Air fares (within UK)	0.20	4	30	25.7
		7.3.4.2 Air fares (international)	2.00	51	70	19.3
		7.3.4.3 School travel	0.00	0	30	35.1
		7.3.4.4 Taxis and hired cars with drivers	1.30	32	1,000	4.6
		7.3.4.5 Other personal travel and transport services	0.20	5	230	9.8
		7.3.4.6 Hire of self-drive cars, vans, bicycles	0.20	4	30	28.0
		7.3.4.7 Car leasing	1.40	35	190	9.7
		7.3.4.8 Water travel, ferries and season tickets	0.20	5	80	25.7

Note: The commodity and service categories are not comparable with those in publications before 2001–02.

The numbering is sequential, it does not use actual COICOP codes.

Table **A1** Components of household expenditure, 2006 (cont.)
based on weighted data and including children's expenditure

Commodity or service			Average weekly expenditure all house- holds (£)	Total weekly expenditure (£ million)	Recording house- holds in sample	Percentage standard error (full method)
8	Communication		11.70	291	6,370	1.5
8.1	Postal services		0.50	12	1,320	5.2
8.2	Telephone and telefax equipment		0.70	18	200	11.3
	8.2.1	Telephone purchase	0.20	4	60	18.9
	8.2.2	Mobile phone purchase	0.50	13	140	13.7
	8.2.3	Answering machine, fax machine, modem purchase	[0.00]	[1]	–	52.2
8.3	Telephone and telefax services		10.50	261	6,330	1.3
	8.3.1	Telephone account	5.70	140	5,970	1.7
	8.3.2	Telephone coin and other payments	0.10	2	130	15.9
	8.3.3	Mobile phone account	3.50	86	2,120	2.4
	8.3.4	Mobile phone – other payments	1.30	32	1,090	4.0
9	Recreation & culture		58.50	1,449	6,580	2.0
9.1	Audio-visual, photographic and information processing equipment		7.10	177	2,070	6.0
	9.1.1	Audio equipment and accessories, CD players	1.90	48	990	8.2
	9.1.1.1	Audio equipment, CD players including in car	1.00	24	160	15.6
	9.1.1.2	Audio accessories e.g. tapes, headphones etc.	0.90	23	870	4.7
	9.1.2	TV, video and computers	4.60	114	1,380	8.5
	9.1.2.1	Purchase of TV and digital decoder	1.40	34	160	22.2
	9.1.2.2	Satellite dish purchase and installation	[0.00]	[0]	–	49.1
	9.1.2.3	Cable TV connection	[0.00]	[0]	–	85.3
	9.1.2.4	Video recorder	[0.00]	[0]	–	46.7
	9.1.2.5	DVD player/recorder	0.10	3	40	22.1
	9.1.2.6	Blank, pre-recorded video cassettes, DVDs	1.10	28	880	4.6
	9.1.2.7	Personal computers, printers and calculators	1.70	43	400	13.2
	9.1.2.8	Spare parts for TV, video, audio	0.10	3	90	18.6
	9.1.2.9	Repair of audio-visual, photographic and information processing	0.10	2	40	21.2
	9.1.3	Photographic, cine and optical equipment	0.60	16	220	15.5
	9.1.3.1	Photographic and cine equipment	0.60	15	160	16.6
	9.1.3.2	Camera films	0.00	1	60	15.3
	9.1.3.3	Optical instruments, binoculars, telescopes, microscopes	[0.00]	[0]	20	32.9
9.2	Other major durables for recreation and culture		1.70	41	150	24.3
	9.2.1	Purchase of boats, trailers and horses	[0.40]	[9]	20	62.4
	9.2.2	Purchase of caravans, mobile homes (including decoration)	0.40	9	20	37.9
	9.2.3	Accessories for boats, horses, caravans and motor caravans	0.10	3	30	48.1
	9.2.4	Musical instruments (purchase and hire)	0.50	13	60	55.4
	9.2.5	Major durables for indoor recreation	[0.00]	[0]	–	59.6
	9.2.6	Maintenance and repair of other major durables	0.10	3	30	29.0
	9.2.7	Purchase of motor caravan (new and second-hand) – outright purchase	[0.20]	[4]	–	56.0
	9.2.8	Purchase of motor caravan (new and second-hand) – loan/HP	–	–	0	–
9.3	Other recreational items and equipment, gardens and pets		10.30	254	4,600	2.7
	9.3.1	Games, toys and hobbies	2.00	49	1,740	3.9
	9.3.2	Computer software and games	1.10	27	370	9.5
	9.3.2.1	Computer software and game cartridges	0.70	18	340	8.7
	9.3.2.2	Computer games consoles	0.30	8	50	21.1
	9.3.3	Equipment for sport, camping and open-air recreation	1.20	29	610	8.9
	9.3.4	Horticultural goods, garden equipment and plants etc.	2.60	64	2,410	4.1
	9.3.4.1	BBQ and swings	0.10	2	50	35.6
	9.3.4.2	Plants, flowers, seeds, fertilisers, insecticides	2.30	57	2,320	4.0
	9.3.4.3	Garden decorative	0.10	3	90	24.2
	9.3.4.4	Artificial flowers, pot pourri	0.10	1	110	15.1
	9.3.5	Pets and pet food	3.50	86	2,470	5.4
	9.3.5.1	Pet food	1.70	41	2,320	2.9
	9.3.5.2	Pet purchase and accessories	0.90	23	710	15.0
	9.3.5.3	Veterinary and other services for pets identified separately	0.90	22	200	12.4

Note: The commodity and service categories are not comparable with those in publications before 2001–02.
The numbering is sequential, it does not use actual COICOP codes.

Table **A1** Components of household expenditure, 2006 (cont.)
based on weighted data and including children's expenditure

Commodity or service				Average weekly expenditure all house-holds (£)	Total weekly expenditure (£ million)	Recording house-holds in sample	Percentage standard error (full method)
9	Recreation & culture (continued)						
	9.4	Recreational and cultural services		18.70	463	6,290	2.6
		9.4.1	Sports admissions, subscriptions, leisure class fees and equipment hire	5.80	143	2,590	5.8
			9.4.1.1 Spectator sports: admission charges	0.50	12	190	13.4
			9.4.1.2 Participant sports (excluding subscriptions)	1.20	30	1,170	5.4
			9.4.1.3 Subscriptions to sports and social clubs	1.90	47	1,080	14.7
			9.4.1.4 Leisure class fees	2.10	51	1,090	5.7
			9.4.1.5 Hire of equipment for sport and open air recreation	0.10	2	40	41.6
		9.4.2	Cinema, theatre and museums etc.	2.00	50	1,070	5.9
			9.4.2.1 Cinemas	0.50	13	580	5.8
			9.4.2.2 Live entertainment: theatre, concerts, shows	1.10	27	350	9.3
			9.4.2.3 Museums, zoological gardens, theme parks, houses and gardens	0.40	11	270	10.7
		9.4.3	TV, video, satellite rental, cable subscriptions, TV licences and Internet	5.80	145	5,870	1.1
			9.4.3.1 TV licences	2.10	52	5,610	0.4
			9.4.3.2 Satellite subscriptions	2.20	55	1,850	2.4
			9.4.3.3 Rent for TV/Satellite/VCR	0.20	6	240	8.1
			9.4.3.4 Cable subscriptions	0.80	20	750	4.7
			9.4.3.5 TV slot meter payments	0.10	1	30	24.2
			9.4.3.6 Video, cassette and CD hire	0.10	3	240	8.6
			9.4.3.7 Internet subscription fees	0.30	9	420	7.3
		9.4.4	Miscellaneous entertainments	1.10	27	1,600	5.3
			9.4.4.1 Admissions to clubs, dances, discos, bingo	0.60	14	780	8.0
			9.4.4.2 Social events and gatherings	0.20	5	340	10.1
			9.4.4.3 Subscriptions for leisure activities and other subscriptions	0.30	8	700	7.9
		9.4.5	Development of film, deposit for film development, passport photos, holiday and school photos	0.40	10	380	12.5
		9.4.6	Gambling payments	3.60	89	3,380	9.1
			9.4.6.1 Football pools stakes	0.00	1	60	18.0
			9.4.6.2 Bingo stakes excluding admission	0.40	10	260	9.6
			9.4.6.3 Lottery	2.10	53	3,010	2.6
			9.4.6.4 Bookmaker, tote, other betting stakes	1.00	25	890	31.0
	9.5	Newspapers, books and stationery		6.60	164	5,960	2.0
		9.5.1	Books	1.60	40	1,590	5.0
		9.5.2	Stationery, diaries, address books, art materials	0.80	19	1,740	4.6
		9.5.3	Cards, calendars, posters and other printed matter	1.20	30	3,080	2.7
		9.5.4	Newspapers	2.00	50	4,490	2.2
		9.5.5	Magazines and periodicals	1.00	26	3,350	2.9
	9.6	Package holidays		14.10	349	1,120	4.6
		9.6.1	Package holidays – UK	0.90	23	210	9.5
		9.6.2	Package holidays – abroad	13.20	326	950	4.8
10	Education			7.20	179	580	11.3
	10.1	Education fees		6.90	170	420	11.8
		10.1.1	Nursery and primary education	1.20	30	80	25.3
		10.1.2	Secondary education	2.30	58	70	19.4
		10.1.3	Sixth form college/college education	0.20	5	40	28.3
		10.1.4	University education	2.20	56	150	14.1
		10.1.5	Other education	0.90	21	110	21.2
	10.2	Payments for school trips, other ad-hoc expenditure		0.40	9	190	15.0
		10.2.1	Nursery and primary education	0.20	4	110	17.8
		10.2.2	Secondary education	0.20	4	60	27.9
		10.2.3	Sixth form college/college education	[0.00]	[0]	–	49.5
		10.2.4	University education	[0.00]	[1]	10	41.3
		10.2.5	Other education	[0.00]	[0]	–	39.8

Note: The commodity and service categories are not comparable with those in publications before 2001–02.
The numbering is sequential, it does not use actual COICOP codes.

Table A1 Components of household expenditure, 2006 (cont.)

based on weighted data and including children's expenditure

				Average weekly expenditure all house-holds (£)	Total weekly expenditure (£ million)	Recording house-holds in sample	Percentage standard error (full method)
Commodity or service							
11	Restaurants & hotels			37.90	939	5,910	2.1
	11.1	Catering services		31.90	790	5,860	2.1
		11.1.1	Restaurant and café meals	12.80	316	4,750	2.3
		11.1.2	Alcoholic drinks (away from home)	8.40	208	3,140	2.8
		11.1.3	Take away meals eaten at home	3.90	96	3,010	2.1
		11.1.4	Other take-away and snack food	4.20	105	3,950	2.4
			11.1.4.1 Hot and cold food	2.90	71	3,400	3.0
			11.1.4.2 Confectionery	0.40	9	2,120	2.5
			11.1.4.3 Ice cream	0.10	4	740	6.0
			11.1.4.4 Soft drinks	0.90	21	2,670	2.5
		11.1.5	Contract catering (food)	0.70	18	40	51.2
		11.1.6	Canteens	1.90	47	2,100	3.5
			11.1.6.1 School meals	0.60	14	760	5.5
			11.1.6.2 Meals bought and eaten at the workplace	1.30	33	1,620	4.3
	11.2	Accommodation services		6.00	149	1,150	4.9
		11.2.1	Holiday in the UK	2.60	64	730	5.6
		11.2.2	Holiday abroad	3.40	85	490	7.2
		11.2.3	Room hire	[0.00]	[1]	20	34.6
12	Miscellaneous goods and services			36.00	893	6,510	1.9
	12.1	Personal care		9.80	244	5,790	1.9
		12.1.1	Hairdressing, beauty treatment	3.20	80	1,720	3.3
		12.1.2	Toilet paper	0.70	18	3,200	1.9
		12.1.3	Toiletries and soap	2.00	50	4,540	1.9
			12.1.3.1 Toiletries (disposable including tampons, lipsyl, toothpaste etc.)	1.20	29	3,880	2.0
			12.1.3.2 Bar of soap, liquid soap, shower gel etc.	0.30	8	1,830	3.9
			12.1.3.3 Toilet requisites (durable including razors, hairbrushes, toothbrushes etc.)	0.50	13	1,610	3.5
		12.1.4	Baby toiletries and accessories (disposable)	0.60	15	1,010	4.6
		12.1.5	Hair products, cosmetics and electrical appliances for personal care	3.20	80	3,620	3.1
			12.1.5.1 Hair products	0.80	19	2,220	3.0
			12.1.5.2 Cosmetics and related accessories	2.20	56	2,680	3.9
			12.1.5.3 Electrical appliances for personal care, including hairdryers, shavers etc.	0.20	6	130	14.2
	12.2	Personal effects		3.10	78	1,850	6.1
		12.2.1	Jewellery, clocks and watches and other personal effects	1.90	46	1,330	8.2
		12.2.2	Leather and travel goods (excluding baby items)	0.90	22	680	10.7
		12.2.3	Sunglasses (non-prescription)	0.10	2	110	16.6
		12.2.4	Baby equipment (excluding prams and pushchairs)	0.10	3	60	21.8
		12.2.5	Prams, pram accessories and pushchairs	0.10	2	30	28.2
		12.2.6	Repairs to personal goods	0.10	2	40	29.6
	12.3	Social protection		2.60	65	330	10.8
		12.3.1	Residential homes	[0.20]	[5]	–	56.7
		12.3.2	Home help	0.30	7	50	26.2
		12.3.3	Nursery, crèche, playschools	0.50	13	100	19.7
		12.3.4	Child care payments	1.60	41	200	12.5

Note: The commodity and service categories are not comparable with those in publications before 2001–02.

The numbering is sequential, it does not use actual COICOP codes.

Table A1 Components of household expenditure, 2006 (cont.)
based on weighted data and including children's expenditure

			Average weekly expenditure all house- holds (£)	Total weekly expenditure (£ million)	Recording house- holds in sample	Percentage standard error (full method)
Commodity or service						
12	Miscellaneous goods and services (continued)					
	12.4	Insurance	15.10	373	5,900	1.5
		12.4.1 Household insurances	5.10	127	5,330	1.4
		12.4.1.1 Structure insurance	2.50	62	4,290	1.6
		12.4.1.2 Contents insurance	2.50	63	5,120	1.6
		12.4.1.3 Insurance for household appliances	0.10	2	100	22.8
		12.4.2 Medical insurance premiums	1.80	44	840	6.3
		12.4.3 Vehicle insurance including boat insurance	8.00	197	4,880	1.5
		12.4.3.1 Vehicle insurance	7.90	197	4,880	1.5
		12.4.3.2 Boat insurance (not home)	[0.00]	[1]	–	84.7
		12.4.4 Non-package holiday, other travel insurance	0.20	4	50	28.2
	12.5	Other services	5.40	133	2,360	8.3
		12.5.1 Moving house	3.10	78	530	7.7
		12.5.1.1 Moving and storage of furniture	0.30	8	220	10.5
		12.5.1.2 Property transaction – purchase and sale	1.50	36	150	10.8
		12.5.1.3 Property transaction – sale only	0.60	15	70	18.0
		12.5.1.4 Property transaction – purchase only	0.60	14	170	12.1
		12.5.1.5 Property transaction – other payments	0.20	5	100	14.5
		12.5.2 Bank, building society, post office, credit card charges	0.40	9	1,030	5.6
		12.5.2.1 Bank and building society charges	0.30	7	820	5.8
		12.5.2.2 Bank and Post Office counter charges	[0.00]	[0]	20	33.4
		12.5.2.3 Annual standing charge for credit cards	0.00	1	250	15.5
		12.5.2.4 Commission travellers' cheques and currency	[0.00]	[0]	10	61.8
		12.5.3 Other services and professional fees	1.90	46	1290	19.5
		12.5.3.1 Other professional fees including court fines	0.40	9	50	25.3
		12.5.3.2 Legal fees	0.40	11	30	48.7
		12.5.3.3 Funeral expenses	[0.40]	[9]	–	73.4
		12.5.3.4 TU and professional organisations	0.60	14	1040	5.3
		12.5.3.5 Other payments for services e.g. photocopying	0.10	3	240	26.7
1–12 All expenditure groups			**378.30**	**9,377**	**6,650**	**1.1**
13	Other expenditure items		77.60	1,923	6,240	3.4
	13.1	Housing: mortgage interest payments, council tax etc.	52.00	1,288	5,750	1.4
		13.1.1 Mortgage interest payments	32.60	807	2,620	2.0
		13.1.2 Mortgage protection premiums	1.80	44	1,370	3.6
		13.1.3 Council tax, domestic rates	17.20	427	5,690	0.8
		13.1.4 Council tax, mortgage (second dwelling)	0.40	9	30	23.3
	13.2	Licences, fines and transfers	2.90	73	4,800	1.9
		13.2.1 Stamp duty, licences and fines (excluding motoring fines)	0.30	7	120	17.0
		13.2.2 Motoring fines	[0.00]	[1]	10	31.7
		13.2.3 Motor vehicle road taxation payments less refunds	2.60	66	4,770	1.2
	13.3	Holiday spending	12.10	301	370	19.9
		13.3.1 Money spent abroad	12.10	300	360	20.0
		13.3.2 Duty free goods bought in UK	[0.00]	[1]	–	59.1

Note: The commodity and service categories are not comparable with those in publications before 2001–02.
The numbering is sequential, it does not use actual COICOP codes.

Table A1 Components of household expenditure, 2006 (cont.)

based on weighted data and including children's expenditure

Commodity or service			Average weekly expenditure all house-holds (£)	Total weekly expenditure (£ million)	Recording house-holds in sample	Percentage standard error (full method)
13	**Other expenditure items (continued)**					
13.4	Money transfers and credit		10.50	261	3,760	5.9
	13.4.1	Money, cash gifts given to children	0.10	2	140	17.2
		13.4.1.1 Money given to children for specific purposes	0.10	2	130	17.4
		13.4.1.2 Cash gifts to children (no specific purpose)	[0.00]	[0]	–	79.4
	13.4.2	Cash gifts and donations	8.60	214	3,050	7.0
		13.4.2.1 Money/presents given to those outside the household	3.40	83	1,290	7.3
		13.4.2.2 Charitable donations and subscriptions	2.10	51	2,050	5.6
		13.4.2.3 Money sent abroad	1.50	38	360	31.0
		13.4.2.4 Maintenance allowance expenditure	1.70	41	170	10.0
	13.4.3	Club instalment payments (child) and interest on credit cards	1.80	45	1,340	5.4
		13.4.3.1 Club instalment payment	[0.00]	[0]	–	103.6
		13.4.3.2 Interest on credit cards	1.80	45	1,340	5.4
Total expenditure			**455.90**	**11,300**	**6,650**	**1.2**
14	**Other items recorded**					
14.1	Life assurance, contributions to pension funds		21.70	539	3,680	3.9
	14.1.1	Life assurance premiums eg mortgage endowment policies	5.80	145	2,580	3.6
	14.1.2	Contributions to pension and superannuation funds etc.	10.60	263	1,990	2.7
	14.1.3	Personal pensions	5.30	131	890	13.8
14.2	Other insurance including Friendly Societies		1.30	31	1,640	4.0
14.3	Income tax, payments less refunds		91.00	2,255	5,240	2.8
	14.3.1	Income tax paid by employees under PAYE	70.10	1,737	3,550	2.3
	14.3.2	Income tax paid direct eg by retired or unoccupied persons	2.00	49	230	17.8
	14.3.3	Income tax paid direct by self-employed	6.00	149	300	10.6
	14.3.4	Income tax deducted at source from income under covenant from investments or from annuities and pensions	10.00	248	3,320	3.8
	14.3.5	Income tax on bonus earnings	3.80	94	1,050	24.4
	14.3.6	Income tax refunds under PAYE	0.20	4	60	29.3
	14.3.7	Income tax refunds other than PAYE	0.70	18	380	10.3
14.4	National insurance contribution		25.40	629	3,490	1.4
	14.4.1	NI contributions paid by employees	25.30	626	3,450	1.4
	14.4.2	NI contributions paid by non-employees	0.10	3	70	21.8
14.5	Purchase or alteration of dwellings (contracted out), mortgages		51.70	1,282	2,830	9.0
	14.5.1	Outright purchase of houses, flats etc. including deposits	[5.40]	[134]	20	64.3
	14.5.2	Capital repayment of mortgage	17.60	437	2,070	2.9
	14.5.3	Central heating installation	1.00	25	140	10.9
	14.5.4	DIY improvements: Double glazing, kitchen units, sheds etc.	1.20	30	110	29.9
	14.5.5	Home improvements – contracted out	19.70	487	1,090	7.4
	14.5.6	Bathroom fittings	0.50	12	100	30.5
	14.5.7	Purchase of materials for capital improvements	0.80	19	70	38.0
	14.5.8	Purchase of second dwelling	5.50	137	60	45.7
14.6	Savings and investments		6.30	156	1,130	9.2
	14.6.1	Savings, investments (excluding AVCs)	5.30	131	830	10.8
	14.6.2	Additional Voluntary Contributions	0.80	19	140	12.3
	14.6.3	Food stamps, other food related expenditure	0.20	5	280	9.9
14.7	Pay off loan to clear other debt		2.60	65	360	7.2
14.8	Windfall receipts from gambling etc.		2.20	53	700	19.4

Note: The commodity and service categories are not comparable with those in publications before 2001–02.
The numbering is sequential, it does not use actual COICOP codes.

Table **A2** **Expenditure on alcoholic drink by place of purchase, 2006**
based on weighted data including children's expenditure

			Average weekly expenditure all households (£)	Total weekly expenditure (£ million)	Recording households in sample
By type of premises					
11	Bought and consumed on licenced premises:				
	11.1.2	Alcoholic drinks (away from home)	8.40	208	3,140
		11.1.2.1 Spirits and liqueurs (away from home)	1.10	26	920
		11.1.2.2 Wine from grape or other fruit (away from home)	1.40	34	1,230
		11.1.2.3 Fortified wine (away from home)	0.00	1	40
		11.1.2.4 Champagne and sparkling wines (away from home)	0.10	3	110
		11.1.2.5 Ciders and perry (away from home)	0.30	7	340
		11.1.2.6 Beer and lager (away from home)	4.70	116	2,480
		11.1.2.7 Alcopops (away from home)	0.20	5	220
		11.1.2.8 Round of drinks (away from home)	0.70	17	280
2	Bought at off-licences (including large supermarket chains):				
	2.1	Alcoholic drinks	6.50	160	3,490
	2.1.1	Spirits and liqueurs (brought home)	1.30	31	900
	2.1.2	Wines, fortified wines (brought home)	3.30	82	2,380
		2.1.2.1 Wine from grape or other fruit (brought home)	2.90	71	2,190
		2.1.2.2 Fortified wine (brought home)	0.20	4	250
		2.1.2.3 Champagne and sparkling wines (brought home)	0.30	7	240
	2.1.3	Beer, lager, ciders and perry (brought home)	1.80	45	1,780
		2.1.3.1 Beer and lager (brought home)	1.60	40	1,570
		2.1.3.2 Ciders and perry (brought home)	0.20	5	390
	2.1.4	Alcopops (brought home)	0.10	2	170
2A	Bought from large supermarket chains:				
	2.1A	Alcoholic drinks	4.20	103	2,760
	2.1.1A	Spirits and liqueurs (brought home)	0.90	22	690
	2.1.2A	Wines, fortified wines (brought home)	2.20	53	1,930
		2.1.2.1A Wine from grape or other fruit (brought home)	1.80	46	1,760
		2.1.2.2A Fortified wine (brought home)	0.10	3	200
		2.1.2.3A Champagne and sparkling wines (brought home)	0.20	5	190
	2.1.3A	Beer, lager, ciders and perry (brought home)	1.10	27	1,240
		2.1.3.1A Beer and lager (brought home)	1.00	24	1,080
		2.1.3.2A Ciders and perry (brought home)	0.10	3	270
	2.1.4A	Alcopops (brought home)	0.00	1	110
2B	Bought from other off-licence outlets:				
	2.1B	Alcoholic drinks	2.30	57	1,550
	2.1.1B	Spirits and liqueurs (brought home)	0.40	9	290
	2.1.2B	Wines, fortified wines (brought home)	1.20	29	890
		2.1.2.1B Wine from grape or other fruit (brought home)	1.00	26	830
		2.1.2.2B Fortified wine (brought home)	0.00	1	60
		2.1.2.3B Champagne and sparkling wines (brought home)	0.10	2	50
	2.1.3B	Beer, lager, ciders and perry (brought home)	0.70	18	800
		2.1.3.1B Beer and lager (brought home)	0.60	16	700
		2.1.3.2B Ciders and perry (brought home)	0.10	2	150
	2.1.4B	Alcopops (brought home)	0.00	1	70

Note: The commodity and service categories are not comparable with those in publications before 2001–02.
      The numbering is sequential, it does not use actual COICOP codes.

Table A3 Expenditure on food and non-alcoholic drinks by place of purchase, 2006

based on weighted data and including children's expenditure

			Large supermarket chains			Other outlets		
			Average weekly expenditure all house-holds (£)	Total weekly expenditure (£ million)	Recording house-holds in sample	Average weekly expenditure all house-holds (£)	Total weekly expenditure (£ million)	Recording house-holds in sample
1	Food and non-alcoholic drinks		33.40	828	6,110	13.50	334	6,130
1.1	Food		30.50	755	6,100	12.40	306	6,080
1.1.1	Bread, rice and cereals		3.00	75	5,720	1.20	30	3,900
	1.1.1.1	Rice	0.20	4	1,150	0.10	2	350
	1.1.1.2	Bread	1.50	38	5,390	0.70	18	3,510
	1.1.1.3	Other breads and cereals	1.40	34	4,500	0.40	10	1,820
1.1.2	Pasta products		0.30	6	2,260	0.10	1	560
1.1.3	Buns, cakes, biscuits etc.		2.20	53	5,110	0.70	18	2,920
	1.1.3.1	Buns, crispbread and biscuits	1.20	30	4,560	0.40	9	2,210
	1.1.3.2	Cakes and puddings	1.00	24	3,550	0.40	9	1,770
1.1.4	Pastry (savoury)		0.50	13	1,950	0.10	3	570
1.1.5	Beef (fresh, chilled or frozen)		0.90	23	2,360	0.70	17	1,230
1.1.6	Pork (fresh, chilled or frozen)		0.40	9	1,220	0.20	5	610
1.1.7	Lamb (fresh, chilled or frozen)		0.40	9	840	0.30	8	520
1.1.8	Poultry (fresh, chilled or frozen)		1.20	30	2,670	0.50	12	1,100
1.1.9	Bacon and ham		0.60	15	2,360	0.20	6	1,010
1.1.10	Other meats and meat preparations		3.70	91	5,150	1.20	30	2,880
	1.1.10.1	Sausages	0.40	10	2,140	0.20	5	1,060
	1.1.10.2	Offal, pate etc.	0.10	2	730	0.00	1	230
	1.1.10.3	Other preserved or processed meat and meat preparations	3.20	79	4,950	1.00	25	2,570
	1.1.10.4	Other fresh, chilled or frozen meat	[0.00]	[0]	10	[0.00]	[0]	20
1.1.11	Fish and fish products		1.60	41	3,680	0.60	14	1,310
	1.1.11.1	Fish (fresh, chilled or frozen)	0.50	13	1,350	0.20	6	480
	1.1.11.2	Seafood, dried, smoked or salted fish	0.40	9	1,160	0.10	3	320
	1.1.11.3	Other preserved or processed fish and seafood	0.80	19	2,880	0.20	5	830
1.1.12	Milk		1.20	29	4,790	1.10	27	3,740
	1.1.12.1	Whole milk	0.30	7	1,490	0.30	8	1,290
	1.1.12.2	Low fat milk	0.80	19	3,860	0.70	18	2,840
	1.1.12.3	Preserved milk	0.10	3	450	0.00	1	150
1.1.13	Cheese and curd		1.20	29	3,980	0.30	8	1,410
1.1.14	Eggs		0.30	8	2,700	0.10	3	1,330
1.1.15	Other milk products		1.40	34	4,370	0.30	7	1,550
	1.1.15.1	Other milk products	0.60	15	3,060	0.10	3	990
	1.1.15.2	Yoghurt	0.80	19	3,180	0.20	4	920
1.1.16	Butter		0.20	6	1,720	0.10	1	480
1.1.17	Margarine, other vegetable fats and peanut butter		0.30	8	2,690	0.10	2	840
1.1.18	Cooking oils and fats		0.20	4	1,220	0.10	2	320
	1.1.18.1	Olive oil	0.10	3	440	0.00	1	80
	1.1.18.2	Edible oils and other edible animal fats	0.10	2	840	0.00	1	250
1.1.19	Fresh fruit		2.30	56	4,880	0.70	16	2,260
	1.1.19.1	Citrus fruits (fresh)	0.40	9	2,400	0.10	2	810
	1.1.19.2	Bananas (fresh)	0.40	9	3,530	0.10	3	1,320
	1.1.19.3	Apples (fresh)	0.40	10	2,850	0.10	3	1,000
	1.1.19.4	Pears (fresh)	0.10	3	1,150	0.00	1	380
	1.1.19.5	Stone fruits (fresh)	0.30	8	1,510	0.10	3	560
	1.1.19.6	Berries (fresh)	0.70	17	2,630	0.20	4	890

Note: The commodity and service categories are not comparable with those in publications before 2001–02.
The numbering is sequential, it does not use actual COICOP codes.

Table $A3$ Expenditure on food and non-alcoholic drinks by place of purchase, 2006 (cont.)

based on weighted data and including children's expenditure

			Large supermarket chains			Other outlets		
			Average weekly expenditure all house-holds (£)	Total weekly expenditure (£ million)	Recording house-holds in sample	Average weekly expenditure all house-holds (£)	Total weekly expenditure (£ million)	Recording house-holds in sample
1		Food and non-alcoholic (continued)						
	1.1.20	Other fresh, chilled or frozen fruits	0.20	6	1,450	0.10	2	440
	1.1.21	Dried fruit and nuts	0.30	8	1,780	0.20	4	700
	1.1.22	Preserved fruit and fruit based products	0.10	3	1,170	0.00	1	320
	1.1.23	Fresh vegetables	2.70	68	5,250	0.80	20	2,700
	1.1.23.1	Leaf and stem vegetables (fresh or chilled)	0.60	15	3,470	0.10	3	1,140
	1.1.23.2	Cabbages (fresh or chilled)	0.30	7	2,710	0.10	3	1,010
	1.1.23.3	Vegetables grown for their fruit (fresh, chilled or frozen)	1.00	24	4,210	0.30	7	1,610
	1.1.23.4	Root crops, non-starchy bulbs and mushrooms (fresh, chilled or frozen)	0.90	21	4,510	0.30	8	1,990
	1.1.24	Dried vegetables and other preserved and processed vegetables	0.50	12	3,570	0.60	16	3,370
	1.1.25	Potatoes	0.50	12	3,340	0.20	5	1,510
	1.1.26	Other tubers and products of tuber vegetables	0.90	22	3,730	0.30	7	1,770
	1.1.27	Sugar and sugar products	0.20	5	1,990	0.10	2	630
	1.1.27.1	Sugar	0.20	4	1,740	0.10	1	560
	1.1.27.2	Other sugar products	0.00	1	450	0.00	0	100
	1.1.28	Jams, marmalades	0.20	4	1,540	0.10	1	470
	1.1.29	Chocolate	0.80	20	2,800	0.50	14	2,110
	1.1.30	Confectionery products	0.30	6	1,990	0.30	6	1,800
	1.1.31	Edible ices and ice cream	0.40	9	1,700	0.10	3	760
	1.1.32	Other food products	1.50	38	4,680	0.50	13	1,920
	1.1.32.1	Sauces, condiments	0.80	21	3,660	0.20	5	1,130
	1.1.32.2	Baker's yeast, dessert preparations, soups	0.60	14	3,050	0.20	5	1,060
	1.1.32.3	Salt, spices, culinary herbs and other food products	0.10	3	1,260	0.10	3	460
1.2		Non-alcoholic drinks	3.00	74	5,270	1.10	28	3,200
	1.2.1	Coffee	0.40	10	1,550	0.10	3	550
	1.2.2	Tea	0.30	7	1,840	0.10	3	770
	1.2.3	Cocoa and powdered chocolate	0.10	2	520	0.00	1	170
	1.2.4	Fruit and vegetable juices (inc. fruit squash)	1.00	24	3,530	0.20	6	1,180
	1.2.5	Mineral or spring waters	0.20	5	1,220	0.10	2	520
	1.2.6	Soft drinks	1.10	26	3,500	0.50	13	2,150

Note: The commodity and service categories are not comparable with those in publications before 2001–02.
The numbering is sequential, it does not use actual COICOP codes.

Table A4 Expenditure on selected items by place of purchase, 2006

based on weighted data and including children's expenditure

			Large supermarket chains			Other outlets		
			Average weekly expenditure all house-holds (£)	Total weekly expenditure (£ million)	Recording house-holds in sample	Average weekly expenditure all house-holds (£)	Total weekly expenditure (£ million)	Recording house-holds in sample
2	Alcoholic drink and tobacco							
	2.2	Tobacco	1.20	29	700	3.50	86	1,440
	2.2.1	Cigarettes	1.10	26	640	3.10	77	1,330
	2.2.2	Cigars and other tobacco products	0.10	3	130	0.30	9	330
	2.2.2.1	Cigars	0.00	0	20	0.00	1	50
	2.2.2.2	Other tobacco	0.10	2	100	0.30	7	280
5	Household goods and services							
	5.5.5	Electrical consumable	0.20	4	650	0.40	11	930
	5.6.1	Cleaning materials	1.60	39	3,880	0.70	18	1,970
7	Transport							
	7.2.2	Petrol, diesel & other motor oils	6.80	167	2,140	11.50	285	3,160
	7.2.2.1	Petrol	5.50	137	1,850	9.00	223	2,710
	7.2.2.2	Diesel oil	1.20	31	400	2.40	60	740
	7.2.2.3	Other motor oils	[0.00]	[0]	10	0.00	1	70
8	Communication							
	8.1	Postal services	–	–	0	0.50	12	1,320
9	Recreation and culture							
	9.3.5.1	Pet food	0.80	21	1,630	0.80	21	1,290
	9.5.2 & 9.5.3	Stationery, diaries, address books, art materials Cards, calendars, posters and other printed matter	0.40	10	1,570	1.60	39	3,090
	9.5.4	Newspapers	0.20	6	1,890	1.80	44	4,100
	9.5.5	Magazines and periodicals	0.30	7	1,550	0.80	19	2,520
12	Miscellaneous goods and services							
	12.1.2	Toilet paper	0.60	14	2,460	0.20	4	920
	12.1.3.1 & 12.1.3.3	Toiletries and other toilet requisites – toothpaste, deodorant, tampons, razors, hairbrushes, toothbrushes	0.90	23	2,980	0.80	20	2,210
	12.1.3.2	Bar of soap, liquid soap, shower gel etc	0.20	4	1,220	0.20	4	710
	12.1.5.2	Cosmetics and related accessories	0.40	11	1,300	1.80	45	1,800

Note: The commodity and service categories are not comparable with those in publications before 2001–02.
The numbering is sequential, it does not use actual COICOP codes.

Table A5 Expenditure on clothing and footwear by place of purchase, 2006

based on weighted data and including children's expenditure

	Large supermarket chains			Clothing chains			Other outlets		
	Average weekly expenditure all house-holds (£)	Total weekly expenditure (£ million)	Recording house-holds in sample	Average weekly expenditure all house-holds (£)	Total weekly expenditure (£ million)	Recording house-holds in sample	Average weekly expenditure all house-holds (£)	Total weekly expenditure (£ million)	Recording house-holds in sample
3 Clothing and footwear	1.50	36	1,490	9.00	223	2,390	12.40	307	3,350
3.1 Clothing	1.30	33	1,420	8.20	202	2,310	9.10	225	2,930
3.1.1 Men's outer garments	0.20	5	240	1.90	46	620	2.50	62	790
3.1.2 Men's under garments	0.10	1	140	0.20	5	230	0.10	3	210
3.1.3 Women's outer garments	0.50	12	450	4.20	105	1,410	3.80	94	1,390
3.1.4 Women's under garments	0.20	4	400	0.70	17	630	0.50	13	520
3.1.5 Boys' outer garments	0.10	2	140	0.20	5	170	0.50	12	300
3.1.6 Girls' outer garments	0.10	3	140	0.30	8	210	0.60	15	370
3.1.7 Infants' outer garments	0.10	3	160	0.20	6	200	0.30	8	290
3.1.8 Children's under garments	0.10	2	220	0.20	4	210	0.20	4	280
3.1.9 Accessories	0.10	1	200	0.30	7	310	0.40	9	590
3.1.9.1 Men's accessories	0.00	0	60	0.10	2	110	0.10	3	190
3.1.9.2 Women's accessories	0.00	1	80	0.20	4	180	0.20	4	250
3.1.9.3 Children's accessories	0.00	0	70	0.00	0	40	0.10	2	190
3.1.10 Haberdashery and clothing hire	0.00	0	40	[0.00]	[0]	20	0.20	5	280
3.2 Footwear	0.10	3	200	0.90	21	480	3.30	82	1,380
3.2.1 Men's	0.00	1	40	0.10	4	90	1.10	28	420
3.2.2 Women's	0.10	2	110	0.60	15	340	1.50	38	770
3.2.3 Children's	0.00	1	70	0.10	2	80	0.60	15	410

Note: The commodity and service categories are not comparable with those in publications before 2001–02.
The numbering system is sequential, it does not use actual COICOP codes.

Table A6 Household expenditure by gross income decile group, 2006

based on weighted data and including children's expenditure

	Lowest ten per cent	Second decile group	Third decile group	Fourth decile group	Fifth decile group	Sixth decile group
Lower boundary of group (£ per week)		143	215	293	384	497
Weighted number of households (thousands)	2,480	2,480	2,480	2,480	2,480	2,480
Total number of households in sample	680	680	700	690	690	680
Total number of persons in sample	930	1,200	1,350	1,500	1,650	1,800
Total number of adults in sample	760	920	1,110	1,130	1,250	1,320
Weighted average number of persons per household	1.4	1.7	1.9	2.1	2.3	2.6
Commodity or service	Average weekly household expenditure (£)					
1 Food & non-alcoholic drinks	24.50	31.40	36.60	40.10	44.60	47.40
2 Alcoholic drinks, tobacco & narcotics	5.30	6.00	8.30	9.20	11.60	11.70
3 Clothing & footwear	6.60	9.10	12.80	15.70	18.10	20.70
4 Housing (net)[1], fuel & power	32.30	35.20	42.50	43.30	45.40	49.90
5 Household goods & services	11.20	14.70	17.60	24.80	23.90	29.50
6 Health	1.80	2.80	4.40	4.40	5.60	5.50
7 Transport	13.90	16.90	33.20	40.50	46.60	55.40
8 Communication	5.70	6.80	8.50	9.40	12.10	12.00
9 Recreation & culture	17.10	25.20	34.70	39.40	51.50	58.20
10 Education	[1.70]	1.50	2.70	2.10	2.40	2.80
11 Restaurants & hotels	10.10	13.60	17.50	23.40	29.00	36.30
12 Miscellaneous goods & services	9.80	14.30	22.20	26.00	28.80	35.80
1–12 All expenditure groups	140.00	177.40	240.90	278.40	319.60	365.20
13 Other expenditure items	15.60	22.40	30.50	54.60	60.60	72.90
Total expenditure	155.60	199.80	271.40	333.00	380.20	438.10
Average weekly expenditure per person (£) Total expenditure	114.60	114.80	142.40	157.00	163.70	166.90

Note: The commodity and service categories are not comparable to those in publications before 2001–02.

1 Excluding mortgage interest payments, council tax and Northern Ireland rates.

Table A6 Household expenditure by gross income decile group, 2006 (cont.)

based on weighted data and including children's expenditure

	Seventh decile group	Eighth decile group	Ninth decile group	Highest ten per cent	All house-holds
Lower boundary of group (£ per week)	624	763	939	1,274	
Weighted number of households (thousands)	2,480	2,480	2,480	2,480	24,790
Total number of households in sample	660	630	640	590	6,650
Total number of persons in sample	1,790	1,880	1,930	1,840	15,850
Total number of adults in sample	1,340	1,380	1,400	1,380	12,000
Weighted average number of persons per household	2.7	2.9	3.0	3.0	2.4
Commodity or service	Average weekly household expenditure (£)				
1 Food & non-alcoholic drinks	51.90	57.80	62.70	71.90	46.90
2 Alcoholic drinks, tobacco & narcotics	13.60	14.90	15.30	15.20	11.10
3 Clothing & footwear	26.00	33.50	39.40	50.50	23.20
4 Housing (net)[1], fuel & power	48.90	52.60	51.10	74.30	47.60
5 Household goods & services	33.60	36.90	46.10	64.40	30.30
6 Health	5.00	6.90	6.40	15.90	5.90
7 Transport	65.40	84.70	107.50	156.20	62.00
8 Communication	13.80	14.80	16.70	17.80	11.70
9 Recreation & culture	67.40	83.70	92.10	115.40	58.50
10 Education	3.30	8.20	15.00	32.60	7.20
11 Restaurants & hotels	44.80	53.30	66.00	84.80	37.90
12 Miscellaneous goods & services	44.10	48.00	57.40	73.80	36.00
1–12 All expenditure groups	417.90	495.10	575.80	772.80	378.30
13 Other expenditure items	89.00	99.00	139.70	191.60	77.60
Total expenditure	**506.90**	**594.10**	**715.50**	**964.40**	**455.90**
Average weekly expenditure per person (£) **Total expenditure**	**190.40**	**205.40**	**240.40**	**317.10**	**192.80**

Note: The commodity and service categories are not comparable with those in publications before 2001–02.

1 Excluding mortgage interest payments, council tax and Northern Ireland rates.

Table A7 Household expenditure as a percentage of total expenditure by gross income decile group, 2006

based on weighted data and including children's expenditure

	Lowest ten per cent	Second decile group	Third decile group	Fourth decile group	Fifth decile group	Sixth decile group
Lower boundary of group (£ per week)		143	215	293	384	497
Weighted number of households (thousands)	2,480	2,480	2,480	2,480	2,480	2,480
Total number of households in sample	680	680	700	690	690	680
Total number of persons in sample	930	1,200	1,350	1,500	1,650	1,800
Total number of adults in sample	760	920	1,110	1,130	1,250	1,320
Weighted average number of persons per household	1.4	1.7	1.9	2.1	2.3	2.6
Commodity or service	Percentage of total expenditure					
1 Food & non-alcoholic drinks	16	16	13	12	12	11
2 Alcoholic drinks, tobacco & narcotics	3	3	3	3	3	3
3 Clothing & footwear	4	5	5	5	5	5
4 Housing (net)[1], fuel & power	21	18	16	13	12	11
5 Household goods & services	7	7	6	7	6	7
6 Health	1	1	2	1	1	1
7 Transport	9	8	12	12	12	13
8 Communication	4	3	3	3	3	3
9 Recreation & culture	11	13	13	12	14	13
10 Education	[1]	1	1	1	1	1
11 Restaurants & hotels	6	7	6	7	8	8
12 Miscellaneous goods & services	6	7	8	8	8	8
1–12 All expenditure groups	90	89	89	84	84	83
13 Other expenditure items	10	11	11	16	16	17
Total expenditure	100	100	100	100	100	100

Note: The commodity and service categories are not comparable to those in publications before 2001–02.
1 Excluding mortgage interest payments, council tax and Northern Ireland rates.

Table A7 Household expenditure as a percentage of total expenditure by gross income decile group, 2006 (cont.)
based on weighted data and including children's expenditure

	Seventh decile group	Eighth decile group	Ninth decile group	Highest ten per cent	All house-holds
Lower boundary of group (£ per week)	624	763	939	1,274	
Weighted number of households (thousands)	2,480	2,480	2,480	2,480	24,790
Total number of households in sample	660	630	640	590	6,650
Total number of persons in sample	1,790	1,880	1,930	1,840	15,850
Total number of adults in sample	1,340	1,380	1,400	1,380	12,000
Weighted average number of persons per household	2.7	2.9	3.0	3.0	2.4
Commodity or service	Percentage of total expenditure				
1 Food & non-alcoholic drinks	10	10	9	7	10
2 Alcoholic drinks, tobacco & narcotics	3	3	2	2	2
3 Clothing & footwear	5	6	6	5	5
4 Housing (net)[1], fuel & power	10	9	7	8	10
5 Household goods & services	7	6	6	7	7
6 Health	1	1	1	2	1
7 Transport	13	14	15	16	14
8 Communication	3	2	2	2	3
9 Recreation & culture	13	14	13	12	13
10 Education	1	1	2	3	2
11 Restaurants & hotels	9	9	9	9	8
12 Miscellaneous goods & services	9	8	8	8	8
1–12 All expenditure groups	82	83	80	80	83
13 Other expenditure items	18	17	20	20	17
Total expenditure	100	100	100	100	100

Note: The commodity and service categories are not comparable to those in publications before 2001–02.
1 Excluding mortgage interest payments, council tax and Northern Ireland rates.

Table A8 Detailed household expenditure by gross income decile group, 2006

based on weighted data and including children's expenditure

	Lowest ten per cent	Second decile group	Third decile group	Fourth decile group	Fifth decile group	Sixth decile group
Lower boundary of group (£ per week)		143	215	293	384	497
Weighted number of households (thousands)	2,480	2,480	2,480	2,480	2,480	2,480
Total number of households in sample	680	680	700	690	690	680
Total number of persons in sample	930	1,200	1,350	1,500	1,650	1,800
Total number of adults in sample	760	920	1,110	1,130	1,250	1,320
Weighted average number of persons per household	1.4	1.7	1.9	2.1	2.3	2.6
Commodity or service	Average weekly household expenditure (£)					
1 Food & non-alcoholic drinks	24.50	31.40	36.60	40.10	44.60	47.40
1.1 Food	22.30	28.70	33.80	36.60	40.80	43.20
1.1.1 Bread, rice and cereals	2.30	2.90	3.30	3.60	4.10	4.60
1.1.2 Pasta products	0.10	0.20	0.20	0.20	0.30	0.30
1.1.3 Buns, cakes, biscuits etc.	1.50	2.10	2.40	2.70	3.00	3.00
1.1.4 Pastry (savoury)	0.30	0.40	0.30	0.50	0.60	0.70
1.1.5 Beef (fresh, chilled or frozen)	0.60	1.00	1.50	1.20	1.50	1.50
1.1.6 Pork (fresh, chilled or frozen)	0.30	0.40	0.40	0.60	0.60	0.50
1.1.7 Lamb (fresh, chilled or frozen)	0.30	0.50	0.60	0.60	0.70	0.60
1.1.8 Poultry (fresh, chilled or frozen)	0.80	1.00	1.10	1.20	1.60	1.60
1.1.9 Bacon and ham	0.40	0.60	0.80	0.80	1.00	0.90
1.1.10 Other meat and meat preparations	2.90	3.50	3.70	4.40	4.70	5.30
1.1.11 Fish and fish products	1.30	1.40	1.90	2.00	1.90	2.00
1.1.12 Milk	1.50	1.80	2.10	2.30	2.40	2.40
1.1.13 Cheese and curd	0.70	0.80	1.10	1.20	1.40	1.50
1.1.14 Eggs	0.30	0.30	0.40	0.40	0.40	0.40
1.1.15 Other milk products	0.80	1.00	1.20	1.40	1.50	1.70
1.1.16 Butter	0.20	0.20	0.30	0.30	0.30	0.20
1.1.17 Margarine, other vegetable fats and peanut butter	0.30	0.30	0.40	0.40	0.40	0.40
1.1.18 Cooking oils and fats	0.20	0.20	0.20	0.20	0.20	0.20
1.1.19 Fresh fruit	1.50	1.80	2.30	2.40	2.50	2.80
1.1.20 Other fresh, chilled or frozen fruits	0.10	0.20	0.30	0.20	0.30	0.30
1.1.21 Dried fruit and nuts	0.20	0.30	0.40	0.40	0.50	0.50
1.1.22 Preserved fruit and fruit based products	0.10	0.10	0.10	0.10	0.10	0.10
1.1.23 Fresh vegetables	1.60	2.10	2.70	2.90	3.20	3.30
1.1.24 Dried vegetables	0.00	0.00	0.00	0.00	0.00	0.00
1.1.25 Other preserved or processed vegetables	0.50	0.60	0.70	0.80	1.00	1.10
1.1.26 Potatoes	0.40	0.50	0.70	0.70	0.80	0.70
1.1.27 Other tubers and products of tuber vegetables	0.60	0.80	0.90	1.00	1.20	1.40
1.1.28 Sugar and sugar products	0.20	0.30	0.30	0.30	0.30	0.30
1.1.29 Jams, marmalades	0.20	0.20	0.30	0.20	0.20	0.20
1.1.30 Chocolate	0.60	1.00	1.00	1.20	1.40	1.40
1.1.31 Confectionery products	0.30	0.40	0.50	0.40	0.50	0.60
1.1.32 Edible ices and ice cream	0.30	0.40	0.40	0.50	0.50	0.60
1.1.33 Other food products	1.00	1.40	1.30	1.50	1.80	1.90
1.2 Non-alcoholic drinks	2.10	2.70	2.80	3.50	3.80	4.10
1.2.1 Coffee	0.30	0.30	0.40	0.50	0.50	0.50
1.2.2 Tea	0.30	0.40	0.40	0.40	0.40	0.40
1.2.3 Cocoa and powdered chocolate	0.10	0.10	0.10	0.10	0.10	0.10
1.2.4 Fruit and vegetable juices (inc. fruit squash)	0.60	0.70	0.60	0.90	0.90	1.10
1.2.5 Mineral or spring waters	0.10	0.10	0.10	0.20	0.20	0.20
1.2.6 Soft drinks (inc. fizzy and ready to drink fruit drinks)	0.80	1.00	1.10	1.40	1.70	1.70

Note: The commodity and service categories are not comparable to those in publications before 2001–02.
   The numbering system is sequential, it does not use actual COICOP codes.

Table A8 Detailed household expenditure by gross income decile group, 2006 (cont.)

based on weighted data and including children's expenditure

		Seventh decile group	Eighth decile group	Ninth decile group	Highest ten per cent	All house-holds
Lower boundary of group (£ per week)		624	763	939	1,274	
Weighted number of households (thousands)		2,480	2,480	2,480	2,480	24,790
Total number of households in sample		660	630	640	590	6,650
Total number of persons in sample		1,790	1,880	1,930	1,840	15,850
Total number of adults in sample		1,340	1,380	1,400	1,380	12,000
Weighted average number of persons per household		2.7	2.9	3.0	3.0	2.4
Commodity or service		Average weekly household expenditure (£)				
1 Food & non-alcoholic drinks		51.90	57.80	62.70	71.90	46.90
1.1 Food		47.20	52.50	57.20	65.70	42.80
1.1.1	Bread, rice and cereals	4.70	5.50	5.70	5.80	4.30
1.1.2	Pasta products	0.40	0.40	0.40	0.50	0.30
1.1.3	Buns, cakes, biscuits etc.	3.20	3.40	3.60	3.90	2.90
1.1.4	Pastry (savoury)	0.80	0.90	1.10	1.20	0.70
1.1.5	Beef (fresh, chilled or frozen)	1.70	2.00	2.20	2.70	1.60
1.1.6	Pork (fresh, chilled or frozen)	0.60	0.70	0.70	0.80	0.60
1.1.7	Lamb (fresh, chilled or frozen)	0.60	0.70	1.00	1.00	0.70
1.1.8	Poultry (fresh, chilled or frozen)	1.90	2.00	2.60	3.10	1.70
1.1.9	Bacon and ham	0.90	1.00	1.00	1.20	0.90
1.1.10	Other meat and meat preparations	5.40	6.00	6.30	7.00	4.90
1.1.11	Fish and fish products	2.30	2.60	2.90	3.70	2.20
1.1.12	Milk	2.50	2.60	2.70	2.60	2.30
1.1.13	Cheese and curd	1.60	2.00	2.00	2.80	1.50
1.1.14	Eggs	0.40	0.50	0.50	0.60	0.40
1.1.15	Other milk products	2.00	2.10	2.30	2.60	1.70
1.1.16	Butter	0.30	0.30	0.40	0.40	0.30
1.1.17	Margarine, other vegetable fats and peanut butter	0.40	0.50	0.50	0.50	0.40
1.1.18	Cooking oils and fats	0.30	0.30	0.30	0.40	0.20
1.1.19	Fresh fruit	3.20	3.40	4.00	5.10	2.90
1.1.20	Other fresh, chilled or frozen fruits	0.30	0.30	0.40	0.60	0.30
1.1.21	Dried fruit and nuts	0.60	0.60	0.70	0.90	0.50
1.1.22	Preserved fruit and fruit based products	0.20	0.20	0.20	0.20	0.10
1.1.23	Fresh vegetables	3.90	4.50	5.10	6.30	3.60
1.1.24	Dried vegetables	0.00	0.00	0.10	0.10	0.00
1.1.25	Other preserved or processed vegetables	1.20	1.40	1.50	1.90	1.10
1.1.26	Potatoes	0.70	0.80	0.90	0.90	0.70
1.1.27	Other tubers and products of tuber vegetables	1.40	1.50	1.60	1.40	1.20
1.1.28	Sugar and sugar products	0.30	0.30	0.30	0.30	0.30
1.1.29	Jams, marmalades	0.20	0.20	0.30	0.30	0.20
1.1.30	Chocolate	1.50	1.70	1.90	2.10	1.40
1.1.31	Confectionery products	0.60	0.70	0.70	0.60	0.50
1.1.32	Edible ices and ice cream	0.50	0.50	0.70	0.70	0.50
1.1.33	Other food products	2.40	2.80	2.70	3.50	2.00
1.2 Non-alcoholic drinks		4.70	5.30	5.50	6.30	4.10
1.2.1	Coffee	0.60	0.60	0.70	0.70	0.50
1.2.2	Tea	0.50	0.50	0.50	0.50	0.40
1.2.3	Cocoa and powdered chocolate	0.10	0.10	0.10	0.10	0.10
1.2.4	Fruit and vegetable juices (inc. fruit squash)	1.40	1.60	1.90	2.30	1.20
1.2.5	Mineral or spring waters	0.30	0.40	0.40	0.50	0.30
1.2.6	Soft drinks	1.80	2.10	2.00	2.20	1.60

Note: The commodity and service categories are not comparable to those in publications before 2001–02.

The numbering system is sequential, it does not use actual COICOP codes.

Table A8 Detailed household expenditure by gross income decile group, 2006 (cont.)

based on weighted data and including children's expenditure

Commodity or service	Lowest ten per cent	Second decile group	Third decile group	Fourth decile group	Fifth decile group	Sixth decile group
	Average weekly household expenditure (£)					
2 Alcoholic drink, tobacco & narcotics	5.30	6.00	8.30	9.20	11.60	11.70
2.1 Alcoholic drinks	2.20	2.60	3.90	4.50	6.10	6.20
2.1.1 Spirits and liqueurs (brought home)	0.50	0.80	1.10	1.20	1.30	1.30
2.1.2 Wines, fortified wines (brought home)	0.80	0.90	1.70	2.00	2.60	2.90
2.1.3 Beer, lager, ciders and perry (brought home)	0.80	0.90	1.10	1.30	2.00	1.90
2.1.4 Alcopops (brought home)	[0.00]	[0.10]	[0.00]	[0.00]	0.10	[0.10]
2.2 Tobacco and narcotics	3.10	3.40	4.40	4.70	5.60	5.50
2.2.1 Cigarettes	2.50	2.90	3.90	4.20	5.10	4.90
2.2.2 Cigars, other tobacco products and narcotics	0.60	0.50	0.50	0.50	0.50	0.50
3 Clothing & footwear	6.60	9.10	12.80	15.70	18.10	20.70
3.1 Clothing	5.40	7.30	10.30	12.10	14.60	16.90
3.1.1 Men's outer garments	1.20	1.10	2.20	2.10	3.60	4.50
3.1.2 Men's under garments	0.20	0.20	0.20	0.30	0.30	0.40
3.1.3 Women's outer garments	2.20	3.00	4.90	5.90	6.10	6.80
3.1.4 Women's under garments	0.50	0.70	0.90	0.90	1.10	1.20
3.1.5 Boy's outer garments (5–15)	0.30	0.50	0.30	0.60	0.70	0.80
3.1.6 Girl's outer garments (5–15)	0.20	0.50	0.50	1.00	1.10	0.90
3.1.7 Infant's outer garments (under 5)	0.30	0.50	0.30	0.40	0.50	0.70
3.1.8 Children's under garments (under 16)	0.10	0.30	0.20	0.30	0.40	0.40
3.1.9 Accessories	0.20	0.20	0.40	0.40	0.40	0.70
3.1.10 Haberdashery and clothing hire	0.10	0.10	0.10	0.10	0.30	0.30
3.1.11 Dry cleaners, laundry and dyeing	0.20	[0.10]	0.20	[0.10]	[0.10]	0.20
3.2 Footwear	1.20	1.80	2.50	3.60	3.50	3.80
4 Housing (net)[1], fuel & power	32.30	35.20	42.50	43.30	45.40	49.90
4.1 Actual rentals for housing	59.90	47.10	32.80	26.40	21.20	21.50
4.1.1 Gross rent	59.90	47.10	32.80	26.40	21.20	21.50
4.1.2 less housing benefit, rebates & allowances rec'd	45.20	32.60	16.00	9.50	3.80	1.80
4.1.3 Net rent	14.70	14.50	16.80	16.90	17.30	19.80
4.1.4 Second dwelling rent	–	–	–	–	–	–
4.2 Maintenance and repair of dwelling	1.60	2.60	5.50	5.50	6.20	7.40
4.3 Water supply and miscellaneous services relating to the dwelling	5.80	5.70	6.20	6.90	6.50	6.80
4.4 Electricity, gas and other fuels	10.20	12.50	14.00	14.00	15.40	15.90
4.4.1 Electricity	4.90	5.80	6.60	6.80	7.30	7.70
4.4.2 Gas	4.50	5.60	6.30	6.40	7.00	7.20
4.4.3 Other fuels	0.80	1.00	1.10	0.80	1.10	1.00

Note: The commodity and service categories are not comparable to those in publications before 2001–02.

The numbering system is sequential, it does not use actual COICOP codes.

1 Excluding mortgage interest payments, council tax and Northern Ireland rates.

Table A8 Detailed household expenditure by gross income decile group, 2006 (cont.)

based on weighted data and including children's expenditure

			Seventh decile group	Eighth decile group	Ninth decile group	Highest ten per cent	All house-holds
Commodity or service			Average weekly household expenditure (£)				
2	Alcoholic drink, tobacco & narcotics		**13.60**	**14.90**	**15.30**	**15.20**	**11.10**
	2.1	Alcoholic drinks	7.70	9.60	10.40	11.50	6.50
		2.1.1 Spirits and liqueurs (brought home)	1.80	1.60	1.40	1.50	1.30
		2.1.2 Wines, fortified wines (brought home)	3.60	5.00	6.20	7.50	3.30
		2.1.3 Beer, lager, ciders and perry (brought home)	2.20	2.90	2.70	2.40	1.80
		2.1.4 Alcopops (brought home)	0.10	0.10	[0.10]	[0.10]	0.10
	2.2	Tobacco and narcotics	5.90	5.30	5.00	3.70	4.60
		2.2.1 Cigarettes	5.50	4.70	4.60	3.40	4.20
		2.2.2 Cigars, other tobacco products and narcotics	0.30	0.60	0.40	0.30	0.50
3	Clothing & footwear		**26.00**	**33.50**	**39.40**	**50.50**	**23.20**
	3.1	Clothing	20.20	27.50	32.70	41.90	18.90
		3.1.1 Men's outer garments	4.50	6.80	9.80	9.80	4.60
		3.1.2 Men's under garments	0.30	0.50	0.70	0.70	0.40
		3.1.3 Women's outer garments	9.10	12.20	13.70	20.70	8.50
		3.1.4 Women's under garments	1.40	2.10	2.00	2.90	1.40
		3.1.5 Boy's outer garments (5–15)	1.10	1.20	1.10	1.10	0.80
		3.1.6 Girl's outer garments (5–15)	1.10	1.70	1.90	1.60	1.00
		3.1.7 Infant's outer garments (under 5)	1.00	1.00	0.80	0.90	0.70
		3.1.8 Children's under garments (under 16)	0.40	0.60	0.60	0.70	0.40
		3.1.9 Accessories	0.70	1.10	1.20	2.00	0.70
		3.1.10 Haberdashery and clothing hire	0.30	0.30	0.40	0.50	0.20
		3.1.11 Dry cleaners, laundry and dyeing	0.30	0.20	0.40	1.10	0.30
	3.2	Footwear	5.80	5.90	6.80	8.60	4.30
4	Housing (net)[1], fuel & power		**48.90**	**52.60**	**51.10**	**74.30**	**47.60**
	4.1	Actual rentals for housing	18.00	18.00	12.60	21.60	27.90
		4.1.1 Gross rent	18.00	17.70	12.60	21.00	27.80
		4.1.2 *less* housing benefit, rebates & allowances rec'd	1.70	0.60	0.10	0.40	11.20
		4.1.3 Net rent	16.40	17.10	12.40	20.60	16.70
		4.1.4 Second dwelling rent	–	[0.30]	–	[0.60]	[0.10]
	4.2	Maintenance and repair of dwelling	9.20	9.50	11.80	20.50	8.00
	4.3	Water supply and miscellaneous services relating to the dwelling	7.00	7.70	7.20	9.60	6.90
	4.4	Electricity, gas and other fuels	16.40	18.00	19.70	22.90	15.90
		4.4.1 Electricity	7.80	8.70	9.30	10.60	7.50
		4.4.2 Gas	7.50	7.90	9.10	10.20	7.20
		4.4.3 Other fuels	1.10	1.50	1.30	2.20	1.20

Note: The commodity and service categories are not comparable to those in publications before 2001–02.

The numbering system is sequential, it does not use actual COICOP codes.

1 Excluding mortgage interest payments, council tax and Northern Ireland rates.

Table A8 Detailed household expenditure by gross income decile group, 2006 (cont.)

based on weighted data and including children's expenditure

	Lowest ten per cent	Second decile group	Third decile group	Fourth decile group	Fifth decile group	Sixth decile group
Commodity or service	Average weekly household expenditure (£)					
5 Household goods & services	11.20	14.70	17.60	24.80	23.90	29.50
5.1 Furniture and furnishings, carpets and other floor coverings	6.40	6.90	9.20	13.10	13.80	16.00
5.1.1 Furniture and furnishings	4.60	4.90	7.10	9.50	9.50	12.90
5.1.2 Floor coverings	1.80	2.00	2.10	3.70	4.30	3.10
5.2 Household textiles	0.40	1.00	1.10	2.20	1.40	1.40
5.3 Household appliances	1.30	1.30	1.60	2.50	1.30	4.50
5.4 Glassware, tableware and household utensils	0.30	0.60	0.90	1.20	1.20	1.30
5.5 Tools and equipment for house and garden	0.60	1.00	1.20	1.50	1.50	1.70
5.6 Goods and services for routine household maintenance	2.20	3.90	3.40	4.30	4.60	4.50
5.6.1 Cleaning materials	1.10	1.40	1.60	1.90	2.10	2.30
5.6.2 Household goods and hardware	0.50	0.70	0.80	1.00	0.90	1.20
5.6.3 Domestic services, carpet cleaning, hire/repair of furniture/furnishings	0.60	1.90	1.00	1.40	1.60	1.10
6 Health	1.80	2.80	4.40	4.40	5.60	5.50
6.1 Medical products, appliances and equipment	1.50	1.40	3.00	2.10	3.10	3.20
6.1.1 Medicines, prescriptions, healthcare products etc.	0.70	0.90	2.30	1.20	1.50	1.80
6.1.2 Spectacles, lenses, accessories and repairs	[0.80]	[0.50]	0.70	[0.90]	1.60	1.50
6.2 Hospital services	[0.30]	1.40	1.30	2.30	2.50	2.30
7 Transport	13.90	16.90	33.20	40.50	46.60	55.40
7.1 Purchase of vehicles	4.60	4.00	12.00	12.30	14.10	19.30
7.1.1 Purchase of new cars and vans	[1.70]	[1.10]	3.50	4.10	4.90	5.60
7.1.2 Purchase of second hand cars or vans	2.80	2.90	8.30	8.00	8.90	12.70
7.1.3 Purchase of motorcycles and other vehicles	[0.20]	[0.00]	[0.10]	[0.10]	[0.20]	[0.90]
7.2 Operation of personal transport	6.40	9.10	15.60	18.80	25.00	28.30
7.2.1 Spares and accessories	[0.30]	0.70	1.00	0.60	1.10	1.70
7.2.2 Petrol, diesel and other motor oils	4.20	5.30	9.60	12.70	16.50	18.40
7.2.3 Repairs and servicing	1.40	2.40	3.70	3.90	4.80	6.00
7.2.4 Other motoring costs	0.50	0.70	1.20	1.70	2.60	2.30
7.3 Transport services	2.90	3.80	5.60	9.40	7.60	7.90
7.3.1 Rail and tube fares	0.60	0.30	0.70	0.60	0.70	1.30
7.3.2 Bus and coach fares	1.00	1.00	1.20	0.80	1.50	1.80
7.3.3 Combined fares	[0.10]	[0.20]	[0.40]	[0.10]	[0.40]	[0.80]
7.3.4 Other travel and transport	1.30	2.30	3.20	7.80	4.90	4.00
8 Communication	5.70	6.80	8.50	9.40	12.10	12.00
8.1 Postal services	0.20	0.40	0.50	0.40	0.50	0.30
8.2 Telephone and telefax equipment	[0.10]	[0.40]	[0.40]	[0.60]	[0.50]	0.70
8.3 Telephone and telefax services	5.40	6.10	7.50	8.40	11.00	11.00

Note: The commodity and service categories are not comparable to those in publications before 2001–02.
     The numbering system is sequential, it does not use actual COICOP codes.

Table A8 Detailed household expenditure by gross income decile group, 2006 (cont.)

based on weighted data and including children's expenditure

Commodity or service	Seventh decile group	Eighth decile group	Ninth decile group	Highest ten per cent	All house-holds
	Average weekly household expenditure (£)				
5 Household goods & services	33.60	36.90	46.10	64.40	30.30
5.1 Furniture and furnishings, carpets and other floor coverings	18.60	20.50	26.20	34.70	16.50
5.1.1 Furniture and furnishings	13.00	14.80	20.30	28.00	12.50
5.1.2 Floor coverings	5.50	5.70	5.80	6.70	4.10
5.2 Household textiles	2.20	2.50	3.20	3.40	1.90
5.3 Household appliances	3.70	3.00	3.90	6.90	3.00
5.4 Glassware, tableware and household utensils	2.00	2.10	2.40	3.60	1.60
5.5 Tools and equipment for house and garden	2.30	3.30	3.30	4.10	2.10
5.6 Goods and services for routine household maintenance	4.70	5.50	7.10	11.70	5.20
5.6.1 Cleaning materials	2.60	2.90	3.40	3.80	2.30
5.6.2 Household goods and hardware	1.30	1.60	1.60	2.20	1.20
5.6.3 Domestic services, carpet cleaning, hire/repair of furniture/furnishings	0.90	1.00	2.10	5.70	1.70
6 Health	5.00	6.90	6.40	15.90	5.90
6.1 Medical products, appliances and equipment	3.30	4.40	4.20	5.10	3.10
6.1.1 Medicines, prescriptions, healthcare products etc.	1.90	2.00	2.30	2.60	1.70
6.1.2 Spectacles, lenses, accessories and repairs	1.40	2.40	1.90	2.50	1.40
6.2 Hospital services	1.70	2.50	2.20	10.80	2.70
7 Transport	65.40	84.70	107.50	156.20	62.00
7.1 Purchase of vehicles	21.60	32.80	44.90	68.70	23.40
7.1.1 Purchase of new cars and vans	6.30	10.70	17.70	27.40	8.30
7.1.2 Purchase of second hand cars or vans	14.60	20.90	26.20	39.80	14.50
7.1.3 Purchase of motorcycles and other vehicles	[0.70]	[1.20]	[1.00]	[1.50]	0.60
7.2 Operation of personal transport	33.60	40.80	47.60	61.10	28.60
7.2.1 Spares and accessories	2.40	2.20	4.10	6.60	2.10
7.2.2 Petrol, diesel and other motor oils	21.90	26.90	29.80	37.10	18.20
7.2.3 Repairs and servicing	6.50	8.30	9.80	12.50	5.90
7.2.4 Other motoring costs	2.80	3.40	3.90	4.90	2.40
7.3 Transport services	10.20	11.10	15.00	26.40	10.00
7.3.1 Rail and tube fares	2.30	2.80	4.00	8.20	2.20
7.3.2 Bus and coach fares	1.90	1.30	1.40	1.20	1.30
7.3.3 Combined fares	0.80	1.90	1.80	3.30	1.00
7.3.4 Other travel and transport	5.10	5.10	7.70	13.60	5.50
8 Communication	13.80	14.80	16.70	17.80	11.70
8.1 Postal services	0.60	0.50	0.70	0.80	0.50
8.2 Telephone and telefax equipment	0.70	1.50	1.00	1.30	0.70
8.3 Telephone and telefax services	12.50	12.70	15.00	15.70	10.50

Note: The commodity and service categories are not comparable to those in publications before 2001–02.
    The numbering system is sequential, it does not use actual COICOP codes.

Table A8 Detailed household expenditure by gross income decile group, 2006 (cont.)

based on weighted data and including children's expenditure

	Lowest ten per cent	Second decile group	Third decile group	Fourth decile group	Fifth decile group	Sixth decile group
Commodity or service	Average weekly household expenditure (£)					
9 Recreation & culture	17.10	25.20	34.70	39.40	51.50	58.20
9.1 Audio-visual, photographic and information processing equipment	1.70	2.40	3.20	4.90	5.20	8.20
9.1.1 Audio equipment and accessories, CD players	0.60	0.60	0.60	1.80	1.20	1.90
9.1.2 TV, video and computers	1.10	1.30	2.30	2.80	3.30	6.10
9.1.3 Photographic, cine and optical equipment	[0.00]	[0.50]	[0.40]	0.30	0.70	0.30
9.2 Other major durables for recreation and culture	[0.10]	[0.60]	[0.40]	[0.40]	[3.20]	[1.20]
9.3 Other recreational items and equipment, gardens and pets	3.30	4.60	6.50	7.80	8.50	10.90
9.3.1 Games, toys and hobbies	0.70	1.00	1.40	1.40	1.70	2.60
9.3.2 Computer software and games	[0.10]	[0.20]	0.50	1.00	1.00	1.10
9.3.3 Equipment for sport, camping and open-air recreation	[0.10]	0.50	0.10	0.50	1.10	0.80
9.3.4 Horticultural goods, garden equipment and plants	0.70	1.00	1.90	2.30	2.00	2.80
9.3.5 Pets and pet food	1.60	1.80	2.60	2.60	2.80	3.60
9.4 Recreational and cultural services	6.70	8.90	11.50	12.90	15.40	17.00
9.4.1 Sports admissions, subscriptions, leisure class fees and equipment hire	0.90	1.60	1.70	2.50	3.30	4.50
9.4.2 Cinema, theatre and museums etc.	0.30	0.70	1.20	1.20	1.30	1.30
9.4.3 TV, video, satellite rental, cable subscriptions, TV licences and the Internet	3.40	3.60	4.20	4.80	5.70	6.20
9.4.4 Miscellaneous entertainments	0.20	0.50	0.60	0.70	0.90	1.00
9.4.5 Development of film, deposit for film development, passport photos, holiday and school photos	[0.10]	0.10	0.60	0.20	0.40	0.40
9.4.6 Gambling payments	1.80	2.40	3.20	3.50	3.90	3.60
9.5 Newspapers, books and stationery	2.80	3.80	4.80	5.60	5.80	6.70
9.5.1 Books	0.40	0.60	0.70	1.00	1.10	1.50
9.5.2 Diaries, address books, cards etc.	0.60	0.90	1.20	1.60	1.60	2.10
9.5.3 Newspapers	1.30	1.80	2.20	2.20	2.10	1.90
9.5.4 Magazines and periodicals	0.50	0.50	0.70	0.80	1.00	1.20
9.6 Package holidays	2.60	4.80	8.20	7.80	13.40	14.20
9.6.1 Package holidays – UK	0.50	0.70	1.60	0.90	1.30	[0.70]
9.6.2 Package holidays – abroad	2.20	4.10	6.60	6.90	12.10	13.50
10 Education	[1.70]	1.50	2.70	2.10	2.40	2.80
10.1 Education fees	[1.60]	[1.30]	2.70	[2.00]	2.00	2.50
10.2 Payments for school trips, other ad-hoc expenditure	[0.10]	[0.20]	[0.00]	[0.20]	0.40	0.30
11 Restaurants & hotels	10.10	13.60	17.50	23.40	29.00	36.30
11.1 Catering services	9.20	12.20	15.20	21.10	25.60	32.00
11.1.1 Restaurant and café meals	3.70	4.90	7.40	8.70	9.90	10.80
11.1.2 Alcoholic drinks (away from home)	2.80	2.80	3.40	5.60	6.20	9.30
11.1.3 Take away meals eaten at home	1.40	1.90	2.10	2.90	3.90	4.30
11.1.4 Other take-away and snack food	1.10	2.20	1.70	2.80	3.70	4.50
11.1.5 Contract catering (food) and canteens	0.20	0.40	0.50	1.10	1.90	3.10
11.2 Accommodation services	0.80	1.30	2.30	2.30	3.50	4.20
11.2.1 Holiday in the UK	[0.40]	0.80	1.90	1.50	1.60	2.30
11.2.2 Holiday abroad	[0.40]	[0.50]	[0.40]	0.80	1.90	1.90
11.2.3 Room hire	–	[0.00]	[0.00]	–	[0.00]	[0.00]

Note: The commodity and service categories are not comparable to those in publications before 2001–02.
The numbering system is sequential, it does not use actual COICOP codes.

Table A8 Detailed household expenditure by gross income decile group, 2006 (cont.)
based on weighted data and including children's expenditure

	Seventh decile group	Eighth decile group	Ninth decile group	Highest ten per cent	All house-holds
Commodity or service	Average weekly household expenditure (£)				
9 Recreation & culture	**67.40**	**83.70**	**92.10**	**115.40**	**58.50**
9.1 Audio-visual, photographic and information processing equipment	8.00	12.30	11.60	14.00	7.10
9.1.1 Audio equipment and accessories, CD players	1.80	3.50	3.60	3.60	1.90
9.1.2 TV, video and computers	5.60	7.70	7.10	8.70	4.60
9.1.3 Photographic, cine and optical equipment	0.60	1.10	0.80	1.80	0.60
9.2 Other major durables for recreation and culture	0.90	1.70	4.60	3.60	1.70
9.3 Other recreational items and equipment, gardens and pets	12.80	14.80	15.00	18.50	10.30
9.3.1 Games, toys and hobbies	2.30	2.90	3.20	2.70	2.00
9.3.2 Computer software and games	1.70	2.00	1.60	1.60	1.10
9.3.3 Equipment for sport, camping and open-air recreation	1.70	1.50	1.80	3.40	1.20
9.3.4 Horticultural goods, garden equipment and plants	2.90	3.00	4.30	5.10	2.60
9.3.5 Pets and pet food	4.30	5.30	4.20	5.70	3.50
9.4 Recreational and cultural services	20.70	27.80	30.50	35.40	18.70
9.4.1 Sports admissions, subscriptions, leisure class fees and equipment hire	6.00	7.10	13.30	16.50	5.80
9.4.2 Cinema, theatre and museums etc.	2.70	3.60	3.70	4.20	2.00
9.4.3 TV, video, satellite rental, cable subscriptions, TV licences and the Internet	6.80	7.10	7.90	8.70	5.80
9.4.4 Miscellaneous entertainments	1.30	1.80	1.40	2.20	1.10
9.4.5 Development of film, deposit for film development, passport photos, holiday and school photos	0.30	0.60	0.60	0.60	0.40
9.4.6 Gambling payments	3.50	7.60	3.60	3.10	3.60
9.5 Newspapers, books and stationery	7.60	8.30	9.30	11.60	6.60
9.5.1 Books	1.80	2.50	2.40	4.00	1.60
9.5.2 Diaries, address books, cards etc.	2.70	2.50	3.00	3.40	2.00
9.5.3 Newspapers	2.00	1.90	2.20	2.60	2.00
9.5.4 Magazines and periodicals	1.10	1.40	1.70	1.60	1.00
9.6 Package holidays	17.40	18.90	21.10	32.40	14.10
9.6.1 Package holidays – UK	[0.60]	1.20	[1.20]	[0.70]	0.90
9.6.2 Package holidays – abroad	16.80	17.70	20.00	31.70	13.20
10 Education	**3.30**	**8.20**	**15.00**	**32.60**	**7.20**
10.1 Education fees	2.90	7.50	14.40	31.80	6.90
10.2 Payments for school trips, other ad-hoc expenditure	0.40	0.60	0.60	[0.80]	0.40
11 Restaurants & hotels	**44.80**	**53.30**	**66.00**	**84.80**	**37.90**
11.1 Catering services	38.90	44.60	55.10	64.60	31.90
11.1.1 Restaurant and café meals	15.00	17.70	20.70	28.70	12.80
11.1.2 Alcoholic drinks (away from home)	10.30	12.70	14.00	16.80	8.40
11.1.3 Take away meals eaten at home	4.90	5.30	5.80	6.20	3.90
11.1.4 Other take-away and snack food	5.00	5.60	7.10	8.60	4.20
11.1.5 Contract catering (food) and canteens	3.80	3.40	7.50	4.40	2.60
11.2 Accommodation services	5.90	8.60	10.90	20.20	6.00
11.2.1 Holiday in the UK	2.80	4.10	4.90	5.60	2.60
11.2.2 Holiday abroad	3.10	4.60	6.00	14.60	3.40
11.2.3 Room hire	[0.00]	[0.00]	[0.10]	[0.00]	[0.00]

Note: The commodity and service categories are not comparable to those in publications before 2001–02.
      The numbering system is sequential, it does not use actual COICOP codes.

Table A8 Detailed household expenditure by gross income decile group, 2006 (cont.)
based on weighted data and including children's expenditure

	Lowest ten per cent	Second decile group	Third decile group	Fourth decile group	Fifth decile group	Sixth decile group
Commodity or service	Average weekly household expenditure (£)					
12 Miscellaneous goods & services	9.80	14.30	22.20	26.00	28.80	35.80
12.1 Personal care	3.50	4.70	6.40	7.00	8.10	9.90
12.1.1 Hairdressing, beauty treatment	1.10	1.50	2.40	2.10	2.80	3.00
12.1.2 Toilet paper	0.40	0.50	0.60	0.70	0.70	0.70
12.1.3 Toiletries and soap	0.80	0.90	1.20	1.50	1.80	2.00
12.1.4 Baby toiletries and accessories (disposable)	0.30	0.40	0.30	0.50	0.50	0.70
12.1.5 Hair products, cosmetics and related electrical appliances	0.90	1.50	1.90	2.30	2.30	3.50
12.2 Personal effects	0.50	0.80	1.40	2.40	1.70	3.30
12.3 Social protection	[0.20]	0.90	[1.40]	1.60	1.30	2.60
12.4 Insurance	4.30	6.10	8.80	11.30	13.40	15.00
12.4.1 Household insurances – structural, contents and appliances	1.90	2.80	3.60	4.00	4.90	5.40
12.4.2 Medical insurance premiums	[0.30]	0.30	0.40	1.20	1.30	1.40
12.4.3 Vehicle insurance including boat insurance	2.10	3.00	4.60	5.80	7.20	8.10
12.4.4 Non-package holiday, other travel insurance	–	[0.00]	[0.20]	[0.20]	[0.00]	[0.10]
12.5 Other services n.e.c.	1.30	1.60	4.20	3.70	4.40	4.90
12.5.1 Moving house	[0.90]	1.30	1.70	2.80	2.60	3.30
12.5.2 Bank, building society, post office, credit card charges	0.30	0.10	0.30	0.30	0.30	0.30
12.5.3 Other services and professional fees	0.10	0.20	2.20	0.60	1.50	1.30
1–12 All expenditure groups	**140.00**	**177.40**	**240.90**	**278.40**	**319.60**	**365.20**
13 Other expenditure items	15.60	22.40	30.50	54.60	60.60	72.90
13.1 Housing: mortgage interest payments, council tax etc.	11.20	13.60	20.40	30.90	41.30	54.00
13.2 Licences, fines and transfers	0.90	1.10	1.90	2.20	2.60	3.00
13.3 Holiday spending	[1.00]	[2.80]	3.30	12.60	8.40	5.80
13.4 Money transfers and credit	2.60	4.90	4.90	8.80	8.30	10.10
13.4.1 Money, cash gifts given to children	[0.00]	[0.10]	[0.10]	[0.00]	[0.10]	[0.10]
13.4.2 Cash gifts and donations	2.10	4.40	4.00	7.20	6.60	8.10
13.4.3 Club instalment payments (child) and interest on credit cards	0.50	0.40	0.90	1.60	1.60	1.90
Total expenditure	**155.60**	**199.80**	**271.40**	**333.00**	**380.20**	**438.10**
14 Other items recorded						
14.1 Life assurance and contributions to pension funds	1.00	1.70	3.20	5.30	10.20	14.80
14.2 Other insurance inc. Friendly Societies	0.20	0.40	0.50	0.80	1.00	1.50
14.3 Income tax, payments less refunds	1.90	3.70	12.10	24.60	41.30	62.40
14.4 National insurance contributions	0.40	0.50	2.30	7.20	14.30	23.70
14.5 Purchase or alteration of dwellings, mortgages	5.00	42.60	42.60	23.80	25.40	63.00
14.6 Savings and investments	0.20	0.70	4.40	3.80	1.90	4.10
14.7 Pay off loan to clear other debt	[0.60]	[0.40]	0.90	1.70	2.40	3.00
14.8 Windfall receipts from gambling etc.	1.00	0.70	2.80	1.70	1.70	2.40

Note: The commodity and service categories are not comparable to those in publications before 2001–02.
The numbering system is sequential, it does not use actual COICOP codes.

Table A8 Detailed household expenditure by gross income decile group, 2006 (cont.)

based on weighted data and including children's expenditure

Commodity or service	Seventh decile group	Eighth decile group	Ninth decile group	Highest ten per cent	All house-holds
	Average weekly household expenditure (£)				
12 Miscellaneous goods & services	44.10	48.00	57.40	73.80	36.00
12.1 Personal care	11.20	13.30	15.20	18.90	9.80
12.1.1 Hairdressing, beauty treatment	3.40	4.10	5.00	7.00	3.20
12.1.2 Toilet paper	0.80	0.90	0.90	1.00	0.70
12.1.3 Toiletries and soap	2.50	2.80	3.10	3.60	2.00
12.1.4 Baby toiletries and accessories (disposable)	0.70	0.80	0.90	0.90	0.60
12.1.5 Hair products, cosmetics and related electrical appliances	3.80	4.60	5.30	6.40	3.20
12.2 Personal effects	4.30	4.50	6.00	6.50	3.10
12.3 Social protection	2.70	3.00	4.60	7.90	2.60
12.4 Insurance	18.20	20.00	23.80	29.70	15.10
12.4.1 Household insurances – structural, contents and appliances	6.10	6.10	7.50	8.90	5.10
12.4.2 Medical insurance premiums	1.80	2.00	3.70	5.50	1.80
12.4.3 Vehicle insurance including boat insurance	10.10	11.40	12.20	15.20	8.00
12.4.4 Non-package holiday, other travel insurance	[0.20]	[0.40]	[0.40]	[0.00]	0.20
12.5 Other services n.e.c.	7.80	7.20	7.80	10.80	5.40
12.5.1 Moving house	3.50	3.30	5.30	6.80	3.10
12.5.2 Bank, building society, post office, credit card charges	0.30	0.40	0.50	0.70	0.40
12.5.3 Other services and professional fees	4.00	3.50	1.90	3.30	1.90
1–12 All expenditure groups	**417.90**	**495.10**	**575.80**	**772.80**	**378.30**
13 Other expenditure items	89.00	99.00	139.70	191.60	77.60
13.1 Housing: mortgage interest payments, council tax etc.	63.70	72.50	94.40	117.80	52.00
13.2 Licences, fines and transfers	3.60	4.10	4.60	5.60	2.90
13.3 Holiday spending	12.00	8.50	20.80	46.20	12.10
13.4 Money transfers and credit	9.70	13.90	20.00	22.10	10.50
13.4.1 Money, cash gifts given to children	[0.10]	[0.20]	[0.10]	0.20	0.10
13.4.2 Cash gifts and donations	7.30	11.00	17.10	18.60	8.60
13.4.3 Club instalment payments (child) & interest on credit cards	2.30	2.70	2.80	3.30	1.80
Total expenditure	**506.90**	**594.10**	**715.50**	**964.40**	**455.90**
14 Other items recorded					
14.1 Life assurance and contributions to pension funds	21.10	28.70	54.40	76.80	21.70
14.2 Other insurance inc. Friendly Societies	1.30	1.60	2.30	2.90	1.30
14.3 Income tax, payments less refunds	87.20	115.30	167.60	393.50	91.00
14.4 National insurance contributions	33.00	43.20	55.20	73.70	25.40
14.5 Purchase or alteration of dwellings, mortgages	46.80	62.50	73.00	132.50	51.70
14.6 Savings and investments	5.20	6.40	13.70	22.50	6.30
14.7 Pay off loan to clear other debt	3.30	4.30	5.90	3.50	2.60
14.8 Windfall receipts from gambling etc.	2.20	5.50	2.00	1.50	2.20

Note: The commodity and service categories are not comparable to those in publications before 2001–02.
The numbering system is sequential, it does not use actual COICOP codes.

Table A9 Household expenditure by disposable income decile group, 2006

based on weighted data and including children's expenditure

	Lowest ten per cent	Second decile group	Third decile group	Fourth decile group	Fifth decile group	Sixth decile group
Lower boundary of group (£ per week)		140	204	268	340	425
Weighted number of households (thousands)	2,480	2,480	2,480	2,480	2,480	2,480
Total number of households in sample	680	690	680	700	690	670
Total number of persons in sample	920	1,170	1,290	1,470	1,660	1,760
Total number of adults in sample	760	900	1,050	1,150	1,250	1,290
Weighted average number of persons per household	1.3	1.7	1.8	2.1	2.3	2.6
Commodity or service	Average weekly household expenditure (£)					
1 Food & non-alcoholic drinks	24.70	30.60	35.80	39.60	44.70	47.40
2 Alcoholic drinks, tobacco & narcotics	5.20	5.90	8.40	9.50	11.00	11.30
3 Clothing & footwear	6.70	9.70	12.60	15.20	18.50	19.40
4 Housing (net)[1], fuel & power	32.80	35.80	40.50	44.30	47.00	50.30
5 Household goods & services	11.00	15.90	18.30	23.30	23.50	28.30
6 Health	1.90	2.80	2.70	4.70	6.60	5.70
7 Transport	14.60	18.40	31.40	39.50	49.70	51.50
8 Communication	5.70	6.80	8.30	9.60	12.10	11.70
9 Recreation & culture	17.30	26.80	33.00	39.80	51.20	55.40
10 Education	[1.90]	0.60	3.10	2.60	1.90	3.70
11 Restaurants & hotels	10.10	13.70	17.50	24.60	29.30	34.20
12 Miscellaneous goods & services	10.30	14.40	22.20	24.50	28.90	35.30
1–12 All expenditure groups	142.20	181.30	234.00	277.20	324.50	354.10
13 Other expenditure items	16.70	22.70	42.40	44.00	61.30	73.60
Total expenditure	**158.90**	**203.90**	**276.40**	**321.20**	**385.80**	**427.70**
Average weekly expenditure per person (£)						
Total expenditure	**117.80**	**120.30**	**149.80**	**154.40**	**164.70**	**165.50**

Note: The commodity and service categories are not comparable to those in publications before 2001–02.
1 Excluding mortgage interest payments, council tax and Northern Ireland rates.

Table A9 Household expenditure by disposable income decile group, 2006 (cont.)

based on weighted data and including children's expenditure

	Seventh decile group	Eighth decile group	Ninth decile group	Highest ten per cent	All house- holds
Lower boundary of group (£ per week)	513	620	751	992	
Weighted number of households (thousands)	2,480	2,480	2,480	2,480	24,790
Total number of households in sample	680	640	630	600	6,650
Total number of persons in sample	1,870	1,900	1,940	1,880	15,850
Total number of adults in sample	1,380	1,400	1,390	1,430	12,000
Weighted average number of persons per household	2.7	2.9	3.0	3.1	2.4
Commodity or service	Average weekly household expenditure (£)				
1 Food & non-alcoholic drinks	52.70	56.70	64.80	71.90	46.90
2 Alcoholic drinks, tobacco & narcotics	14.40	14.60	15.30	15.60	11.10
3 Clothing & footwear	26.10	32.20	42.10	49.80	23.20
4 Housing (net)[1], fuel & power	45.80	50.60	56.20	72.20	47.60
5 Household goods & services	38.60	33.70	45.10	65.10	30.30
6 Health	5.60	5.80	6.90	15.90	5.90
7 Transport	68.10	83.50	108.00	155.50	62.00
8 Communication	13.70	14.70	17.00	17.90	11.70
9 Recreation & culture	69.30	80.10	97.60	114.30	58.50
10 Education	4.80	6.30	11.70	35.70	7.20
11 Restaurants & hotels	44.30	54.10	66.70	84.40	37.90
12 Miscellaneous goods & services	45.70	45.50	58.50	74.80	36.00
1–12 All expenditure groups	428.90	478.00	589.90	773.30	378.30
13 Other expenditure items	93.00	97.70	154.10	170.40	77.60
Total expenditure	**521.80**	**575.70**	**743.90**	**943.70**	**455.90**
Average weekly expenditure per person (£) **Total expenditure**	**192.80**	**197.50**	**245.70**	**304.60**	**192.80**

Note: The commodity and service categories are not comparable to those in publications before 2001–02.

1 Excluding mortgage interest payments, council tax and Northern Ireland rates.

Table A10 Household expenditure as a percentage of total expenditure by disposable income decile group, 2006

based on weighted data and including children's expenditure

	Lowest ten per cent	Second decile group	Third decile group	Fourth decile group	Fifth decile group	Sixth decile group
Lower boundary of group (£ per week)		140	204	268	340	425
Weighted number of households (thousands)	2,480	2,480	2,480	2,480	2,480	2,480
Total number of households in sample	680	690	680	700	690	670
Total number of persons in sample	920	1,170	1,290	1,470	1,660	1,760
Total number of adults in sample	760	900	1,050	1,150	1,250	1,290
Weighted average number of persons per household	1.3	1.7	1.8	2.1	2.3	2.6
Commodity or service	Percentage of total expenditure					
1 Food & non-alcoholic drinks	16	15	13	12	12	11
2 Alcoholic drinks, tobacco & narcotics	3	3	3	3	3	3
3 Clothing & footwear	4	5	5	5	5	5
4 Housing (net)[1], fuel & power	21	18	15	14	12	12
5 Household goods & services	7	8	7	7	6	7
6 Health	1	1	1	1	2	1
7 Transport	9	9	11	12	13	12
8 Communication	4	3	3	3	3	3
9 Recreation & culture	11	13	12	12	13	13
10 Education	[1]	0	1	1	0	1
11 Restaurants & hotels	6	7	6	8	8	8
12 Miscellaneous goods & services	6	7	8	8	7	8
1–12 All expenditure groups	89	89	85	86	84	83
13 Other expenditure items	11	11	15	14	16	17
Total expenditure	**100**	**100**	**100**	**100**	**100**	**100**

Note: The commodity and service categories are not comparable to those in publications before 2001–02.
1 Excluding mortgage interest payments, council tax and Northern Ireland rates.

Table A10 Household expenditure as a percentage of total expenditure by disposable income decile group, 2006 (cont.)

based on weighted data and including children's expenditure

	Seventh decile group	Eighth decile group	Ninth decile group	Highest ten per cent	All house-holds
Lower boundary of group (£ per week)	513	620	751	992	
Weighted number of households (thousands)	2,480	2,480	2,480	2,480	24,790
Total number of households in sample	680	640	630	600	6,650
Total number of persons in sample	1,870	1,900	1,940	1,880	15,850
Total number of adults in sample	1,380	1,400	1,390	1,430	12,000
Weighted average number of persons per household	2.7	2.9	3.0	3.1	2.4
Commodity or service	Percentage of total expenditure				
1 Food & non-alcoholic drinks	10	10	9	8	10
2 Alcoholic drinks, tobacco & narcotics	3	3	2	2	2
3 Clothing & footwear	5	6	6	5	5
4 Housing (net)[1], fuel & power	9	9	8	8	10
5 Household goods & services	7	6	6	7	7
6 Health	1	1	1	2	1
7 Transport	13	15	15	16	14
8 Communication	3	3	2	2	3
9 Recreation & culture	13	14	13	12	13
10 Education	1	1	2	4	2
11 Restaurants & hotels	8	9	9	9	8
12 Miscellaneous goods & services	9	8	8	8	8
1–12 All expenditure groups	82	83	79	82	83
13 Other expenditure items	18	17	21	18	17
Total expenditure	100	100	100	100	100

Note: The commodity and service categories are not comparable to those in publications before 2001–02.

1 Excluding mortgage interest payments, council tax and Northern Ireland rates.

Table A11 Household expenditure by age of household reference person, 2006
based on weighted data and including children's expenditure

	Less than 30	30 to 49	50 to 64	65 to 74	75 or over	All house- holds
Weighted number of households (thousands)	2,450	9,610	6,430	3,190	3,100	24,790
Total number of households in sample	610	2,580	1,710	940	810	6,650
Total number of persons in sample	1,440	7,910	3,720	1,600	1,180	15,850
Total number of adults in sample	1,050	4,840	3,350	1,580	1,180	12,000
Weighted average number of persons per household	2.3	3.0	2.2	1.7	1.4	2.4
Commodity or service	Average weekly household expenditure (£)					
1 Food & non-alcoholic drinks	34.90	52.40	52.20	42.60	32.70	46.90
2 Alcoholic drinks, tobacco & narcotics	10.70	13.00	12.70	9.00	4.60	11.10
3 Clothing & footwear	26.40	30.30	23.30	14.80	7.40	23.20
4 Housing (net)[1], fuel & power	75.40	51.70	43.20	35.70	34.00	47.60
5 Household goods & services	28.60	35.10	32.60	23.90	18.30	30.30
6 Health	2.10	4.90	8.80	5.40	6.50	5.90
7 Transport	52.90	79.10	70.30	45.10	16.80	62.00
8 Communication	13.90	14.30	11.80	7.70	6.10	11.70
9 Recreation & culture	47.30	68.10	67.80	51.30	25.70	58.50
10 Education	6.40	10.00	9.10	[2.10]	[0.80]	7.20
11 Restaurants & hotels	40.00	47.00	42.60	24.10	12.50	37.90
12 Miscellaneous goods & services	33.50	43.30	38.00	26.80	20.90	36.00
1–12 All expenditure groups	372.20	448.90	412.30	288.50	186.40	378.30
13 Other expenditure items	64.50	105.20	84.30	41.60	25.40	77.60
Total expenditure	**436.60**	**554.10**	**496.60**	**330.10**	**211.80**	**455.90**
Average weekly expenditure per person (£)						
Total expenditure	**186.30**	**186.70**	**221.60**	**193.00**	**147.30**	**192.80**

Note: The commodity and service categories are not comparable to those in publications before 2001–02.

1 Excluding mortgage interest payments, council tax and Northern Ireland rates.

Table A12 Household expenditure as a percentage of total expenditure by age of household reference person, 2006

based on weighted data and including children's expenditure

	Less than 30	30 to 49	50 to 64	65 to 74	75 or over	All house-holds
Weighted number of households (thousands)	2,450	9,610	6,430	3,190	3,100	24,790
Total number of households in sample	610	2,580	1,710	940	810	6,650
Total number of persons in sample	1,440	7,910	3,720	1,600	1,180	15,850
Total number of adults in sample	1,050	4,840	3,350	1,580	1,180	12,000
Weighted average number of persons per household	2.3	3.0	2.2	1.7	1.4	2.4
Commodity or service	Percentage of total expenditure					
1 Food & non-alcoholic drinks	8	9	11	13	15	10
2 Alcoholic drinks, tobacco & narcotics	2	2	3	3	2	2
3 Clothing & footwear	6	5	5	4	3	5
4 Housing (net)[1], fuel & power	17	9	9	11	16	10
5 Household goods & services	7	6	7	7	9	7
6 Health	0	1	2	2	3	1
7 Transport	12	14	14	14	8	14
8 Communication	3	3	2	2	3	3
9 Recreation & culture	11	12	14	16	12	13
10 Education	1	2	2	[1]	[0]	2
11 Restaurants & hotels	9	8	9	7	6	8
12 Miscellaneous goods & services	8	8	8	8	10	8
1–12 All expenditure groups	85	81	83	87	88	83
13 Other expenditure items	15	19	17	13	12	17
Total expenditure	100	100	100	100	100	100

Note: The commodity and service categories are not comparable to those in publications before 2001–02.

1 Excluding mortgage interest payments, council tax and Northern Ireland rates.

Table A13 Detailed household expenditure by age of household reference person, 2006

based on weighted data and including children's expenditure

	Less than 30	30 to 49	50 to 64	65 to 74	75 or over	All house-holds
Weighted number of households (thousands)	2,450	9,610	6,430	3,190	3,100	24,790
Total number of households in sample	610	2,580	1,710	940	810	6,650
Total number of persons in sample	1,440	7,910	3,720	1,600	1,180	15,850
Total number of adults in sample	1,050	4,840	3,350	1,580	1,180	12,000
Weighted average number of persons per household	2.3	3.0	2.2	1.7	1.4	2.4

Commodity or service	Average weekly household expenditure (£)					
1 Food & non-alcoholic drinks	34.90	52.40	52.20	42.60	32.70	46.90
1.1 Food	31.50	47.40	47.80	39.60	30.50	42.80
1.1.1 Bread, rice and cereals	3.40	5.00	4.60	3.50	2.60	4.30
1.1.2 Pasta products	0.50	0.40	0.30	0.10	0.10	0.30
1.1.3 Buns, cakes, biscuits etc.	1.70	3.20	3.10	2.80	2.60	2.90
1.1.4 Pastry (savoury)	0.80	0.90	0.70	0.40	0.20	0.70
1.1.5 Beef (fresh, chilled or frozen)	1.10	1.60	2.00	1.80	1.10	1.60
1.1.6 Pork (fresh, chilled or frozen)	0.40	0.50	0.70	0.70	0.50	0.60
1.1.7 Lamb (fresh, chilled or frozen)	0.40	0.60	0.70	0.80	0.60	0.70
1.1.8 Poultry (fresh, chilled or frozen)	1.50	2.00	2.00	1.40	0.80	1.70
1.1.9 Bacon and ham	0.50	0.80	1.10	0.90	0.70	0.90
1.1.10 Other meat and meat preparations	3.30	5.60	5.30	4.50	3.60	4.90
1.1.11 Fish and fish products	1.40	2.00	2.70	2.40	2.10	2.20
1.1.12 Milk	1.70	2.50	2.40	2.10	1.90	2.30
1.1.13 Cheese and curd	1.20	1.80	1.70	1.30	0.80	1.50
1.1.14 Eggs	0.30	0.50	0.50	0.50	0.40	0.40
1.1.15 Other milk products	1.10	1.90	1.80	1.50	1.10	1.70
1.1.16 Butter	0.10	0.30	0.30	0.40	0.30	0.30
1.1.17 Margarine, other vegetable fats and peanut butter	0.30	0.40	0.50	0.50	0.40	0.40
1.1.18 Cooking oils and fats	0.20	0.20	0.30	0.20	0.10	0.20
1.1.19 Fresh fruit	1.90	3.00	3.40	3.00	2.40	2.90
1.1.20 Other fresh, chilled or frozen fruits	0.20	0.30	0.40	0.30	0.20	0.30
1.1.21 Dried fruit and nuts	0.30	0.50	0.60	0.60	0.40	0.50
1.1.22 Preserved fruit and fruit based products	0.10	0.10	0.20	0.20	0.20	0.10
1.1.23 Fresh vegetables	2.80	3.80	4.20	3.30	2.30	3.60
1.1.24 Dried vegetables	0.00	0.00	0.00	0.00	0.00	0.00
1.1.25 Other preserved or processed vegetables	0.90	1.30	1.20	0.80	0.50	1.10
1.1.26 Potatoes	0.40	0.70	0.90	0.80	0.60	0.70
1.1.27 Other tubers and products of tuber vegetables	1.00	1.60	1.20	0.70	0.50	1.20
1.1.28 Sugar and sugar products	0.20	0.30	0.30	0.30	0.30	0.30
1.1.29 Jams, marmalades	0.10	0.20	0.30	0.30	0.30	0.20
1.1.30 Chocolate	0.90	1.70	1.40	1.20	0.90	1.40
1.1.31 Confectionery products	0.30	0.60	0.50	0.50	0.40	0.50
1.1.32 Edible ices and ice cream	0.40	0.60	0.50	0.40	0.30	0.50
1.1.33 Other food products	2.10	2.50	2.00	1.50	1.20	2.00
1.2 Non-alcoholic drinks	3.50	5.00	4.40	3.00	2.20	4.10
1.2.1 Coffee	0.20	0.50	0.70	0.50	0.30	0.50
1.2.2 Tea	0.20	0.40	0.50	0.50	0.50	0.40
1.2.3 Cocoa and powdered chocolate	0.10	0.10	0.10	0.10	0.10	0.10
1.2.4 Fruit and vegetable juices (inc. fruit squash)	1.10	1.50	1.20	0.80	0.60	1.20
1.2.5 Mineral or spring waters	0.30	0.30	0.30	0.20	0.10	0.30
1.2.6 Soft drinks (inc. fizzy and ready to drink fruit drinks)	1.50	2.10	1.60	1.00	0.60	1.60

Note: The commodity and service categories are not comparable to those in publications before 2001–02.
The numbering system is sequential, it does not use actual COICOP codes.

Table **A13** Detailed household expenditure by age of household reference person, 2006 (cont.)
based on weighted data and including children's expenditure

	Less than 30	30 to 49	50 to 64	65 to 74	75 or over	All house-holds
Commodity or service	Average weekly household expenditure (£)					
2 Alcoholic drink, tobacco & narcotics	**10.70**	**13.00**	**12.70**	**9.00**	**4.60**	**11.10**
2.1 Alcoholic drinks	5.00	7.60	7.40	5.70	3.20	6.50
2.1.1 Spirits and liqueurs (brought home)	0.70	1.10	1.60	1.50	1.40	1.30
2.1.2 Wines, fortified wines (brought home)	2.10	4.00	3.80	3.00	1.40	3.30
2.1.3 Beer, lager, ciders and perry (brought home)	2.10	2.30	2.00	1.10	0.50	1.80
2.1.4 Alcopops (brought home)	0.20	0.10	0.10	[0.00]	[0.00]	0.10
2.2 Tobacco and narcotics	5.70	5.40	5.30	3.40	1.40	4.60
2.2.1 Cigarettes	5.20	4.90	4.70	2.90	1.30	4.20
2.2.2 Cigars, other tobacco products and narcotics	0.60	0.50	0.60	0.50	[0.10]	0.50
3 Clothing & footwear	**26.40**	**30.30**	**23.30**	**14.80**	**7.40**	**23.20**
3.1 Clothing	21.60	24.20	19.40	12.20	6.00	18.90
3.1.1 Men's outer garments	6.40	5.90	4.40	2.60	1.20	4.60
3.1.2 Men's under garments	0.40	0.40	0.50	0.40	0.20	0.40
3.1.3 Women's outer garments	9.60	9.70	9.80	6.40	3.00	8.50
3.1.4 Women's under garments	1.60	1.40	1.60	1.20	0.80	1.40
3.1.5 Boy's outer garments (5–15)	0.40	1.60	0.30	[0.20]	[0.00]	0.80
3.1.6 Girl's outer garments (5–15)	0.40	2.00	0.70	0.20	[0.10]	1.00
3.1.7 Infant's outer garments (under 5)	1.30	1.00	0.40	0.20	[0.10]	0.70
3.1.8 Children's under garments (under 16)	0.40	0.70	0.30	0.20	[0.00]	0.40
3.1.9 Accessories	0.80	1.00	0.70	0.40	[0.20]	0.70
3.1.10 Haberdashery, clothing materials and clothing hire	[0.10]	0.30	0.30	0.20	0.10	0.20
3.1.11 Dry cleaners, laundry and dyeing	[0.20]	0.30	0.40	0.20	0.30	0.30
3.2 Footwear	4.80	6.10	3.90	2.60	1.40	4.30
4 Housing (net)[1], fuel & power	**75.40**	**51.70**	**43.20**	**35.70**	**34.00**	**47.60**
4.1 Actual rentals for housing	69.00	29.30	19.40	16.10	20.90	27.90
4.1.1 Gross rent	69.00	29.20	19.20	16.10	20.90	27.80
4.1.2 *less* housing benefit, rebates & allowances rec'd	17.00	9.80	10.00	10.60	13.80	11.20
4.1.3 Net rent	51.90	19.40	9.20	5.50	7.10	16.70
4.1.4 Second dwelling rent	[0.00]	[0.10]	[0.20]	–	–	[0.10]
4.2 Maintenance and repair of dwelling	5.30	8.80	9.00	7.90	5.50	8.00
4.3 Water supply and miscellaneous services relating to the dwelling	6.40	6.80	7.30	6.60	7.30	6.90
4.4 Electricity, gas and other fuels	11.70	16.60	17.40	15.70	14.10	15.90
4.4.1 Electricity	6.10	8.00	8.20	7.20	6.30	7.50
4.4.2 Gas	5.30	7.40	7.70	7.30	6.50	7.20
4.4.3 Other fuels	0.30	1.20	1.50	1.20	1.40	1.20

Note: The commodity and service categories are not comparable to those in publications before 2001–02.
    The numbering system is sequential, it does not use actual COICOP codes.
1 Excluding mortgage interest payments, council tax and Northern Ireland rates.

Table A13 Detailed household expenditure by age of household reference person, 2006 (cont.)

based on weighted data and including children's expenditure

	Less than 30	30 to 49	50 to 64	65 to 74	75 or over	All house-holds
Commodity or service	Average weekly household expenditure (£)					
5 Household goods & services	**28.60**	**35.10**	**32.60**	**23.90**	**18.30**	**30.30**
5.1 Furniture and furnishings and floor coverings	20.30	19.90	17.10	11.60	7.20	16.50
5.1.1 Furniture and furnishings	16.20	14.80	12.70	8.30	6.00	12.50
5.1.2 Floor coverings	4.10	5.00	4.40	3.20	1.30	4.10
5.2 Household textiles	1.40	2.20	2.00	1.70	1.30	1.90
5.3 Household appliances	1.00	3.70	3.40	2.50	2.20	3.00
5.4 Glassware, tableware and household utensils	1.70	1.80	1.80	1.20	0.60	1.60
5.5 Tools and equipment for house and garden	1.30	2.40	2.50	1.80	1.10	2.10
5.6 Goods and services for routine household maintenance	2.90	5.20	5.80	5.10	5.90	5.20
5.6.1 Cleaning materials	1.60	2.60	2.60	2.10	1.30	2.30
5.6.2 Household goods and hardware	0.80	1.30	1.30	1.10	0.70	1.20
5.6.3 Domestic services, carpet cleaning, hire/repair of furniture/furnishings	0.50	1.30	1.90	1.80	3.80	1.70
6 Health	**2.10**	**4.90**	**8.80**	**5.40**	**6.50**	**5.90**
6.1 Medical products, appliances and equipment	1.40	3.00	3.80	2.90	3.80	3.10
6.1.1 Medicines, prescriptions and healthcare products	1.00	1.70	2.00	1.60	2.00	1.70
6.1.2 Spectacles, lenses, accessories and repairs	0.40	1.30	1.80	1.30	1.80	1.40
6.2 Hospital services	0.70	1.90	5.00	2.50	2.70	2.70
7 Transport	**52.90**	**79.10**	**70.30**	**45.10**	**16.80**	**62.00**
7.1 Purchase of vehicles	15.90	31.60	26.20	17.60	4.50	23.40
7.1.1 Purchase of new cars and vans	3.30	9.80	10.70	8.60	[2.70]	8.30
7.1.2 Purchase of second hand cars or vans	12.20	21.00	14.70	8.80	1.70	14.50
7.1.3 Purchase of motorcycles and other vehicles	[0.50]	0.80	[0.70]	[0.20]	[0.10]	0.60
7.2 Operation of personal transport	23.80	35.60	33.70	20.50	8.60	28.60
7.2.1 Spares and accessories	1.30	2.40	3.00	1.30	0.40	2.10
7.2.2 Petrol, diesel and other motor oils	15.60	23.00	21.20	13.10	4.70	18.20
7.2.3 Repairs and servicing	5.00	7.20	6.60	4.70	2.70	5.90
7.2.4 Other motoring costs	1.90	3.00	2.90	1.50	0.80	2.40
7.3 Transport services	13.20	11.90	10.40	7.00	3.70	10.00
7.3.1 Rail and tube fares	2.80	3.20	1.90	0.60	0.40	2.20
7.3.2 Bus and coach fares	2.20	1.70	1.40	0.40	0.30	1.30
7.3.3 Combined fares	2.90	1.10	1.00	[0.20]	[0.00]	1.00
7.3.4 Other travel and transport	5.20	5.90	6.10	5.80	3.00	5.50
8 Communication	**13.90**	**14.30**	**11.80**	**7.70**	**6.10**	**11.70**
8.1 Postal services	0.40	0.50	0.50	0.60	0.60	0.50
8.2 Telephone and telefax equipment	1.00	1.00	0.80	[0.20]	[0.10]	0.70
8.3 Telephone and telefax services	12.50	12.90	10.50	6.90	5.40	10.50

Note: The commodity and service categories are not comparable to those in publications before 2001–02.

The numbering system is sequential, it does not use actual COICOP codes.

Table A13 Detailed household expenditure by age of household reference person, 2006 (cont.)

based on weighted data and including children's expenditure

Commodity or service	Less than 30	30 to 49	50 to 64	65 to 74	75 or over	All house-holds
	Average weekly household expenditure (£)					
9 Recreation & culture	47.30	68.10	67.80	51.30	25.70	58.50
9.1 Audio-visual, photographic and information processing equipment	8.80	8.50	8.30	3.80	2.50	7.10
9.1.1 Audio equipment and accessories, CD players	2.60	2.50	2.00	0.80	0.50	1.90
9.1.2 TV, video and computers	6.00	5.40	5.20	2.40	2.00	4.60
9.1.3 Photographic, cine and optical equipment	[0.10]	0.70	1.10	0.50	[0.10]	0.60
9.2 Other major durables for recreation and culture	[0.60]	2.20	2.00	[1.70]	[0.00]	1.70
9.3 Other recreational items and equipment, gardens and pets	7.90	12.40	12.00	8.40	3.80	10.30
9.3.1 Games, toys and hobbies	1.50	2.90	1.90	1.50	0.30	2.00
9.3.2 Computer software and games	1.40	1.80	0.90	[0.20]	[0.00]	1.10
9.3.3 Equipment for sport, camping and open-air recreation	1.00	1.60	1.20	0.70	[0.20]	1.20
9.3.4 Horticultural goods, garden equipment and plants	1.10	2.50	3.40	2.70	2.10	2.60
9.3.5 Pets and pet food	2.90	3.60	4.70	3.30	1.10	3.50
9.4 Recreational and cultural services	15.80	23.00	21.20	14.20	6.90	18.70
9.4.1 Sports admissions, subscriptions, leisure class fees and equipment hire	4.40	8.60	5.70	3.30	0.70	5.80
9.4.2 Cinema, theatre and museums etc.	2.10	2.50	2.30	1.30	0.70	2.00
9.4.3 TV, video, satellite rental, cable subscriptions, TV licences and the Internet	5.80	7.20	6.40	4.70	1.60	5.80
9.4.4 Miscellaneous entertainments	1.10	1.40	1.10	0.80	0.50	1.10
9.4.5 Development of film, deposit for film development, passport photos, holiday and school photos	0.80	0.50	0.40	0.20	[0.10]	0.40
9.4.6 Gambling payments	1.60	2.90	5.40	3.90	3.20	3.60
9.5 Newspapers, books and stationery	4.40	6.80	8.00	6.70	5.20	6.60
9.5.1 Books	1.60	1.80	1.90	1.20	0.70	1.60
9.5.2 Diaries, address books, cards etc.	1.20	2.30	2.30	1.60	1.00	2.00
9.5.3 Newspapers	0.60	1.40	2.60	3.00	2.90	2.00
9.5.4 Magazines and periodicals	0.90	1.20	1.10	0.90	0.60	1.00
9.6 Package holidays	9.90	15.20	16.20	16.60	7.20	14.10
9.6.1 Package holidays – UK	[0.20]	0.70	0.90	1.80	1.20	0.90
9.6.2 Package holidays – abroad	9.60	14.40	15.30	14.80	5.90	13.20
10 Education	6.40	10.00	9.10	[2.10]	[0.80]	7.20
10.1 Education fees	6.30	9.30	8.80	[2.00]	[0.70]	6.90
10.2 Payments for school trips, other ad-hoc expenditure	[0.00]	0.60	0.30	[0.00]	[0.10]	0.40
11 Restaurants & hotels	40.00	47.00	42.60	24.10	12.50	37.90
11.1 Catering services	37.00	39.70	35.00	19.00	10.30	31.90
11.1.1 Restaurant and café meals	11.80	14.30	14.40	11.10	6.80	12.80
11.1.2 Alcoholic drinks (away from home)	12.00	9.60	10.00	5.20	1.70	8.40
11.1.3 Take away meals eaten at home	5.60	5.60	3.30	1.50	0.90	3.90
11.1.4 Other take-away and snack food	5.40	6.70	3.60	0.90	0.30	4.20
11.1.5 Contract catering (food) and canteens	[2.20]	[3.50]	[3.70]	[0.20]	[0.60]	2.60
11.2 Accommodation services	3.00	7.30	7.60	5.20	2.20	6.00
11.2.1 Holiday in the UK	0.70	2.90	3.20	2.90	1.40	2.60
11.2.2 Holiday abroad	2.30	4.30	4.30	2.30	[0.80]	3.40
11.2.3 Room hire	[0.00]	[0.00]	[0.00]	–	–	[0.00]

Note: The commodity and service categories are not comparable to those in publications before 2001–02.
The numbering system is sequential, it does not use actual COICOP codes.

Table A13 Detailed household expenditure by age of household reference person, 2006 (cont.)

based on weighted data and including children's expenditure

Commodity or service	Less than 30	30 to 49	50 to 64	65 to 74	75 or over	All house-holds
	Average weekly household expenditure (£)					
12 Miscellaneous goods & services	33.50	43.30	38.00	26.80	20.90	36.00
12.1 Personal care	9.30	11.60	10.40	7.90	5.40	9.80
12.1.1 Hairdressing, beauty treatment	2.30	3.30	3.70	3.30	2.70	3.20
12.1.2 Toilet paper	0.60	0.80	0.80	0.60	0.50	0.70
12.1.3 Toiletries and soap	1.90	2.50	2.10	1.50	1.00	2.00
12.1.4 Baby toiletries and accessories (disposable)	1.20	0.90	0.30	0.10	0.10	0.60
12.1.5 Hair products, cosmetics and related electrical appliances	3.30	4.00	3.40	2.50	1.10	3.20
12.2 Personal effects	3.20	4.20	3.30	1.80	1.00	3.10
12.3 Social protection	3.20	4.40	1.00	[0.30]	2.60	2.60
12.4 Insurance	12.00	16.70	17.10	13.40	9.90	15.10
12.4.1 Household insurances – structural, contents and appliances	2.90	5.60	5.80	5.10	4.00	5.10
12.4.2 Medical insurance premiums	0.30	1.10	2.40	2.80	2.70	1.80
12.4.3 Vehicle insurance including boat insurance	8.80	9.70	8.60	5.40	3.10	8.00
12.4.4 Non-package holiday, other travel insurance	–	0.20	[0.30]	[0.10]	[0.00]	0.20
12.5 Other services	5.80	6.40	6.30	3.30	2.10	5.40
12.5.1 Moving house	4.60	3.90	2.70	2.30	1.40	3.10
12.5.2 Bank, building society, post office, credit card charges	0.40	0.50	0.30	0.20	0.10	0.40
12.5.3 Other services and professional fees	0.70	2.00	3.20	0.80	0.60	1.90
1–12 All expenditure groups	372.20	448.90	412.30	288.50	186.40	378.30
13 Other expenditure items	64.50	105.20	84.30	41.60	25.40	77.60
13.1 Housing: mortgage interest payments, council tax etc.	49.20	79.30	45.00	22.00	14.80	52.00
13.2 Licences, fines and transfers	2.10	3.40	3.40	2.90	1.30	2.90
13.3 Holiday spending	7.90	10.40	23.60	8.00	[1.30]	12.10
13.4 Money transfers and credit	5.30	12.10	12.30	8.80	8.00	10.50
13.4.1 Money, cash gifts given to children	[0.00]	0.20	[0.00]	[0.00]	[0.00]	0.10
13.4.2 Cash gifts and donations	2.90	9.30	10.40	8.20	7.80	8.60
13.4.3 Club instalment payments (child) and interest on credit cards	2.30	2.60	1.90	0.60	0.20	1.80
Total expenditure	436.60	554.10	496.60	330.10	211.80	455.90
14 Other items recorded						
14.1 Life assurance & contributions to pension funds	10.10	30.80	30.10	5.60	2.10	21.70
14.2 Other insurance inc. Friendly Societies	0.70	1.70	1.50	0.90	0.40	1.30
14.3 Income tax, payments less refunds	72.20	124.80	104.50	47.10	18.30	91.00
14.4 National insurance contributions	30.10	38.20	27.70	2.60	[0.60]	25.40
14.5 Purchase or alteration of dwellings, mortgages	24.90	64.40	64.90	30.20	28.30	51.70
14.6 Savings and investments	4.50	8.20	7.50	1.90	3.70	6.30
14.7 Pay off loan to clear other debt	3.80	4.00	1.90	[1.40]	[0.20]	2.60
14.8 Windfall receipts from gambling etc.	1.50	1.70	3.30	1.70	2.10	2.20

Note: The commodity and service categories are not comparable to those in publications before 2001–02.
    The numbering system is sequential, it does not use actual COICOP codes.

Table A14 Household expenditure by gross income quintile group where the household reference person is aged under 30, 2006

based on weighted data and including children's expenditure

	Lowest twenty per cent	Second quintile group	Third quintile group	Fourth quintile group	Highest twenty per cent	All house-holds
Lower boundary of group (£ per week)[1]		215	384	624	939	
Weighted number of households (thousands)	530	390	610	570	350	2,450
Total number of households in sample	150	110	150	130	70	610
Total number of persons in sample	330	250	380	320	170	1,440
Total number of adults in sample	190	160	270	270	150	1,050
Weighted average number of persons per household	2.2	2.2	2.5	2.3	2.6	2.3
Commodity or service	Average weekly household expenditure (£)					
1 Food & non-alcoholic drinks	26.80	28.00	31.50	42.40	48.70	34.90
2 Alcoholic drinks, tobacco & narcotics	7.30	11.60	10.70	12.90	11.30	10.70
3 Clothing & footwear	11.90	21.70	19.70	42.90	38.20	26.40
4 Housing (net)[2], fuel & power	46.90	77.00	70.00	80.50	117.70	75.40
5 Household goods & services	11.80	17.10	25.60	44.30	46.40	28.60
6 Health	0.70	1.40	2.70	2.60	2.80	2.10
7 Transport	16.30	27.20	46.00	69.50	121.70	52.90
8 Communication	7.10	11.70	13.80	18.00	19.90	13.90
9 Recreation & culture	19.30	30.10	47.50	72.40	67.60	47.30
10 Education	[5.20]	[11.80]	[6.50]	[3.70]	[6.10]	6.40
11 Restaurants & hotels	18.00	28.00	35.30	55.50	69.70	40.00
12 Miscellaneous goods & services	9.80	22.40	29.20	51.70	59.70	33.50
1–12 All expenditure groups	181.10	287.90	338.60	496.50	609.90	372.20
13 Other expenditure items	10.00	35.60	73.50	92.30	117.70	64.50
Total expenditure	**191.10**	**323.50**	**412.10**	**588.80**	**727.70**	**436.60**
Average weekly expenditure per person (£)						
Total expenditure	**87.40**	**147.00**	**165.70**	**256.30**	**283.40**	**186.30**

Note: The commodity and service categories are not comparable to those in publications before 2001–02.

1 Lower boundary of 2006 gross income quintile groups (£ per week).

2 Excluding mortgage interest payments, council tax and Northern Ireland rates.

Table A15 Household expenditure by gross income quintile group where the household reference person is aged under 30 to 49, 2006

based on weighted data and including children's expenditure

	Lowest twenty per cent	Second quintile group	Third quintile group	Fourth quintile group	Highest twenty per cent	All house-holds
Lower boundary of group (£ per week)[1]		215	384	624	939	
Weighted number of households (thousands)	970	1,290	2,020	2,530	2,800	9,610
Total number of households in sample	270	360	570	680	710	2,580
Total number of persons in sample	620	1,010	1,740	2,190	2,360	7,910
Total number of adults in sample	350	550	1,030	1,380	1,540	4,840
Weighted average number of persons per household	2.2	2.7	3.0	3.1	3.2	3.0
Commodity or service	Average weekly household expenditure (£)					
1 Food & non-alcoholic drinks	31.70	39.10	48.10	55.80	65.60	52.40
2 Alcoholic drinks, tobacco & narcotics	7.80	10.30	12.00	14.30	15.40	13.00
3 Clothing & footwear	11.90	20.70	22.40	30.60	46.40	30.30
4 Housing (net)[2], fuel & power	38.60	52.60	48.10	50.20	59.70	51.70
5 Household goods & services	11.70	20.00	27.90	32.70	57.60	35.10
6 Health	2.00	3.00	3.20	5.00	7.80	4.90
7 Transport	19.50	49.40	54.70	79.60	130.40	79.10
8 Communication	8.90	12.40	12.80	14.80	17.60	14.30
9 Recreation & culture	24.50	39.20	49.60	76.10	102.50	68.10
10 Education	4.40	3.80	2.10	5.00	24.90	10.00
11 Restaurants & hotels	17.50	26.20	34.10	46.40	76.50	47.00
12 Miscellaneous goods & services	12.70	27.50	35.80	46.70	63.40	43.30
1–12 All expenditure groups	191.20	304.20	351.00	457.30	667.80	448.90
13 Other expenditure items	24.00	55.90	78.20	104.10	176.50	105.20
Total expenditure	**215.20**	**360.10**	**429.20**	**561.40**	**844.30**	**554.10**
Average weekly expenditure per person (£) **Total expenditure**	**96.60**	**132.70**	**145.20**	**178.70**	**264.30**	**186.70**

Note: The commodity and service categories are not comparable to those in publications before 2001–02.

1 Lower boundary of 2006 gross income quintile groups (£ per week).

2 Excluding mortgage interest payments, council tax and Northern Ireland rates.

Table A16 Household expenditure by gross income quintile group where the household reference person is aged 50 to 64, 2006

based on weighted data and including children's expenditure

	Lowest twenty per cent	Second quintile group	Third quintile group	Fourth quintile group	Highest twenty per cent	All house-holds
Lower boundary of group (£ per week)[1]		215	384	624	939	
Weighted number of households (thousands)	1,070	1,110	1,310	1,370	1,560	6,430
Total number of households in sample	300	310	360	350	380	1,710
Total number of persons in sample	430	570	770	870	1,090	3,720
Total number of adults in sample	400	520	700	790	950	3,350
Weighted average number of persons per household	1.5	1.8	2.1	2.5	2.9	2.2
Commodity or service			Average weekly household expenditure (£)			
1 Food & non-alcoholic drinks	30.40	40.30	48.20	57.20	74.70	52.20
2 Alcoholic drinks, tobacco & narcotics	6.90	9.70	12.90	15.80	15.90	12.70
3 Clothing & footwear	7.00	14.70	18.30	23.60	44.70	23.30
4 Housing (net)[2], fuel & power	32.70	38.90	40.50	42.40	56.40	43.20
5 Household goods & services	14.20	27.30	24.00	36.80	52.50	32.60
6 Health	2.20	4.20	7.40	7.40	18.90	8.80
7 Transport	23.90	40.50	52.20	71.40	137.60	70.30
8 Communication	6.70	9.10	11.50	13.00	16.60	11.80
9 Recreation & culture	26.10	41.00	62.70	77.90	110.90	67.80
10 Education	[0.80]	[1.60]	[3.40]	7.30	26.50	9.10
11 Restaurants & hotels	13.40	20.30	34.00	50.20	78.90	42.60
12 Miscellaneous goods & services	12.00	26.10	26.80	44.90	67.50	38.00
1–12 All expenditure groups	176.40	273.80	341.90	448.00	701.10	412.30
13 Other expenditure items	24.60	55.20	59.10	86.10	165.70	84.30
Total expenditure	201.00	329.00	400.90	534.10	866.80	496.60
Average weekly expenditure per person (£) Total expenditure	136.60	178.90	187.90	211.10	299.80	221.60

Note: The commodity and service categories are not comparable to those in publications before 2001–02.
1 Lower boundary of 2006 gross income quintile groups (£ per week).
2 Excluding mortgage interest payments, council tax and Northern Ireland rates.

Table A17 Household expenditure by gross income quintile group where the household reference person is aged 65 to 74, 2006

based on weighted data and including children's expenditure

	Lowest twenty per cent	Second quintile group	Third quintile group	Fourth quintile group	Highest twenty per cent	All house-holds
Lower boundary of group (£ per week)[1]		215	384	624	939	
Weighted number of households (thousands)	940	1,070	640	340	200	3,190
Total number of households in sample	270	320	190	100	50	940
Total number of persons in sample	330	560	390	210	110	1,600
Total number of adults in sample	330	550	380	210	110	1,580
Weighted average number of persons per household	1.2	1.7	2.0	2.1	2.2	1.7
Commodity or service	Average weekly household expenditure (£)					
1 Food & non-alcoholic drinks	28.70	41.10	49.60	57.60	68.80	42.60
2 Alcoholic drinks, tobacco & narcotics	5.50	8.30	11.10	12.90	16.10	9.00
3 Clothing & footwear	7.30	11.20	15.30	29.20	43.70	14.80
4 Housing (net)[2], fuel & power	29.30	32.90	40.50	40.90	57.00	35.70
5 Household goods & services	11.80	21.60	26.30	38.30	60.30	23.90
6 Health	3.00	3.10	8.00	8.60	14.40	5.40
7 Transport	14.80	40.50	53.60	76.70	131.10	45.10
8 Communication	5.40	6.90	8.90	10.60	13.70	7.70
9 Recreation & culture	25.30	43.60	66.70	79.10	116.70	51.30
10 Education	[0.00]	[0.10]	[0.00]	[5.00]	[24.10]	[2.10]
11 Restaurants & hotels	9.30	19.70	29.30	49.30	57.80	24.10
12 Miscellaneous goods & services	14.10	21.30	30.50	36.80	86.40	26.80
1–12 All expenditure groups	154.60	250.20	339.80	444.80	690.10	288.50
13 Other expenditure items	21.40	30.40	52.70	72.00	109.30	41.60
Total expenditure	**176.10**	**280.70**	**392.50**	**516.80**	**799.40**	**330.10**
Average weekly expenditure per person (£) **Total expenditure**	**142.90**	**163.70**	**195.00**	**241.80**	**358.00**	**193.00**

Note: The commodity and service categories are not comparable to those in publications before 2001–02.

1 Lower boundary of 2006 gross income quintile groups (£ per week).

2 Excluding mortgage interest payments, council tax and Northern Ireland rates.

Table A18 Household expenditure by gross income quintile group where the household reference person is aged 75 or over, 2006

based on weighted data and including children's expenditure

	Lowest twenty per cent	Second quintile group	Third quintile group	Fourth quintile group	Highest twenty per cent	All house-holds
Lower boundary of group (£ per week)[1]		215	384	624	939	
Weighted number of households (thousands)	1,460	1,090	370	140	50	3,100
Total number of households in sample	370	290	100	40	10	810
Total number of persons in sample	420	460	190	80	30	1,180
Total number of adults in sample	420	460	190	80	30	1,180
Weighted average number of persons per household	1.1	1.6	1.8	2.2	2.4	1.4
Commodity or service	Average weekly household expenditure (£)					
1 Food & non-alcoholic drinks	23.60	36.60	43.80	57.90	[62.00]	32.70
2 Alcoholic drinks, tobacco & narcotics	2.70	5.50	7.90	8.10	[8.80]	4.60
3 Clothing & footwear	4.70	6.40	13.30	21.20	[25.00]	7.40
4 Housing (net)[2], fuel & power	29.50	33.00	46.70	45.20	[66.10]	34.00
5 Household goods & services	14.10	17.40	32.10	22.70	[50.30]	18.30
6 Health	2.70	8.60	12.30	15.00	[3.40]	6.50
7 Transport	6.50	18.00	30.80	47.60	[105.70]	16.80
8 Communication	4.40	5.60	12.00	11.30	[7.60]	6.10
9 Recreation & culture	13.30	26.60	46.70	47.20	[153.90]	25.70
10 Education	[0.00]	[0.60]	[0.20]	[12.80]	[0.00]	[0.80]
11 Restaurants & hotels	6.20	11.80	21.20	57.80	[20.00]	12.50
12 Miscellaneous goods & services	11.00	21.20	40.60	46.30	[89.90]	20.90
1–12 All expenditure groups	118.50	191.40	307.70	393.10	[592.70]	186.40
13 Other expenditure items	13.30	28.30	44.50	49.10	[112.00]	25.40
Total expenditure	**131.80**	**219.80**	**352.20**	**442.20**	**[704.60]**	**211.80**
Average weekly expenditure per person (£)						
Total expenditure	**117.00**	**138.10**	**194.20**	**204.90**	**[298.70]**	**147.30**

Note: The commodity and service categories are not comparable to those in publications before 2001–02.

1 Lower boundary of 2006 gross income quintile groups (£ per week).

2 Excluding mortgage interest payments, council tax and Northern Ireland rates.

Table A19 Household expenditure by economic activity status of the household reference person, 2006

based on weighted data and including children's expenditure

	Employees			Self-employed	All in employment[1]
	Full-time	Part-time	All		
Weighted number of households (thousands)	10,830	2,150	12,970	2,060	15,060
Total number of households in sample	2,810	580	3,390	550	3,950
Total number of persons in sample	7,620	1,480	9,090	1,570	10,680
Total number of adults in sample	5,530	1,000	6,540	1,110	7,660
Weighted average number of persons per household	2.7	2.6	2.6	2.8	2.7
Commodity or service	Average weekly household expenditure (£)				
1 Food & non-alcoholic drinks	52.90	45.60	51.70	56.70	52.30
2 Alcoholic drinks, tobacco & narcotics	13.00	10.80	12.60	14.90	12.90
3 Clothing & footwear	30.40	26.00	29.70	31.70	29.90
4 Housing (net)[2], fuel & power	54.30	52.80	54.00	53.10	53.90
5 Household goods & services	38.20	27.20	36.40	37.80	36.50
6 Health	6.40	3.70	5.90	5.70	5.90
7 Transport	83.30	62.30	79.80	84.50	80.40
8 Communication	13.90	12.70	13.70	17.00	14.10
9 Recreation & culture	74.10	55.00	70.90	76.20	71.60
10 Education	10.00	5.70	9.30	15.10	10.10
11 Restaurants & hotels	51.00	39.50	49.10	49.20	49.10
12 Miscellaneous goods & services	46.70	37.00	45.10	44.20	44.90
1–12 All expenditure groups	474.20	378.20	458.30	486.10	461.60
13 Other expenditure items	113.80	71.50	106.80	116.20	108.00
Total expenditure	**588.00**	**449.80**	**565.10**	**602.40**	**569.70**
Average weekly expenditure per person (£)					
Total expenditure	**220.90**	**174.50**	**213.40**	**218.80**	**214.00**

Note: The commodity and service categories are not comparable to those in publications before 2001–02.

1 Includes households where the household reference person was on a Government supported training scheme.

2 Excluding mortgage interest payments, council tax and Northern Ireland rates.

Table A19 Household expenditure by economic activity status of the household reference person, 2006 (cont.)

based on weighted data and including children's expenditure

	Unemployed	All economically active[1]	Economically inactive			All households
			Retired	Other	All	
Weighted number of households (thousands)	450	15,510	6,220	3,060	9,280	24,790
Total number of households in sample	120	4,060	1,740	840	2,580	6,650
Total number of persons in sample	260	10,940	2,730	2,180	4,910	15,850
Total number of adults in sample	170	7,830	2,710	1,470	4,180	12,000
Weighted average number of persons per household	2.2	2.6	1.6	2.6	1.9	2.4
Commodity or service	Average weekly household expenditure (£)					
1 Food & non-alcoholic drinks	30.70	51.70	37.10	42.40	38.90	46.90
2 Alcoholic drinks, tobacco & narcotics	7.90	12.80	6.60	11.90	8.30	11.10
3 Clothing & footwear	10.60	29.40	10.40	18.30	13.00	23.20
4 Housing (net)[2], fuel & power	45.50	53.60	34.50	43.50	37.40	47.60
5 Household goods & services	13.20	35.90	19.90	22.90	20.90	30.30
6 Health	0.90	5.70	7.40	3.50	6.10	5.90
7 Transport	33.00	79.00	29.90	41.40	33.70	62.00
8 Communication	7.50	13.90	6.70	10.80	8.10	11.70
9 Recreation & culture	27.70	70.30	37.90	40.50	38.70	58.50
10 Education	[2.20]	9.90	1.50	5.40	2.80	7.20
11 Restaurants & hotels	15.60	48.10	17.40	27.70	20.80	37.90
12 Miscellaneous goods & services	14.10	44.00	22.50	22.70	22.60	36.00
1–12 All expenditure groups	208.90	454.30	231.80	291.00	251.30	378.30
13 Other expenditure items	27.10	105.70	30.90	30.20	30.70	77.60
Total expenditure	**236.00**	**560.00**	**262.70**	**321.20**	**282.00**	**455.90**
Average weekly expenditure per person (£)						
Total expenditure	**109.40**	**211.60**	**168.50**	**125.00**	**149.00**	**192.80**

Note: The commodity and service categories are not comparable to those in publications before 2001–02.

1 Includes households where the household reference person was on a Government supported training scheme.

2 Excluding mortgage interest payments, council tax and Northern Ireland rates.

Table A20 Household expenditure by gross income quintile group: the household reference person is a full-time employee, 2006

based on weighted data and including children's expenditure

	Lowest twenty per cent	Second quintile group	Third quintile group	Fourth quintile group	Highest twenty per cent	All house-holds
Lower boundary of group (£ per week)[1]		215	384	624	939	
Weighted number of households (thousands)	50	960	2,570	3,440	3,810	10,830
Total number of households in sample	20	260	700	900	940	2,810
Total number of persons in sample	30	440	1,720	2,540	2,890	7,620
Total number of adults in sample	20	340	1,220	1,840	2,110	5,530
Weighted average number of persons per household	1.9	1.7	2.4	2.8	3.0	2.7
Commodity or service			Average weekly household expenditure (£)			
1 Food & non-alcoholic drinks	[27.40]	29.40	42.40	52.90	66.20	52.90
2 Alcoholic drinks, tobacco & narcotics	[7.90]	9.70	10.80	13.70	14.70	13.00
3 Clothing & footwear	[10.10]	17.30	19.10	27.90	43.90	30.40
4 Housing (net)[2], fuel & power	[68.50]	52.20	47.40	49.50	63.60	54.30
5 Household goods & services	[7.30]	19.80	25.40	35.70	54.20	38.20
6 Health	[2.30]	4.40	4.20	5.70	9.00	6.40
7 Transport	[29.20]	35.80	49.40	74.40	126.90	83.30
8 Communication	[9.70]	9.40	11.50	13.60	16.90	13.90
9 Recreation & culture	[29.10]	29.40	50.00	75.20	101.10	74.10
10 Education	–	[5.10]	2.60	5.00	21.00	10.00
11 Restaurants & hotels	[35.50]	24.10	31.70	46.10	75.50	51.00
12 Miscellaneous goods & services	[17.10]	26.40	29.80	46.10	64.20	46.70
1–12 All expenditure groups	[244.00]	263.10	324.30	445.90	657.30	474.20
13 Other expenditure items	[32.40]	57.90	71.80	101.20	168.90	113.80
Total expenditure	[276.40]	321.00	396.10	547.00	826.20	588.00
Average weekly expenditure per person (£) Total expenditure	[148.70]	189.70	164.90	197.90	275.50	220.90

Note: The commodity and service categories are not comparable to those in publications before 2001–02.

1 Lower boundary of 2006 gross income quintile groups (£ per week).

2 Excluding mortgage interest payments, council tax and Northern Ireland rates.

Table A21 Household expenditure by gross income quintile group: the household reference person is self-employed, 2006

based on weighted data and including children's expenditure

		Lowest twenty per cent	Second quintile group	Third quintile group	Fourth quintile group	Highest twenty per cent	All house-holds
Lower boundary of group (£ per week)[1]			215	384	624	939	
Weighted number of households (thousands)		200	320	480	510	560	2,060
Total number of households in sample		60	90	140	130	140	550
Total number of persons in sample		110	220	400	390	450	1,570
Total number of adults in sample		80	150	280	280	310	1,110
Weighted average number of persons per household		2.0	2.5	2.8	2.9	3.0	2.8
Commodity or service		Average weekly household expenditure (£)					
1	Food & non-alcoholic drinks	33.70	46.20	53.50	61.70	69.10	56.70
2	Alcoholic drinks, tobacco & narcotics	7.30	12.80	15.10	15.60	18.10	14.90
3	Clothing & footwear	12.40	23.70	21.30	32.80	51.20	31.70
4	Housing (net)[2], fuel & power	47.20	50.30	50.10	54.10	58.40	53.10
5	Household goods & services	20.00	24.40	32.50	34.30	59.60	37.80
6	Health	1.30	6.50	5.00	4.50	8.70	5.70
7	Transport	47.20	63.90	53.60	85.90	134.90	84.50
8	Communication	10.10	14.10	16.50	18.80	19.80	17.00
9	Recreation & culture	42.00	47.00	66.30	83.30	107.10	76.20
10	Education	[5.40]	[3.70]	[7.20]	[11.50]	35.20	15.10
11	Restaurants & hotels	30.20	31.30	36.00	54.80	72.60	49.20
12	Miscellaneous goods & services	20.90	33.50	39.50	42.90	63.90	44.20
1–12	All expenditure groups	277.60	357.20	396.60	500.20	698.60	486.10
13	Other expenditure items	83.30	70.30	101.90	102.00	179.50	116.20
Total expenditure		**360.90**	**427.60**	**498.60**	**602.30**	**878.10**	**602.40**
Average weekly expenditure per person (£) **Total expenditure**		**177.40**	**173.00**	**176.50**	**208.80**	**293.60**	**218.80**

Note: The commodity and service categories are not comparable to those in publications before 2001–02.

1 Lower boundary of 2006 gross income quintile groups (£ per week).

2 Excluding mortgage interest payments, council tax and Northern Ireland rates.

Table **A22** Household expenditure by number of persons working, 2006
based on weighted data and including children's expenditure

	Number of persons working					All house-holds
	None	One	Two	Three	Four or more	
Weighted number of households (thousands)	8,500	6,980	7,480	1,410	420	24,790
Total number of households in sample	2,370	1,910	1,960	310	90	6,650
Total number of persons in sample	4,140	4,290	5,850	1,150	420	15,850
Total number of adults in sample	3,510	3,030	4,180	930	360	12,000
Weighted average number of persons per household	1.7	2.2	2.9	3.6	4.6	2.4
Weighted average age of head of household	65	46	43	48	48	52
Employment status of the household reference person[1]:						
– % working full-time or self-employed	0	67	88	86	91	51
– % working part-time	0	19	9	12	7	9
– % not working	100	14	2	3	2	41
Commodity or service	Average weekly household expenditure (£)					
1 Food & non-alcoholic drinks	35.80	42.00	57.60	71.10	80.70	46.90
2 Alcoholic drinks, tobacco & narcotics	7.40	10.50	14.40	17.80	16.90	11.10
3 Clothing & footwear	11.40	20.60	33.10	44.80	60.10	23.20
4 Housing (net)[2], fuel & power	35.60	51.20	54.30	60.30	65.60	47.60
5 Household goods & services	19.50	28.70	43.30	33.00	32.90	30.30
6 Health	4.70	4.70	7.90	6.60	8.00	5.90
7 Transport	28.10	57.80	88.20	121.10	152.40	62.00
8 Communication	7.00	11.60	15.00	20.90	21.10	11.70
9 Recreation & culture	35.10	53.10	81.40	92.50	98.20	58.50
10 Education	1.70	9.90	10.70	9.70	[4.10]	7.20
11 Restaurants & hotels	17.40	34.20	55.30	74.60	80.20	37.90
12 Miscellaneous goods & services	20.80	33.20	50.90	55.60	59.30	36.00
1–12 All expenditure groups	224.60	357.50	512.10	608.00	679.50	378.30
13 Other expenditure items	28.60	80.70	125.50	95.90	102.60	77.60
Total expenditure	**253.20**	**438.20**	**637.60**	**703.90**	**782.10**	**455.90**
Average weekly expenditure per person (£) **Total expenditure**	**146.60**	**201.50**	**219.40**	**195.20**	**170.40**	**192.80**

Note: The commodity and service categories are not comparable to those in publications before 2001–02.

1 Excludes households where the household reference person was on a Government-supported training scheme.

2 Excluding mortgage interest payments, council tax and Northern Ireland rates.

Table **A23** Household expenditure by age at which the household reference person completed continuous full-time education, 2006

based on weighted data and including children's expenditure

	Aged 14 and under	Aged 15	Aged 16	Aged 17 and under 19	Aged 19 and under 22	Aged 22 or over
Weighted number of households (thousands)	2,500	5,050	7,110	4,610	2,570	2,770
Total number of households in sample	690	1,410	1,930	1,270	640	670
Total number of persons in sample	1,140	2,920	5,180	3,240	1,660	1,630
Total number of adults in sample	1,070	2,580	3,600	2,290	1,160	1,220
Weighted average number of persons per household	1.6	2.1	2.7	2.5	2.5	2.4
Weighted average age of head of household	76	60	47	47	44	44
Commodity or service	\multicolumn{6}{c}{Average weekly household expenditure (£)}

Commodity or service	Aged 14 and under	Aged 15	Aged 16	Aged 17 and under 19	Aged 19 and under 22	Aged 22 or over
1 Food & non-alcoholic drinks	34.40	43.50	48.30	49.90	49.60	53.60
2 Alcoholic drinks, tobacco & narcotics	5.70	10.90	12.90	11.80	10.30	11.80
3 Clothing & footwear	8.10	16.60	24.80	26.70	30.60	30.20
4 Housing (net)[1], fuel & power	33.00	36.90	44.10	53.50	61.20	61.80
5 Household goods & services	16.70	25.30	27.90	34.20	36.00	47.30
6 Health	3.70	4.20	6.50	6.70	6.30	7.60
7 Transport	19.30	44.60	62.80	64.80	89.90	102.10
8 Communication	6.70	9.60	12.40	12.70	14.40	14.40
9 Recreation & culture	26.00	52.10	58.90	69.60	67.90	72.40
10 Education	[0.10]	1.60	3.30	8.50	10.50	26.70
11 Restaurants & hotels	12.70	27.80	38.70	42.20	49.70	57.60
12 Miscellaneous goods & services	15.60	26.60	36.10	42.10	45.30	53.80
1–12 All expenditure groups	181.80	299.80	376.60	422.80	471.60	539.20
13 Other expenditure items	23.30	47.80	75.70	88.70	109.20	146.40
Total expenditure	**205.10**	**347.60**	**452.30**	**511.50**	**580.90**	**685.60**
Average weekly expenditure per person (£) **Total expenditure**	**127.60**	**167.10**	**170.00**	**203.60**	**230.30**	**287.30**

Note: The commodity and service categories are not comparable to those in publications before 2001–02.

1 Excluding mortgage interest payments, council tax and Northern Ireland rates.

Table A24 Household expenditure by socio-economic classification of the household reference person, 2006

based on weighted data and including children's expenditure

	Large employers & higher managerial	Higher profes-sional	Lower managerial and professional	Inter-mediate	Small employers	Lower super-visory
Weighted number of households (thousands)	1,200	1,820	4,520	1,460	1,560	1,580
Total number of households in sample	310	470	1,170	380	430	420
Total number of persons in sample	900	1,230	3,100	910	1,240	1,140
Total number of adults in sample	610	900	2,270	670	870	810
Weighted average number of persons per household	2.8	2.5	2.6	2.5	2.8	2.7
Commodity or service	Average weekly household expenditure (£)					
1 Food & non-alcoholic drinks	65.20	54.50	55.30	44.70	53.90	47.00
2 Alcoholic drinks, tobacco & narcotics	13.60	12.10	13.00	11.60	13.70	14.80
3 Clothing & footwear	40.30	37.70	32.90	22.90	27.80	22.30
4 Housing (net)[3], fuel & power	59.50	58.30	54.20	52.20	51.50	49.30
5 Household goods & services	60.70	43.60	41.40	31.50	33.40	28.20
6 Health	5.90	10.60	6.40	4.50	4.10	4.10
7 Transport	135.10	94.90	94.10	64.70	75.30	58.30
8 Communication	14.50	15.10	14.80	12.80	16.40	12.90
9 Recreation & culture	99.60	85.10	77.10	66.10	68.50	57.60
10 Education	30.00	18.80	10.90	2.10	8.10	1.90
11 Restaurants & hotels	70.90	66.00	53.80	39.70	43.20	38.90
12 Miscellaneous goods & services	59.50	59.20	49.80	41.00	38.80	35.60
1–12 All expenditure groups	654.80	555.90	503.70	393.80	434.80	370.90
13 Other expenditure items	167.60	128.40	130.80	93.40	103.70	79.70
Total expenditure	**822.40**	**684.40**	**634.50**	**487.30**	**538.50**	**450.60**
Average weekly expenditure per person (£) **Total expenditure**	**293.80**	**270.80**	**240.00**	**198.80**	**191.00**	**169.40**

Note: The commodity and service categories are not comparable to those in publications before 2001–02.

1 Includes those who have never worked.

2 Includes those who are economically inactive.

3 Excludes mortgage interest payments, council tax and Northern Ireland rates.

Table A24 Household expenditure by socio-economic classification of the household reference person, 2006 (cont.)

based on weighted data and including children's expenditure

	Semi-routine	Routine	Long-term unem-ployed[1]	Students	Occupation not stated[2]	All house-holds
Weighted number of households (thousands)	1,810	1,570	480	310	8,460	24,790
Total number of households in sample	490	430	130	70	2,360	6,650
Total number of persons in sample	1,290	1,190	380	180	4,300	15,850
Total number of adults in sample	900	840	210	150	3,770	12,000
Weighted average number of persons per household	2.6	2.8	2.8	2.7	1.8	2.4
Commodity or service	Average weekly household expenditure (£)					
1 Food & non-alcoholic drinks	44.20	47.00	37.60	38.80	38.60	46.90
2 Alcoholic drinks, tobacco & narcotics	12.20	12.50	9.80	7.30	8.10	11.10
3 Clothing & footwear	22.80	22.20	13.70	44.90	12.00	23.20
4 Housing (net)[3], fuel & power	50.90	49.80	41.50	97.40	35.50	47.60
5 Household goods & services	23.10	24.00	20.70	9.80	20.70	30.30
6 Health	5.90	3.20	0.90	2.10	6.30	5.90
7 Transport	47.80	52.10	40.90	43.10	32.00	62.00
8 Communication	12.00	11.50	9.80	14.70	7.70	11.70
9 Recreation & culture	50.40	56.00	28.20	37.80	38.60	58.50
10 Education	2.90	2.90	[0.40]	[39.50]	2.20	7.20
11 Restaurants & hotels	31.30	36.90	19.10	43.30	19.60	37.90
12 Miscellaneous goods & services	35.80	27.30	15.00	19.80	22.50	36.00
1–12 All expenditure groups	339.20	345.50	237.50	398.50	243.80	378.30
13 Other expenditure items	56.90	65.00	19.30	26.60	29.40	77.60
Total expenditure	**396.10**	**410.50**	**256.80**	**425.00**	**273.30**	**455.90**
Average weekly expenditure per person (£)						
Total expenditure	**150.00**	**149.20**	**92.20**	**159.30**	**152.00**	**192.80**

Note: The commodity and service categories are not comparable to those in publications before 2001–02.

1 Includes those who have never worked.

2 Includes those who are economically inactive.

3 Excludes mortgage interest payments, council tax and Northern Ireland rates.

Table **A25** **Expenditure by household composition, 2006**
based on weighted data and including children's expenditure

	Retired households				Non-retired	
	State pension[1]		Other retired		One person	One man and one woman
	One person	One man and one woman	One person	One man and one woman		
Weighted number of households (thousands)	680	500	2,500	2,080	3,760	5,050
Total number of households in sample	190	150	670	620	960	1,320
Total number of persons in sample	190	290	670	1,230	960	2,640
Total number of adults in sample	190	290	670	1,230	960	2,640
Weighted average number of persons per household	1.0	2.0	1.0	2.0	1.0	2.0
Commodity or service	Average weekly household expenditure (£)					
1 Food & non-alcoholic drinks	21.90	41.70	25.40	50.10	24.10	48.60
2 Alcoholic drinks, tobacco & narcotics	2.20	7.60	4.60	9.30	7.80	13.80
3 Clothing & footwear	5.20	9.10	6.70	15.70	11.40	25.80
4 Housing (net)[2], fuel & power	28.50	35.90	31.00	38.10	41.60	51.70
5 Household goods & services	11.70	16.10	17.00	26.20	19.10	42.40
6 Health	2.40	3.50	4.30	9.10	3.00	7.90
7 Transport	7.60	30.20	17.70	47.50	37.50	77.40
8 Communication	4.40	6.10	5.40	8.50	8.80	12.30
9 Recreation & culture	16.00	35.40	24.10	57.60	33.60	72.50
10 Education	–	–	[1.20]	[0.90]	2.00	4.60
11 Restaurants & hotels	6.70	13.80	10.30	27.10	24.70	50.20
12 Miscellaneous goods & services	12.40	18.40	18.80	29.80	21.20	41.20
1–12 All expenditure groups	119.10	217.80	166.40	319.90	234.80	448.50
13 Other expenditure items	19.00	23.90	23.50	42.70	62.30	105.50
Total expenditure	**138.10**	**241.70**	**190.00**	**362.60**	**297.10**	**554.00**
Average weekly expenditure per person (£) **Total expenditure**	**138.10**	**120.90**	**190.00**	**181.30**	**297.10**	**277.00**

Note: The commodity and service categories are not comparable to those in publications before 2001–02.

1 Mainly dependent on state pension and not economically active – see definitions in Appendix B.

2 Excluding mortgage interest payments, council tax and Northern Ireland rates.

Table A25 Expenditure by household composition, 2006 (cont.)
based on weighted data and including children's expenditure

| | Retired and non-retired households | | | | | | |
| | One adult | | Two adults | | | Three or more adults | |
	with one child	with two or more children	with one child	with two children	with three or more children	without children	with children
Weighted number of households (thousands)	760	700	1,870	2,090	850	2,380	990
Total number of households in sample	230	220	520	610	270	490	260
Total number of persons in sample	470	770	1,550	2,430	1,450	1,620	1,280
Total number of adults in sample	230	220	1,040	1,210	540	1,620	870
Weighted average number of persons per household	2.0	3.4	3.0	4.0	5.4	3.3	4.9
Commodity or service	Average weekly household expenditure (£)						
1 Food & non-alcoholic drinks	33.20	43.60	54.20	68.70	74.10	65.50	79.90
2 Alcoholic drinks, tobacco & narcotics	7.90	7.40	13.40	14.20	12.50	15.00	20.50
3 Clothing & footwear	16.80	22.10	31.70	35.70	40.90	38.10	46.50
4 Housing (net)[2], fuel & power	41.50	46.80	54.30	51.80	50.60	65.30	60.70
5 Household goods & services	18.10	21.20	37.80	46.90	34.50	29.80	39.10
6 Health	2.00	2.10	4.70	5.60	3.50	11.00	6.40
7 Transport	25.50	31.10	77.40	90.10	95.20	109.10	97.60
8 Communication	9.10	12.10	13.80	14.60	17.30	18.40	21.20
9 Recreation & culture	33.30	53.40	60.70	89.50	83.90	80.20	94.60
10 Education	3.40	12.50	12.80	17.20	38.20	12.20	8.90
11 Restaurants & hotels	17.20	23.00	42.40	52.30	48.70	62.90	67.60
12 Miscellaneous goods & services	20.60	32.70	53.40	54.70	46.80	47.60	57.30
1–12 All expenditure groups	228.70	308.00	456.90	541.50	546.10	555.00	600.30
13 Other expenditure items	43.30	57.90	115.90	127.00	118.40	78.30	100.20
Total expenditure	271.90	365.90	572.80	668.60	664.50	633.30	700.50
Average weekly expenditure per person (£)							
Total expenditure	136.00	106.60	190.90	167.10	123.40	190.30	142.70

Note: The commodity and service categories are not comparable to those in publications before 2001–02.

1 Mainly dependent on state pension and not economically active – see defintions in Appendix B.

2 Excluding mortgage interest payments, council tax and Northern Ireland rates.

Table A26 Expenditure of one person retired households mainly dependent on state pensions[1] by gross income quintile group, 2006

based on weighted data

	Lowest twenty per cent	Second quintile group	Third quintile group	Fourth quintile group	Highest twenty per cent	All house-holds
Lower boundary of group (£ per week)[2]		215	384	624	939	
Weighted number of households (thousands)	610	60	–	0	0	680
Total number of households in sample	170	20	–	0	0	190
Total number of persons in sample	170	20	–	0	0	190
Total number of adults in sample	170	20	–	0	0	190
Weighted average number of persons per household	1.0	1.0	1.0	0	0	1.0
Commodity or service	Average weekly household expenditure (£)					
1 Food & non-alcoholic drinks	21.60	[23.60]	[32.00]	–	–	21.90
2 Alcoholic drinks, tobacco & narcotics	2.10	[2.50]	[4.70]	–	–	2.20
3 Clothing & footwear	5.30	[5.80]	–	–	–	5.20
4 Housing (net)[3], fuel & power	29.10	[24.90]	[12.90]	–	–	28.50
5 Household goods & services	11.50	[14.00]	[4.10]	–	–	11.70
6 Health	1.50	[10.90]	[4.20]	–	–	2.40
7 Transport	7.40	[10.10]	[6.10]	–	–	7.60
8 Communication	4.30	[4.90]	[3.40]	–	–	4.40
9 Recreation & culture	15.80	[19.10]	[4.20]	–	–	16.00
10 Education	–	–	–	–	–	–
11 Restaurants & hotels	6.90	[5.30]	–	–	–	6.70
12 Miscellaneous goods & services	12.30	[13.60]	[13.30]	–	–	12.40
1–12 All expenditure groups	117.90	[134.90]	[84.90]	–	–	119.10
13 Other expenditure items	18.10	[29.90]	[1.50]	–	–	19.00
Total expenditure	136.00	[164.80]	[86.30]	–	–	138.10
Average weekly expenditure per person (£) Total expenditure	136.00	[164.80]	[86.30]	–	–	138.10

Note: The commodity and service categories are not comparable to those in publications before 2001–02.

1 Mainly dependent on state pension and not economically active – see definitions in Appendix B.

2 Lower boundary of 2006 gross income quintile groups (£ per week).

3 Excluding mortgage interest payments, council tax and Northern Ireland rates.

Table A27 Expenditure of one person retired households not mainly dependent on state pensions by gross income quintile group, 2006

based on weighted data

	Lowest twenty per cent	Second quintile group	Third quintile group	Fourth quintile group	Highest twenty per cent	All house-holds
Lower boundary of group (£ per week)[1]		215	384	624	939	
Weighted number of households (thousands)	1,490	750	190	60	10	2,500
Total number of households in sample	400	200	50	20	–	670
Total number of persons in sample	400	200	50	20	–	670
Total number of adults in sample	400	200	50	20	–	670
Weighted average number of persons per household	1.0	1.0	1.0	1.0	1.0	1.0
Commodity or service	Average weekly household expenditure (£)					
1 Food & non-alcoholic drinks	23.20	27.30	32.40	[32.00]	[24.50]	25.40
2 Alcoholic drinks, tobacco & narcotics	3.80	5.50	7.20	[6.50]	[8.70]	4.60
3 Clothing & footwear	5.50	7.00	11.90	[13.90]	[10.90]	6.70
4 Housing (net)[2] fuel & power	28.50	31.60	44.30	[43.10]	[41.30]	31.00
5 Household goods & services	12.90	20.50	29.60	[33.40]	[18.30]	17.00
6 Health	2.70	6.90	7.50	[2.00]	[0.30]	4.30
7 Transport	7.20	23.30	51.80	[86.70]	[79.50]	17.70
8 Communication	4.90	5.70	8.00	[7.30]	[5.90]	5.40
9 Recreation & culture	15.90	24.30	55.00	[40.20]	[458.80]	24.10
10 Education	[0.00]	[0.60]	[0.40]	[39.50]	–	[1.20]
11 Restaurants & hotels	6.50	12.20	22.90	[35.30]	[31.80]	10.30
12 Miscellaneous goods & services	10.50	21.90	59.10	[53.90]	[19.40]	18.80
1–12 All expenditure groups	121.60	186.70	330.10	[393.90]	[699.40]	166.40
13 Other expenditure items	13.10	29.80	60.50	[52.10]	[187.00]	23.50
Total expenditure	**134.70**	**216.50**	**390.60**	**[446.00]**	**[886.40]**	**190.00**
Average weekly expenditure per person (£)						
Total expenditure	**134.70**	**216.50**	**390.60**	**[446.00]**	**[886.40]**	**190.00**

Note: The commodity and service categories are not comparable to those in publications before 2001–02.

1 Lower boundary of 2006 gross income quintile groups (£ per week).

2 Excluding mortgage interest payments, council tax and Northern Ireland rates.

Table A28 Expenditure of one person non-retired households by gross income quintile group, 2006

based on weighted data

	Lowest twenty per cent	Second quintile group	Third quintile group	Fourth quintile group	Highest twenty per cent	All house-holds
Lower boundary of group (£ per week)[1]		215	384	624	939	
Weighted number of households (thousands)	1,110	1,000	890	490	270	3,760
Total number of households in sample	290	260	230	120	60	960
Total number of persons in sample	290	260	230	120	60	960
Total number of adults in sample	290	260	230	120	60	960
Weighted average number of persons per household	1.0	1.0	1.0	1.0	1.0	1.0
Commodity or service	Average weekly household expenditure (£)					
1 Food & non-alcoholic drinks	19.20	21.60	27.00	31.60	29.70	24.10
2 Alcoholic drinks, tobacco & narcotics	7.00	8.00	7.10	10.30	8.60	7.80
3 Clothing & footwear	5.40	11.80	10.90	19.10	22.80	11.40
4 Housing (net)[2], fuel & power	32.10	46.50	39.00	43.50	66.90	41.60
5 Household goods & services	11.60	17.00	15.80	35.00	38.80	19.10
6 Health	1.60	3.40	3.20	3.10	7.00	3.00
7 Transport	18.60	35.10	41.60	60.80	68.40	37.50
8 Communication	6.40	9.20	8.70	11.10	13.40	8.80
9 Recreation & culture	18.50	26.90	38.20	61.00	55.50	33.60
10 Education	[0.50]	[1.20]	[0.70]	[3.90]	[11.80]	2.00
11 Restaurants & hotels	12.00	17.80	29.50	40.40	57.90	24.70
12 Miscellaneous goods & services	8.30	18.20	21.50	46.60	37.70	21.20
1–12 All expenditure groups	141.30	216.80	243.30	366.50	418.50	234.80
13 Other expenditure items	21.20	46.30	71.50	102.40	187.20	62.30
Total expenditure	**162.50**	**263.10**	**314.80**	**468.90**	**605.70**	**297.10**
Average weekly expenditure per person (£) **Total expenditure**	**162.50**	**263.10**	**314.80**	**468.90**	**605.70**	**297.10**

Note: The commodity and service categories are not comparable to those in publications before 2001–02.

1 Lower boundary of 2006 gross income quintile groups (£ per week).

2 Excluding mortgage interest payments, council tax and Northern Ireland rates.

Table A29 Expenditure of one adult households with children by gross income quintile group, 2006

based on weighted data and including children's expenditure

	Lowest twenty per cent	Second quintile group	Third quintile group	Fourth quintile group	Highest twenty per cent	All house-holds
Lower boundary of group (£ per week)[1]		215	384	624	939	
Weighted number of households (thousands)	660	390	260	100	50	1,460
Total number of households in sample	210	130	90	30	10	460
Total number of persons in sample	530	360	240	70	40	1,240
Total number of adults in sample	210	130	90	30	10	460
Weighted average number of persons per household	2.6	2.8	2.8	2.4	2.8	2.7
Commodity or service	Average weekly household expenditure (£)					
1 Food & non-alcoholic drinks	33.00	39.40	46.40	42.10	[45.40]	38.20
2 Alcoholic drinks, tobacco & narcotics	6.90	7.70	9.60	[9.10]	[4.00]	7.70
3 Clothing & footwear	13.20	16.00	30.90	38.70	[27.00]	19.30
4 Housing (net)[2], fuel & power	39.30	53.10	39.90	51.20	[44.70]	44.10
5 Household goods & services	15.90	13.80	28.60	33.40	[39.20]	19.60
6 Health	1.50	1.30	2.20	[2.30]	[15.30]	2.10
7 Transport	14.30	30.60	38.30	60.40	[77.20]	28.20
8 Communication	7.20	12.20	14.00	15.10	[15.20]	10.60
9 Recreation & culture	25.00	38.20	51.20	123.30	[116.30]	43.00
10 Education	1.90	[1.70]	[5.50]	[6.90]	[150.70]	7.70
11 Restaurants & hotels	13.30	20.70	26.40	31.90	[46.20]	20.00
12 Miscellaneous goods & services	12.90	24.90	41.80	36.80	[115.60]	26.40
1–12 All expenditure groups	184.40	259.50	334.70	451.20	[696.80]	266.70
13 Other expenditure items	12.80	55.40	76.40	113.40	[247.60]	50.30
Total expenditure	**197.20**	**314.90**	**411.20**	**564.60**	**[944.40]**	**317.00**
Average weekly expenditure per person (£)						
Total expenditure	**76.60**	**111.70**	**144.40**	**231.70**	**[333.20]**	**118.00**

Note: The commodity and service categories are not comparable to those in publications before 2001–02.

1 Lower boundary of 2006 gross income quintile groups (£ per week).

2 Excluding mortgage interest payments, council tax and Northern Ireland rates.

Table A30 Expenditure of two adult households with children by gross income quintile group, 2006

based on weighted data and including children's expenditure

	Lowest twenty per cent	Second quintile group	Third quintile group	Fourth quintile group	Highest twenty per cent	All house-holds
Lower boundary of group (£ per week)[1]		215	384	624	939	
Weighted number of households (thousands)	210	530	1,110	1,430	1,530	4,810
Total number of households in sample	60	160	330	420	440	1,390
Total number of persons in sample	220	640	1,280	1,600	1,690	5,430
Total number of adults in sample	120	320	650	830	870	2,790
Weighted average number of persons per household	3.8	4.0	3.9	3.8	3.8	3.9
Commodity or service	Average weekly household expenditure (£)					
1 Food & non-alcoholic drinks	49.40	53.80	54.60	63.40	77.00	64.00
2 Alcoholic drinks, tobacco & narcotics	10.50	12.50	14.50	12.60	14.70	13.60
3 Clothing & footwear	17.10	29.70	24.10	32.50	49.90	35.10
4 Housing (net)[2], fuel & power	43.70	56.60	51.00	47.50	58.30	52.60
5 Household goods & services	9.70	26.70	36.90	36.20	58.20	41.20
6 Health	0.70	1.90	3.50	4.20	8.20	4.90
7 Transport	27.70	56.00	59.70	75.50	133.70	86.10
8 Communication	9.10	13.60	14.10	14.40	16.90	14.80
9 Recreation & culture	26.60	44.50	54.80	82.50	107.30	77.30
10 Education	[15.40]	4.70	3.00	7.10	48.00	19.20
11 Restaurants & hotels	29.70	29.20	33.70	43.30	71.30	47.80
12 Miscellaneous goods & services	15.10	33.20	36.70	53.40	76.00	52.80
1–12 All expenditure groups	254.90	362.40	386.70	472.60	719.40	509.40
13 Other expenditure items	31.40	56.20	82.00	112.30	193.00	121.20
Total expenditure	**286.40**	**418.60**	**468.60**	**584.90**	**912.40**	**630.60**
Average weekly expenditure per person (£) **Total expenditure**	**76.00**	**103.70**	**121.40**	**152.70**	**238.60**	**163.50**

Note: The commodity and service categories are not comparable to those in publications before 2001–02.

1 Lower boundary of 2006 gross income quintile groups (£ per week).

2 Excluding mortgage interest payments, council tax and Northern Ireland rates.

Table A31 Expenditure of one man one woman non-retired households by gross income quintile group, 2006
based on weighted data

	Lowest twenty per cent	Second quintile group	Third quintile group	Fourth quintile group	Highest twenty per cent	All house- holds
Lower boundary of group (£ per week)[1]		215	384	624	939	
Weighted number of households (thousands)	300	590	1,130	1,500	1,530	5,050
Total number of households in sample	90	170	300	390	380	1,320
Total number of persons in sample	170	330	610	770	760	2,640
Total number of adults in sample	170	330	610	770	760	2,640
Weighted average number of persons per household	2.0	2.0	2.0	2.0	2.0	2.0
Commodity or service	Average weekly household expenditure (£)					
1 Food & non-alcoholic drinks	40.00	45.50	45.60	47.70	54.50	48.60
2 Alcoholic drinks, tobacco & narcotics	9.50	12.60	12.80	14.50	15.30	13.80
3 Clothing & footwear	8.90	14.30	18.30	24.00	40.90	25.80
4 Housing (net)[2], fuel & power	38.20	43.20	49.70	48.90	61.90	51.70
5 Household goods & services	14.20	33.60	27.40	37.60	67.00	42.40
6 Health	4.30	5.50	7.60	7.70	9.90	7.90
7 Transport	33.40	51.00	47.70	70.80	124.90	77.40
8 Communication	7.70	8.80	11.60	12.80	14.80	12.30
9 Recreation & culture	35.90	49.90	65.20	71.20	95.20	72.50
10 Education	[0.00]	[2.20]	[1.40]	3.20	10.40	4.60
11 Restaurants & hotels	18.10	26.30	35.90	44.80	81.70	50.20
12 Miscellaneous goods & services	17.70	34.40	28.80	39.30	59.50	41.20
1–12 All expenditure groups	228.00	327.40	352.00	422.40	636.10	448.50
13 Other expenditure items	30.00	71.40	61.70	89.80	181.50	105.50
Total expenditure	**258.00**	**398.80**	**413.70**	**512.20**	**817.60**	**554.00**
Average weekly expenditure per person (£) **Total expenditure**	**129.00**	**199.40**	**206.90**	**256.10**	**408.80**	**277.00**

Note: The commodity and service categories are not comparable to those in publications before 2001–02.
1 Lower boundary of 2006 gross income quintile groups (£ per week).
2 Excluding mortgage interest payments, council tax and Northern Ireland rates.

Table A32 Expenditure of one man one woman retired households mainly dependent on state pensions[1] by gross income quintile group, 2006

based on weighted data

	Lowest twenty per cent	Second quintile group	Third quintile group	Fourth quintile group	Highest twenty per cent	All house-holds
Lower boundary of group (£ per week)[2]		215	384	624	939	
Weighted number of households (thousands)	230	250	10	0	0	500
Total number of households in sample	70	80	–	0	0	150
Total number of persons in sample	140	150	–	0	0	290
Total number of adults in sample	140	150	–	0	0	290
Weighted average number of persons per household	2.0	2.0	2.0	0	0	2.0
Commodity or service	Average weekly household expenditure (£)					
1 Food & non-alcoholic drinks	41.60	41.80	[42.10]	–	–	41.70
2 Alcoholic drinks, tobacco & narcotics	6.10	8.50	[16.90]	–	–	7.60
3 Clothing & footwear	8.50	9.70	[9.50]	–	–	9.10
4 Housing (net)[3], fuel & power	37.50	34.60	[32.30]	–	–	35.90
5 Household goods & services	12.40	20.30	[2.70]	–	–	16.10
6 Health	2.70	3.60	[15.50]	–	–	3.50
7 Transport	28.10	31.90	[34.90]	–	–	30.20
8 Communication	6.00	6.10	[6.40]	–	–	6.10
9 Recreation & culture	34.10	37.50	[18.60]	–	–	35.40
10 Education	–	–	–	–	–	–
11 Restaurants & hotels	11.30	16.10	[13.90]	–	–	13.80
12 Miscellaneous goods & services	17.90	18.90	[15.90]	–	–	18.40
1–12 All expenditure groups	206.10	228.90	[208.60]	–	–	217.80
13 Other expenditure items	22.20	25.90	[17.20]	–	–	23.90
Total expenditure	**228.30**	**254.80**	**[225.80]**	**–**	**–**	**241.70**
Average weekly expenditure per person (£) **Total expenditure**	**114.20**	**127.40**	**[112.90]**	**–**	**–**	**120.90**

Note: The commodity and service categories are not comparable to those in publications before 2001–02.

1 Mainly dependent on state pensions and not economically active – see definitions in Appendix B.

2 Lower boundary of 2006 gross income quintile groups (£ per week).

3 Excluding mortgage interest payments, council tax and Northern Ireland rates.

Table A33 Expenditure of one man one woman retired households not mainly dependent on state pensions by gross income quintile group, 2006

based on weighted data

	Lowest twenty per cent	Second quintile group	Third quintile group	Fourth quintile group	Highest twenty per cent	All house-holds
Lower boundary of group (£ per week)[1]		215	384	624	939	
Weighted number of households (thousands)	160	990	570	250	110	2,080
Total number of households in sample	40	290	180	70	30	620
Total number of persons in sample	90	590	350	150	60	1,230
Total number of adults in sample	90	590	350	150	60	1,230
Weighted average number of persons per household	2.0	2.0	2.0	2.0	2.0	2.0
Commodity or service	Average weekly household expenditure (£)					
1 Food & non-alcoholic drinks	40.50	47.40	49.70	60.00	68.90	50.10
2 Alcoholic drinks, tobacco & narcotics	6.70	7.70	9.30	14.80	15.60	9.30
3 Clothing & footwear	6.00	11.90	16.20	28.80	[31.00]	15.70
4 Housing (net)[2], fuel & power	30.10	33.70	42.10	44.30	53.90	38.10
5 Household goods & services	23.30	21.30	28.50	36.90	38.60	26.20
6 Health	8.30	5.60	10.70	15.70	19.60	9.10
7 Transport	14.80	35.60	46.30	76.70	144.50	47.50
8 Communication	7.20	6.60	11.20	10.40	9.60	8.50
9 Recreation & culture	26.60	44.50	60.60	82.00	151.50	57.60
10 Education	–	[0.30]	–	[5.50]	[1.60]	[0.90]
11 Restaurants & hotels	8.30	19.00	28.40	60.00	45.40	27.10
12 Miscellaneous goods & services	19.00	22.50	28.30	44.50	88.10	29.80
1–12 All expenditure groups	191.00	256.10	331.20	479.70	668.20	319.90
13 Other expenditure items	33.70	29.80	47.20	72.60	81.90	42.70
Total expenditure	**224.60**	**285.90**	**378.40**	**552.20**	**750.00**	**362.60**
Average weekly expenditure per person (£) **Total expenditure**	**112.30**	**143.00**	**189.20**	**276.10**	**375.00**	**181.30**

Note: The commodity and service categories are not comparable to those in publications before 2001–02.

1 Lower boundary of 2006 gross income quintile groups (£ per week).

2 Excluding mortgage interest payments, council tax and Northern Ireland rates.

Table A34 Household expenditure by tenure, 2006
based on weighted data and including children's expenditure

	Owners			Social rented from		
	Owned outright	Buying with a mortgage[1]	All	Council[2]	Registered Social Landlord[3]	All
Weighted number of households (thousands)	7,830	9,850	17,690	2,680	1,610	4,290
Total number of households in sample	2,170	2,630	4,800	730	420	1,150
Total number of persons in sample	4,200	7,480	11,680	1,620	930	2,540
Total number of adults in sample	3,910	5,120	9,040	1,120	630	1,740
Weighted average number of persons per household	1.9	2.8	2.4	2.2	2.2	2.2
Commodity or service	Average weekly household expenditure (£)					
1 Food & non-alcoholic drinks	46.20	55.20	51.20	34.30	34.60	34.40
2 Alcoholic drinks, tobacco & narcotics	8.60	12.80	11.00	11.90	10.10	11.30
3 Clothing & footwear	18.80	31.40	25.80	12.60	15.20	13.50
4 Housing (net)[6], fuel & power	35.40	36.60	36.00	46.30	51.20	48.10
5 Household goods & services	30.40	41.20	36.40	13.40	17.20	14.80
6 Health	9.00	5.90	7.30	1.50	3.30	2.20
7 Transport	60.10	84.10	73.50	24.40	24.40	24.40
8 Communication	9.30	14.50	12.20	9.30	9.60	9.40
9 Recreation & culture	59.50	75.70	68.60	29.10	30.30	29.60
10 Education	5.90	10.60	8.50	0.40	1.10	0.70
11 Restaurants & hotels	34.00	49.30	42.50	19.30	19.20	19.30
12 Miscellaneous goods & services	36.60	48.50	43.20	12.80	14.30	13.30
1–12 All expenditure groups	353.90	465.70	416.20	215.30	230.30	220.90
13 Other expenditure items	48.30	140.80	99.80	13.50	13.20	13.40
Total expenditure	**402.20**	**606.50**	**516.00**	**228.70**	**243.50**	**234.30**
Average weekly expenditure per person (£)						
Total expenditure	**206.30**	**218.20**	**213.90**	**104.20**	**111.30**	**106.90**

Note: The commodity and service categories are not comparable to those in publications before 2001–02.

1 Including shared owners (who own part of the equity and pay mortgage, part rent).

2 "Council" includes local authorities, New Towns and Scottish Homes, but see note 3 below.

3 Formerly Housing Associations.

Table $A34$ Household expenditure by tenure, 2006 (cont.)
based on weighted data and including children's expenditure

	Private rented[4]				All tenures
	Rent free	Rent paid unfurn-ished[5]	Rent paid, furnished	All	
Weighted number of households (thousands)	310	1,830	670	2,810	24,790
Total number of households in sample	90	460	150	700	6,650
Total number of persons in sample	170	1,090	360	1,620	15,850
Total number of adults in sample	140	790	300	1,230	12,000
Weighted average number of persons per household	2.0	2.3	2.5	2.3	2.4
Commodity or service	Average weekly household expenditure (£)				
1 Food & non-alcoholic drinks	37.40	39.30	38.10	38.80	46.90
2 Alcoholic drinks, tobacco & narcotics	7.60	12.10	13.30	11.90	11.10
3 Clothing & footwear	19.30	18.20	33.40	21.90	23.20
4 Housing (net)[6], fuel & power	22.70	121.70	158.00	119.40	47.60
5 Household goods & services	15.10	17.90	7.20	15.10	30.30
6 Health	2.60	3.00	2.20	2.80	5.90
7 Transport	35.30	50.10	46.40	47.60	62.00
8 Communication	8.50	12.90	13.40	12.50	11.70
9 Recreation & culture	31.50	41.70	35.70	39.10	58.50
10 Education	[3.10]	8.40	13.30	[9.00]	7.20
11 Restaurants & hotels	22.60	37.00	43.80	37.00	37.90
12 Miscellaneous goods & services	26.80	26.30	22.10	25.40	36.00
1–12 All expenditure groups	232.40	388.50	426.90	380.40	378.30
13 Other expenditure items	34.50	37.30	32.00	35.70	77.60
Total expenditure	**266.90**	**425.70**	**458.90**	**416.20**	**455.90**
Average weekly expenditure per person (£) **Total expenditure**	**136.20**	**182.90**	**183.80**	**178.80**	**192.80**

Note: The commodity and service categories are not comparable to those in publications before 2001–02.
4 All tenants whose accommodation goes with the job of someone in the household are allocated to "rented privately",
even if the landlord is a local authority or housing association or Housing Action Trust, or if the accommodation is rent free.
Squatters are also included in this category.
5 'Unfurnished' includes the answers: 'partly furnished'.
6 Excluding mortgage interest payments, council tax and Northern Ireland rates.

Table A35 Household expenditure by UK countries and Government Office Regions, 2006
based on weighted data and including children's expenditure

		North East	North West	Yorkshire and The Humber	East Midlands	West Midlands	East	London
Weighted number of households (thousands)		1,100	2,810	2,110	1,720	2,180	2,260	2,950
Total number of households in sample		280	700	550	500	540	590	540
Total number of persons in sample		620	1,630	1,300	1,240	1,310	1,410	1,280
Total number of adults in sample		510	1,230	980	920	990	1,050	940
Weighted average number of persons per household		2.2	2.3	2.3	2.4	2.4	2.4	2.5
Commodity or service		Average weekly household expenditure (£)						
1	Food & non-alcoholic drinks	40.20	42.80	46.40	48.10	47.10	48.20	50.50
2	Alcoholic drinks, tobacco & narcotics	10.70	11.50	10.80	10.40	10.90	10.00	10.30
3	Clothing & footwear	20.90	20.10	24.30	21.20	23.50	24.50	27.70
4	Housing (net)[1], fuel & power	37.60	41.60	39.80	40.40	42.30	52.00	70.00
5	Household goods & services	27.70	27.50	34.30	30.30	25.40	30.90	29.40
6	Health	3.60	9.50	6.00	6.60	5.40	6.30	5.60
7	Transport	43.60	50.50	53.60	59.00	55.80	65.40	68.30
8	Communication	9.60	10.80	10.60	11.90	11.20	12.40	14.90
9	Recreation & culture	49.70	60.80	60.10	66.30	51.90	64.80	46.50
10	Education	[1.60]	6.50	8.30	4.70	6.50	5.90	14.40
11	Restaurants & hotels	32.30	33.60	39.60	36.80	34.40	38.80	47.00
12	Miscellaneous goods & services	27.60	33.50	32.30	34.00	33.10	44.00	38.00
1–12	All expenditure groups	305.20	348.70	365.90	369.90	347.40	403.10	422.50
13	Other expenditure items	54.30	72.90	58.50	68.60	64.90	84.10	115.50
Total expenditure		**359.50**	**421.70**	**424.40**	**438.50**	**412.30**	**487.20**	**538.00**
Average weekly expenditure per person (£) **Total expenditure**		**161.60**	**179.50**	**182.20**	**180.40**	**172.10**	**202.70**	**216.00**

Note: The commodity and service categories are not comparable to those in publications before 2001–02.
1 Excluding mortgage interest payments, council tax and Northern Ireland rates.

Table A35 Household expenditure by UK countries and Government Office Regions, 2006 (cont.)

based on weighted data and including children's expenditure

	South East	South West	England	Wales	Scotland	Northern Ireland	United Kingdom
Weighted number of households (thousands)	3,490	2,220	20,830	1,230	2,090	640	24,790
Total number of households in sample	890	580	5,170	310	580	590	6,650
Total number of persons in sample	2,120	1,300	12,220	720	1,370	1,540	15,850
Total number of adults in sample	1,610	1,040	9,280	560	1,040	1,130	12,000
Weighted average number of persons per household	2.3	2.2	2.4	2.4	2.4	2.7	2.4
Commodity or service	Average weekly household expenditure (£)						
1 Food & non-alcoholic drinks	49.20	45.60	47.00	42.30	46.90	53.60	46.90
2 Alcoholic drinks, tobacco & narcotics	10.60	10.60	10.70	12.50	13.90	14.10	11.10
3 Clothing & footwear	21.50	18.70	22.60	23.50	25.90	33.50	23.20
4 Housing (net)[1], fuel & power	52.50	45.20	48.50	46.00	39.40	46.20	47.60
5 Household goods & services	35.50	30.40	30.50	26.20	30.10	31.10	30.30
6 Health	6.50	5.10	6.30	4.20	3.10	4.20	5.90
7 Transport	77.30	70.30	62.40	58.60	60.20	61.50	62.00
8 Communication	11.60	10.90	11.70	10.90	11.60	13.80	11.70
9 Recreation & culture	64.40	60.20	58.60	52.60	63.70	47.50	58.50
10 Education	8.30	7.00	7.70	3.70	5.70	3.80	7.20
11 Restaurants & hotels	37.60	34.60	37.70	35.40	40.30	40.70	37.90
12 Miscellaneous goods & services	42.90	34.50	36.50	30.50	34.50	34.60	36.00
1–12 All expenditure groups	417.80	373.00	380.30	346.40	375.40	384.50	378.30
13 Other expenditure items	94.00	73.20	80.10	58.30	68.60	63.00	77.60
Total expenditure	**511.80**	**446.20**	**460.30**	**404.70**	**444.00**	**447.50**	**455.90**
Average weekly expenditure per person (£)							
Total expenditure	**222.60**	**200.80**	**195.40**	**171.70**	**188.00**	**168.60**	**192.80**

Note: The commodity and service categories are not comparable to those in publications before 2001–02.
1 Excluding mortgage interest payments, council tax and Northern Ireland rates.

Table A36 Household expenditure as a percentage of total expenditure by UK countries and Government Office Regions, 2006

based on weighted data and including children's expenditure

	North East	North West	Yorkshire and The Humber	East Midlands	West Midlands	East	London
Weighted number of households (thousands)	1,100	2,810	2,110	1,720	2,180	2,260	2,950
Total number of households in sample	280	700	550	500	540	590	540
Total number of persons in sample	620	1,630	1,300	1,240	1,310	1,410	1,280
Total number of adults in sample	510	1,230	980	920	990	1,050	940
Weighted average number of persons per household	2.2	2.3	2.3	2.4	2.4	2.4	2.5
Commodity or service	Percentage of total expenditure						
1 Food & non-alcoholic drinks	11	10	11	11	11	10	9
2 Alcoholic drinks, tobacco & narcotics	3	3	3	2	3	2	2
3 Clothing & footwear	6	5	6	5	6	5	5
4 Housing (net)[1], fuel & power	10	10	9	9	10	11	13
5 Household goods & services	8	7	8	7	6	6	5
6 Health	1	2	1	2	1	1	1
7 Transport	12	12	13	13	14	13	13
8 Communication	3	3	2	3	3	3	3
9 Recreation & culture	14	14	14	15	13	13	9
10 Education	[0]	2	2	1	2	1	3
11 Restaurants & hotels	9	8	9	8	8	8	9
12 Miscellaneous goods & services	8	8	8	8	8	9	7
1–12 All expenditure groups	85	83	86	84	84	83	79
13 Other expenditure items	15	17	14	16	16	17	21
Total expenditure	100	100	100	100	100	100	100

Note: The commodity and service categories are not comparable to those in publications before 2001–02.
1 Excluding mortgage interest payments, council tax and Northern Ireland rates.

Table **A36** **Household expenditure as a percentage of total expenditure**
by UK countries and Government Office Regions, 2006 (cont.)
based on weighted data and including children's expenditure

	South East	South West	England	Wales	Scotland	Northern Ireland	United Kingdom
Weighted number of households (thousands)	3,490	2,220	20,830	1,230	2,090	640	24,790
Total number of households in sample	890	580	5,170	310	580	590	6,650
Total number of persons in sample	2,120	1,300	12,220	720	1,370	1,540	15,850
Total number of adults in sample	1,610	1,040	9,280	560	1,040	1,130	12,000
Weighted average number of persons per household	2.3	2.2	2.4	2.4	2.4	2.7	2.4
Commodity or service				Percentage of total expenditure			
1 Food & non-alcoholic drinks	10	10	10	10	11	12	10
2 Alcoholic drinks, tobacco & narcotics	2	2	2	3	3	3	2
3 Clothing & footwear	4	4	5	6	6	7	5
4 Housing (net)[1], fuel & power	10	10	11	11	9	10	10
5 Household goods & services	7	7	7	6	7	7	7
6 Health	1	1	1	1	1	1	1
7 Transport	15	16	14	14	14	14	14
8 Communication	2	2	3	3	3	3	3
9 Recreation & culture	13	13	13	13	14	11	13
10 Education	2	2	2	1	1	1	2
11 Restaurants & hotels	7	8	8	9	9	9	8
12 Miscellaneous goods & services	8	8	8	8	8	8	8
1–12 All expenditure groups	82	84	83	86	85	86	83
13 Other expenditure items	18	16	17	14	15	14	17
Total expenditure	**100**	**100**	**100**	**100**	**100**	**100**	**100**

Note: The commodity and service categories are not comparable to those in publications before 2001–02.
1 Excluding mortgage interest payments, council tax and Northern Ireland rates.

Table A37 Detailed household expenditure by UK countries and Government Office Regions, 2006

based on weighted data and including children's expenditure

	North East	North West	Yorkshire and The Humber	East Midlands	West Midlands	East	London
Weighted number of households (thousands)	1,100	2,810	2,110	1,720	2,180	2,260	2,950
Total number of households in sample	280	700	550	500	540	590	540
Total number of persons in sample	620	1,630	1,300	1,240	1,310	1,410	1,280
Total number of adults in sample	510	1,230	980	920	990	1,050	940
Weighted average number of persons per household	2.2	2.3	2.3	2.4	2.4	2.4	2.5
Commodity or service	Average weekly household expenditure (£)						
1 Food & non-alcoholic drinks	40.20	42.80	46.40	48.10	47.10	48.20	50.50
1.1 Food	36.90	39.20	42.60	43.90	42.90	44.20	45.80
1.1.1 Bread, rice and cereals	3.90	4.00	4.30	4.50	4.40	4.30	4.40
1.1.2 Pasta products	0.20	0.30	0.30	0.30	0.30	0.30	0.40
1.1.3 Buns, cakes, biscuits etc.	2.60	2.50	3.00	3.00	2.90	3.10	2.80
1.1.4 Pastry (savoury)	0.60	0.70	0.70	0.60	0.60	0.70	0.60
1.1.5 Beef (fresh, chilled or frozen)	1.40	1.40	1.60	1.50	1.80	1.70	1.50
1.1.6 Pork (fresh, chilled or frozen)	0.40	0.60	0.70	0.60	0.60	0.60	0.60
1.1.7 Lamb (fresh, chilled or frozen)	0.20	0.70	0.60	0.60	0.80	0.70	1.00
1.1.8 Poultry (fresh, chilled or frozen)	1.20	1.60	1.60	1.60	1.70	1.80	1.90
1.1.9 Bacon and ham	0.90	0.90	1.00	0.90	1.00	0.90	0.70
1.1.10 Other meat and meat preparations	5.10	4.90	5.00	5.10	5.00	4.90	4.50
1.1.11 Fish and fish products	1.60	2.30	2.20	2.20	2.00	2.40	2.80
1.1.12 Milk	2.40	2.10	2.40	2.40	2.30	2.30	2.10
1.1.13 Cheese and curd	1.10	1.30	1.30	1.60	1.70	1.60	1.60
1.1.14 Eggs	0.40	0.40	0.50	0.50	0.40	0.40	0.50
1.1.15 Other milk products	1.30	1.50	1.60	1.80	1.60	1.70	1.80
1.1.16 Butter	0.30	0.20	0.30	0.30	0.30	0.30	0.30
1.1.17 Margarine, other vegetable fats and peanut butter	0.40	0.40	0.40	0.50	0.50	0.50	0.40
1.1.18 Cooking oils and fats	0.20	0.20	0.20	0.30	0.20	0.20	0.40
1.1.19 Fresh fruit	2.20	2.40	2.80	2.70	2.70	3.00	3.80
1.1.20 Other fresh, chilled or frozen fruits	0.20	0.30	0.30	0.30	0.30	0.30	0.50
1.1.21 Dried fruit and nuts	0.40	0.40	0.40	0.60	0.40	0.60	0.60
1.1.22 Preserved fruit and fruit based products	0.20	0.10	0.10	0.10	0.20	0.20	0.10
1.1.23 Fresh vegetables	2.70	3.00	3.10	3.70	3.40	3.80	4.60
1.1.24 Dried vegetables and other preserved or processed vegetables	0.90	1.00	1.10	1.20	1.00	1.10	1.30
1.1.25 Potatoes	0.60	0.70	0.70	0.60	0.70	0.70	0.60
1.1.26 Other tubers and products of tuber vegetables	1.10	1.10	1.20	1.30	1.30	1.10	1.00
1.1.27 Sugar and sugar products	0.20	0.20	0.30	0.30	0.30	0.30	0.30
1.1.28 Jams, marmalades	0.20	0.20	0.20	0.20	0.20	0.30	0.20
1.1.29 Chocolate	1.50	1.10	1.50	1.50	1.40	1.40	1.40
1.1.30 Confectionery products	0.50	0.50	0.70	0.60	0.50	0.50	0.50
1.1.31 Edible ices and ice cream	0.40	0.50	0.50	0.50	0.50	0.50	0.50
1.1.32 Other food products	1.50	1.80	2.10	2.00	1.90	2.00	2.40
1.2 Non-alcoholic drinks	3.30	3.70	3.80	4.20	4.20	4.00	4.60
1.2.1 Coffee	0.50	0.40	0.50	0.50	0.50	0.60	0.50
1.2.2 Tea	0.40	0.40	0.40	0.50	0.40	0.40	0.50
1.2.3 Cocoa and powdered chocolate	0.10	0.10	0.10	0.10	0.10	0.10	0.10
1.2.4 Fruit and vegetable juices (inc. fruit squash)	0.80	1.00	1.00	1.30	1.20	1.20	1.50
1.2.5 Mineral or spring waters	0.20	0.20	0.20	0.20	0.20	0.30	0.50
1.2.6 Soft drinks (inc. fizzy and ready to drink fruit drinks)	1.30	1.50	1.50	1.60	1.70	1.50	1.60

Note: The commodity and service categories are not comparable to those in publications before 2001–02.

The numbering system is sequential, it does not use actual COICOP codes.

Table A37 Detailed household expenditure by UK countries and Government Office Regions, 2006 (cont.)
based on weighted data and including children's expenditure

	South East	South West	England	Wales	Scotland	Northern Ireland	United Kingdom
Weighted number of households (thousands)	3,490	2,220	20,830	1,230	2,090	640	24,790
Total number of households in sample	890	580	5,170	310	580	590	6,650
Total number of persons in sample	2,120	1,300	12,220	720	1,370	1,540	15,850
Total number of adults in sample	1,610	1,040	9,280	560	1,040	1,130	12,000
Weighted average number of persons per household	2.3	2.2	2.4	2.4	2.4	2.7	2.4
Commodity or service	Average weekly household expenditure (£)						
1 Food & non-alcoholic drinks	49.20	45.60	47.00	42.30	46.90	53.60	46.90
1.1 Food	45.00	41.90	42.90	38.60	42.20	48.80	42.80
1.1.1 Bread, rice and cereals	4.10	4.10	4.20	4.00	4.40	5.50	4.30
1.1.2 Pasta products	0.30	0.30	0.30	0.30	0.40	0.30	0.30
1.1.3 Buns, cakes, biscuits etc.	3.00	2.90	2.90	2.50	3.00	3.90	2.90
1.1.4 Pastry (savoury)	0.70	0.60	0.70	0.60	0.70	0.70	0.70
1.1.5 Beef (fresh, chilled or frozen)	1.50	1.40	1.50	1.50	1.80	3.10	1.60
1.1.6 Pork (fresh, chilled or frozen)	0.60	0.60	0.60	0.50	0.40	0.70	0.60
1.1.7 Lamb (fresh, chilled or frozen)	0.70	0.60	0.70	0.70	0.40	0.40	0.70
1.1.8 Poultry (fresh, chilled or frozen)	1.90	1.60	1.70	1.50	1.70	2.20	1.70
1.1.9 Bacon and ham	0.70	0.80	0.80	0.90	0.90	1.20	0.90
1.1.10 Other meat and meat preparations	5.00	4.40	4.80	4.60	5.60	5.80	4.90
1.1.11 Fish and fish products	2.30	2.00	2.30	1.60	2.10	1.60	2.20
1.1.12 Milk	2.20	2.20	2.30	2.30	2.20	2.80	2.30
1.1.13 Cheese and curd	1.80	1.70	1.60	1.30	1.30	1.30	1.50
1.1.14 Eggs	0.50	0.40	0.50	0.40	0.40	0.50	0.40
1.1.15 Other milk products	1.80	1.90	1.70	1.40	1.60	1.80	1.70
1.1.16 Butter	0.30	0.30	0.30	0.20	0.40	0.30	0.30
1.1.17 Margarine, other vegetable fats and peanut butter	0.50	0.40	0.40	0.40	0.40	0.50	0.40
1.1.18 Cooking oils and fats	0.20	0.20	0.30	0.20	0.20	0.20	0.20
1.1.19 Fresh fruit	3.40	3.00	3.00	2.50	2.50	2.80	2.90
1.1.20 Other fresh, chilled or frozen fruits	0.30	0.20	0.30	0.20	0.40	0.30	0.30
1.1.21 Dried fruit and nuts	0.60	0.60	0.50	0.50	0.30	0.30	0.50
1.1.22 Preserved fruit and fruit based products	0.10	0.20	0.10	0.10	0.10	0.20	0.10
1.1.23 Fresh vegetables	4.30	3.80	3.70	2.90	2.60	2.90	3.60
1.1.24 Dried vegetables and other preserved or processed vegetables	1.20	1.20	1.10	1.00	1.10	1.20	1.10
1.1.25 Potatoes	0.70	0.70	0.70	0.80	0.70	1.40	0.70
1.1.26 Other tubers and products of tuber vegetables	1.10	1.20	1.10	1.30	1.40	1.50	1.20
1.1.27 Sugar and sugar products	0.30	0.30	0.30	0.30	0.30	0.20	0.30
1.1.28 Jams, marmalades	0.20	0.20	0.20	0.20	0.20	0.30	0.20
1.1.29 Chocolate	1.40	1.30	1.30	1.30	1.50	1.60	1.40
1.1.30 Confectionery products	0.50	0.40	0.50	0.60	0.60	0.60	0.50
1.1.31 Edible ices and ice cream	0.50	0.50	0.50	0.50	0.50	0.60	0.50
1.1.32 Other food products	2.10	1.80	2.00	1.80	2.30	2.20	2.00
1.2 Non-alcoholic drinks	4.20	3.70	4.00	3.70	4.70	4.80	4.10
1.2.1 Coffee	0.60	0.50	0.50	0.40	0.50	0.40	0.50
1.2.2 Tea	0.50	0.40	0.40	0.40	0.40	0.50	0.40
1.2.3 Cocoa and powdered chocolate	0.10	0.10	0.10	0.10	0.10	0.00	0.10
1.2.4 Fruit and vegetable juices (inc. fruit squash)	1.30	1.20	1.20	0.90	1.10	1.10	1.20
1.2.5 Mineral or spring waters	0.30	0.20	0.30	0.20	0.30	0.30	0.30
1.2.6 Soft drinks (inc. fizzy and ready to drink fruit drinks)	1.40	1.20	1.50	1.60	2.30	2.40	1.60

Note: The commodity and service categories are not comparable to those in publications before 2001–02.
The numbering system is sequential, it does not use actual COICOP codes.

Table **A37** Detailed household expenditure by UK countries and Government Office Regions, 2006 (cont.)

based on weighted data and including children's expenditure

Commodity or service	North East	North West	Yorkshire and The Humber	East Midlands	West Midlands	East	London
	Average weekly household expenditure (£)						
2 Alcoholic drink, tobacco & narcotics	**10.70**	**11.50**	**10.80**	**10.40**	**10.90**	**10.00**	**10.30**
2.1 Alcoholic drinks	6.30	6.70	6.10	6.30	6.40	6.10	5.80
2.1.1 Spirits and liqueurs (brought home)	1.20	1.40	0.90	1.30	1.40	1.00	1.00
2.1.2 Wines, fortified wines (brought home)	3.00	2.90	2.80	3.20	3.00	3.60	3.50
2.1.3 Beer, lager, ciders and perry (brought home)	2.00	2.30	2.20	1.60	1.90	1.40	1.30
2.1.4 Alcopops (brought home)	[0.10]	0.10	[0.10]	[0.10]	[0.10]	0.10	[0.00]
2.2 Tobacco and narcotics	4.40	4.90	4.80	4.10	4.50	3.90	4.50
2.2.1 Cigarettes	4.00	4.50	4.40	3.90	4.00	3.40	3.90
2.2.2 Cigars, other tobacco products and narcotics	[0.40]	0.40	0.40	[0.10]	0.50	0.50	0.60
3 Clothing & footwear	**20.90**	**20.10**	**24.30**	**21.20**	**23.50**	**24.50**	**27.70**
3.1 Clothing	17.10	16.20	20.30	16.60	18.70	20.00	22.40
3.1.1 Men's outer garments	4.50	3.80	4.70	3.90	4.90	5.70	5.60
3.1.2 Men's under garments	0.50	0.40	0.40	0.40	0.30	0.30	0.40
3.1.3 Women's outer garments	7.10	6.80	9.60	6.90	8.70	8.50	10.10
3.1.4 Women's under garments	1.20	1.20	1.50	1.20	1.10	1.50	1.80
3.1.5 Boys' outer garments (5–15)	[0.30]	1.00	0.90	0.80	0.60	0.80	0.30
3.1.6 Girls' outer garments (5–15)	1.20	1.20	0.90	1.30	0.90	0.90	1.00
3.1.7 Infants' outer garments (under 5)	[0.70]	0.60	0.50	0.70	0.70	0.70	0.70
3.1.8 Children's under garments (under 16)	0.50	0.40	0.50	0.40	0.30	0.50	0.40
3.1.9 Accessories	0.80	0.60	0.90	0.50	0.70	0.70	1.10
3.1.10 Haberdashery, clothing materials and clothing hire	[0.20]	0.10	0.20	0.40	0.10	0.20	0.20
3.1.11 Dry cleaners, laundry and dyeing	[0.10]	0.20	0.20	[0.20]	0.40	0.30	0.60
3.2 Footwear	3.80	3.90	4.00	4.60	4.80	4.50	5.30
4 Housing (net)[1], fuel & power	**37.60**	**41.60**	**39.80**	**40.40**	**42.30**	**52.00**	**70.00**
4.1 Actual rentals for housing	22.20	23.70	19.70	22.30	25.30	24.40	60.20
4.1.1 Gross rent	21.70	23.70	19.70	21.70	25.30	24.40	60.20
4.1.2 *less* housing benefit, rebates & allowances rec'd	10.50	11.60	9.50	8.40	10.10	8.30	22.50
4.1.3 Net rent	11.20	12.00	10.20	13.30	15.20	16.00	37.70
4.1.4 Second dwelling rent	[0.40]	–	–	[0.60]	–	–	–
4.2 Maintenance and repair of dwelling	5.70	7.30	7.60	5.60	4.80	12.10	8.50
4.3 Water supply and miscellaneous services relating to the dwelling	5.80	6.60	6.40	6.10	6.40	7.60	9.40
4.4 Electricity, gas and other fuels	14.40	15.70	15.60	14.90	15.90	16.30	14.50
4.4.1 Electricity	6.60	7.30	7.00	7.00	7.50	7.50	6.90
4.4.2 Gas	7.20	7.90	7.60	7.30	7.70	6.70	7.50
4.4.3 Other fuels	[0.70]	[0.50]	1.00	[0.60]	0.60	2.00	[0.00]

Note: The commodity and service categories are not comparable to those in publications before 2001–02.

The numbering system is sequential, it does not use actual COICOP codes.

1 Excluding mortgage interest payments, council tax and Northern Ireland rates.

Table A37 Detailed household expenditure by UK countries and Government Office Regions, 2006 (cont.)

based on weighted data and including children's expenditure

			South East	South West	England	Wales	Scotland	Northern Ireland	United Kingdom
Commodity or service			Average weekly household expenditure (£)						
2	Alcoholic drink, tobacco & narcotics		10.60	10.60	10.70	12.50	13.90	14.10	11.10
2.1	Alcoholic drinks		6.90	7.00	6.40	6.40	7.30	5.60	6.50
	2.1.1	Spirits and liqueurs (brought home)	1.20	1.00	1.20	1.30	2.30	1.10	1.30
	2.1.2	Wines, fortified wines (brought home)	3.80	4.20	3.40	2.70	3.10	2.80	3.30
	2.1.3	Beer, lager, ciders and perry (brought home)	1.70	1.70	1.80	2.20	1.90	1.50	1.80
	2.1.4	Alcopops (brought home)	[0.10]	[0.10]	0.10	[0.10]	[0.10]	0.20	0.10
2.2	Tobacco and narcotics		3.70	3.60	4.20	6.10	6.60	8.40	4.60
	2.2.1	Cigarettes	3.20	3.10	3.80	5.60	5.80	8.10	4.20
	2.2.2	Cigars, other tobacco products and narcotics	0.50	0.50	0.50	0.50	0.80	0.30	0.50
3	Clothing & footwear		21.50	18.70	22.60	23.50	25.90	33.50	23.20
3.1	Clothing		17.70	15.40	18.40	19.30	21.30	26.50	18.90
	3.1.1	Men's outer garments	3.90	3.10	4.50	4.80	4.80	6.80	4.60
	3.1.2	Men's under garments	0.40	0.50	0.40	0.40	0.30	0.40	0.40
	3.1.3	Women's outer garments	8.20	7.40	8.30	8.90	9.20	11.80	8.50
	3.1.4	Women's under garments	1.50	1.20	1.40	0.90	1.30	1.40	1.40
	3.1.5	Boys' outer garments (5–15)	0.70	0.50	0.70	0.90	1.30	1.70	0.80
	3.1.6	Girls' outer garments (5–15)	0.90	0.80	1.00	1.00	1.40	1.70	1.00
	3.1.7	Infants' outer garments (under 5)	0.50	0.60	0.60	0.70	1.00	0.80	0.70
	3.1.8	Children's under garments (under 16)	0.30	0.30	0.40	0.50	0.70	0.50	0.40
	3.1.9	Accessories	0.50	0.70	0.70	0.70	0.80	0.60	0.70
	3.1.10	Haberdashery, clothing materials and clothing hire	0.30	0.20	0.20	[0.20]	0.30	0.50	0.20
	3.1.11	Dry cleaners, laundry and dyeing	0.40	[0.10]	0.30	[0.20]	[0.20]	0.30	0.30
3.2	Footwear		3.80	3.30	4.20	4.20	4.70	7.00	4.30
4	Housing (net)[1], fuel & power		52.50	45.20	48.50	46.00	39.40	46.20	47.60
4.1	Actual rentals for housing		28.30	23.20	29.20	24.10	19.50	20.00	27.90
	4.1.1	Gross rent	28.10	23.20	29.10	24.10	19.50	20.00	27.80
	4.1.2	*less* housing benefit, rebates & allowances rec'd	9.30	8.00	11.30	10.10	10.80	8.80	11.20
	4.1.3	Net rent	18.80	15.20	17.80	14.00	8.70	11.30	16.70
	4.1.4	Second dwelling rent	[0.20]	[0.00]	[0.10]	–	–	–	[0.10]
4.2	Maintenance and repair of dwelling		9.80	7.30	7.90	8.50	7.00	11.40	8.00
4.3	Water supply and miscellaneous services relating to the dwelling		7.60	7.20	7.20	6.80	6.50	0.20	6.90
4.4	Electricity, gas and other fuels		16.00	15.50	15.50	16.70	17.20	23.30	15.90
	4.4.1	Electricity	7.90	8.00	7.40	7.80	8.70	9.20	7.50
	4.4.2	Gas	7.60	6.00	7.30	6.60	7.40	1.60	7.20
	4.4.3	Other fuels	0.50	1.50	0.80	2.20	1.20	12.50	1.20

Note: The commodity and service categories are not comparable to those in publications before 2001–02.
        The numbering system is sequential, it does not use actual COICOP codes.
1 Excluding mortgage interest payments, council tax and Northern Ireland rates.

Table A37 Detailed household expenditure by UK countries and Government Office Regions, 2006 (cont.)

based on weighted data and including children's expenditure

	North East	North West	Yorkshire and The Humber	East Midlands	West Midlands	East	London
Commodity or service	Average weekly household expenditure (£)						
5 Household goods & services	**27.70**	**27.50**	**34.30**	**30.30**	**25.40**	**30.90**	**29.40**
5.1 Furniture and furnishings, carpets and other floor coverings	17.10	15.20	19.80	15.70	12.10	16.30	15.90
5.1.1 Furniture and furnishings	11.40	10.70	14.30	11.60	9.10	12.20	13.60
5.1.2 Floor coverings	5.70	4.50	5.50	4.10	3.00	4.10	2.30
5.2 Household textiles	2.00	1.40	2.40	1.40	1.50	2.50	2.20
5.3 Household appliances	1.30	3.20	2.80	4.20	3.10	3.30	2.80
5.4 Glassware, tableware and household utensils	1.10	1.40	1.60	1.50	1.20	1.50	1.80
5.5 Tools and equipment for house and garden	1.80	1.80	2.40	2.20	2.50	2.30	1.40
5.6 Goods and services for routine household maintenance	4.30	4.40	5.20	5.40	5.00	5.10	5.40
5.6.1 Cleaning materials	2.40	1.90	2.50	2.40	2.30	2.40	2.20
5.6.2 Household goods and hardware	0.80	1.00	1.20	1.20	1.10	1.10	1.10
5.6.3 Domestic services, carpet cleaning and hire/repair of furniture/furnishings	1.10	1.60	1.50	1.80	1.60	1.60	2.10
6 Health	**3.60**	**9.50**	**6.00**	**6.60**	**5.40**	**6.30**	**5.60**
6.1 Medical products, appliances and equipment	2.40	2.50	4.00	3.40	2.40	3.70	2.90
6.1.1 Medicines, prescriptions, healthcare products and equipment	1.40	1.40	1.90	1.40	1.50	1.80	1.70
6.1.2 Spectacles, lenses, accessories and repairs	[0.90]	1.20	2.00	2.00	1.00	1.90	1.20
6.2 Hospital services	1.30	6.90	2.00	3.30	3.00	2.50	2.70
7 Transport	**43.60**	**50.50**	**53.60**	**59.00**	**55.80**	**65.40**	**68.30**
7.1 Purchase of vehicles	15.30	18.00	19.10	18.70	18.20	23.80	23.80
7.1.1 Purchase of new cars and vans	[4.60]	9.40	5.50	5.10	8.00	8.80	[5.50]
7.1.2 Purchase of second hand cars or vans	10.10	8.30	12.50	13.40	9.80	14.30	17.40
7.1.3 Purchase of motorcycles and other vehicles	[0.70]	[0.30]	[1.10]	[0.30]	[0.40]	[0.70]	[0.90]
7.2 Operation of personal transport	22.30	23.00	26.60	32.40	29.50	34.60	22.90
7.2.1 Spares and accessories	[1.60]	1.10	2.80	3.20	2.70	2.90	1.20
7.2.2 Petrol, diesel and other motor oils	15.10	15.40	16.30	20.00	18.70	20.50	13.90
7.2.3 Repairs and servicing	4.00	4.10	5.00	6.50	5.50	7.60	5.60
7.2.4 Other motoring costs	1.60	2.40	2.50	2.70	2.50	3.60	2.20
7.3 Transport services	6.00	9.50	7.80	7.90	8.20	7.00	21.60
7.3.1 Rail and tube fares	1.20	1.30	1.10	1.10	1.30	3.40	3.60
7.3.2 Bus and coach fares	1.60	1.10	1.80	1.30	1.60	0.80	2.00
7.3.3 Combined fares	[0.10]	[0.00]	[0.20]	[0.10]	[0.10]	[0.50]	6.70
7.3.4 Other travel and transport	3.10	7.10	4.70	5.40	5.20	2.20	9.20
8 Communication	**9.60**	**10.80**	**10.60**	**11.90**	**11.20**	**12.40**	**14.90**
8.1 Postal services	0.30	0.60	0.50	0.30	0.40	0.40	0.50
8.2 Telephone and telefax equipment	[0.90]	[0.50]	[0.60]	1.20	[0.80]	1.20	[0.50]
8.3 Telephone and telefax services	8.40	9.70	9.60	10.40	10.10	10.70	13.80

Note: The commodity and service categories are not comparable to those in publications before 2001–02.
       The numbering system is sequential, it does not use actual COICOP codes.

Table A37 Detailed household expenditure by UK countries and Government Office Regions, 2006 (cont.)

based on weighted data and including children's expenditure

Commodity or service	South East	South West	England	Wales	Scotland	Northern Ireland	United Kingdom
	Average weekly household expenditure (£)						
5 Household goods & services	**35.50**	**30.40**	**30.50**	**26.20**	**30.10**	**31.10**	**30.30**
5.1 Furniture and furnishings, carpets and other floor coverings	19.90	15.80	16.50	14.60	17.00	18.20	16.50
5.1.1 Furniture and furnishings	15.50	12.50	12.60	9.40	12.60	14.70	12.50
5.1.2 Floor coverings	4.40	3.30	4.00	5.30	4.40	3.50	4.10
5.2 Household textiles	2.00	1.30	1.90	2.10	1.80	2.40	1.90
5.3 Household appliances	3.70	3.30	3.20	1.90	2.40	2.20	3.00
5.4 Glassware, tableware and household utensils	1.70	2.00	1.60	1.40	1.50	1.50	1.60
5.5 Tools and equipment for house and garden	2.10	2.20	2.10	1.80	2.30	1.80	2.10
5.6 Goods and services for routine household maintenance	6.10	5.80	5.30	4.40	5.10	5.00	5.20
5.6.1 Cleaning materials	2.70	2.20	2.30	2.20	2.10	2.40	2.30
5.6.2 Household goods and hardware	1.70	1.10	1.20	1.00	1.10	1.20	1.20
5.6.3 Domestic services, carpet cleaning and hire/repair of furniture/furnishings	1.70	2.50	1.80	1.20	1.90	1.50	1.70
6 Health	**6.50**	**5.10**	**6.30**	**4.20**	**3.10**	**4.20**	**5.90**
6.1 Medical products, appliances and equipment	4.30	2.90	3.20	3.10	2.00	3.10	3.10
6.1.1 Medicines, prescriptions, healthcare products and equipment	2.40	1.80	1.80	1.50	1.40	1.40	1.70
6.1.2 Spectacles, lenses, accessories and repairs	1.90	1.10	1.50	[1.60]	0.60	1.70	1.40
6.2 Hospital services	2.10	2.20	3.00	[1.10]	1.20	1.20	2.70
7 Transport	**77.30**	**70.30**	**62.40**	**58.60**	**60.20**	**61.50**	**62.00**
7.1 Purchase of vehicles	32.90	30.30	23.30	21.90	26.30	20.30	23.40
7.1.1 Purchase of new cars and vans	11.80	12.10	8.30	12.00	6.50	7.60	8.30
7.1.2 Purchase of second hand cars or vans	20.60	17.90	14.40	9.40	19.00	12.50	14.50
7.1.3 Purchase of motorcycles and other vehicles	[0.60]	[0.30]	0.60	[0.60]	[0.70]	[0.20]	0.60
7.2 Operation of personal transport	33.40	31.00	28.60	30.20	26.80	32.00	28.60
7.2.1 Spares and accessories	2.20	2.10	2.10	2.30	1.20	1.70	2.10
7.2.2 Petrol, diesel and other motor oils	20.30	20.60	17.90	21.20	18.30	22.90	18.20
7.2.3 Repairs and servicing	8.40	6.10	6.10	4.90	5.30	5.80	5.90
7.2.4 Other motoring costs	2.40	2.40	2.50	1.80	2.00	1.70	2.40
7.3 Transport services	11.00	8.90	10.50	6.40	7.10	9.20	10.00
7.3.1 Rail and tube fares	4.40	1.60	2.40	0.60	1.60	0.60	2.20
7.3.2 Bus and coach fares	0.80	1.00	1.30	1.00	1.70	1.00	1.30
7.3.3 Combined fares	0.60	[0.00]	1.20	[0.00]	[0.10]	[0.10]	1.00
7.3.4 Other travel and transport	5.20	6.20	5.70	4.80	3.70	7.60	5.50
8 Communication	**11.60**	**10.90**	**11.70**	**10.90**	**11.60**	**13.80**	**11.70**
8.1 Postal services	0.60	0.50	0.50	0.60	0.60	0.60	0.50
8.2 Telephone and telefax equipment	0.60	[0.60]	0.70	[0.70]	[0.80]	[0.80]	0.70
8.3 Telephone and telefax services	10.50	9.90	10.60	9.60	10.20	12.40	10.50

Note: The commodity and service categories are not comparable to those in publications before 2001–02.
The numbering system is sequential, it does not use actual COICOP codes.

Table A37 Detailed household expenditure by UK countries and Government Office Regions, 2006 (cont.)

based on weighted data and including children's expenditure

	North East	North West	Yorkshire and The Humber	East Midlands	West Midlands	East	London
Commodity or service	Average weekly household expenditure (£)						
9 Recreation & culture	49.70	60.80	60.10	66.30	51.90	64.80	46.50
9.1 Audio-visual, photographic and information processing equipment	4.70	9.10	5.70	8.20	6.50	7.40	5.40
9.1.1 Audio equipment and accessories, CD players	1.90	2.10	1.80	3.40	1.20	1.50	2.40
9.1.2 TV, video and computers	2.20	6.80	3.50	3.90	4.40	5.40	2.50
9.1.3 Photographic, cine and optical equipment	[0.60]	[0.10]	0.40	[0.90]	[0.90]	0.40	[0.50]
9.2 Other major durables for recreation and culture	[0.10]	[3.70]	[0.40]	[5.30]	1.00	2.00	[0.10]
9.3 Other recreational items and equipment, gardens and pets	7.30	9.00	11.10	11.90	9.20	12.00	7.30
9.3.1 Games, toys and hobbies	1.80	1.60	2.20	2.60	2.00	2.10	1.30
9.3.2 Computer software and games	[0.80]	1.50	1.10	0.80	0.90	1.20	0.80
9.3.3 Equipment for sport, camping and open-air recreation	0.60	0.80	1.00	1.20	1.20	1.30	1.10
9.3.4 Horticultural goods, garden equipment and plants	1.60	2.30	2.90	2.30	1.90	2.60	2.50
9.3.5 Pets and pet food	2.50	2.80	4.00	4.90	3.20	4.80	1.60
9.4 Recreational and cultural services	17.40	17.70	20.20	23.00	15.60	19.20	18.20
9.4.1 Sports admissions, subscriptions, leisure class fees and equipment hire	3.80	4.20	6.60	9.10	4.00	6.30	6.40
9.4.2 Cinema, theatre and museums etc.	1.50	2.00	2.40	2.60	1.80	1.90	2.10
9.4.3 TV, video, satellite rental, cable subscriptions, TV licences and the Internet	5.60	5.90	6.10	6.20	5.20	6.30	5.70
9.4.4 Miscellaneous entertainments	0.80	0.90	1.10	1.40	0.90	1.20	1.10
9.4.5 Development of film, deposit for film development, passport photos, holiday and school photos	[0.90]	0.20	0.30	0.70	0.40	0.40	0.30
9.4.6 Gambling payments	4.70	4.50	3.60	3.00	3.40	3.00	2.40
9.5 Newspapers, books and stationery	5.80	5.90	6.90	6.40	6.00	6.80	6.90
9.5.1 Books	1.10	1.50	1.70	1.40	1.50	1.60	2.20
9.5.2 Diaries, address books, cards etc.	1.60	1.70	2.00	2.20	1.80	2.10	1.70
9.5.3 Newspapers	2.40	1.90	2.00	1.80	1.80	1.90	2.00
9.5.4 Magazines and periodicals	0.70	0.90	1.30	1.00	0.90	1.20	1.00
9.6 Package holidays	14.50	15.40	15.80	11.60	13.60	17.40	8.70
9.6.1 Package holidays – UK	[0.90]	0.80	1.70	1.30	[1.10]	1.90	[0.60]
9.6.2 Package holidays – abroad	13.60	14.60	14.10	10.30	12.60	15.60	8.10
10 Education	[1.60]	6.50	8.30	4.70	6.50	5.90	14.40
10.1 Education fees	[1.30]	6.00	7.90	4.30	6.20	5.70	14.30
10.2 Payments for school trips, other ad-hoc expenditure	[0.30]	[0.50]	[0.40]	[0.40]	[0.30]	[0.20]	[0.20]
11 Restaurants & hotels	32.30	33.60	39.60	36.80	34.40	38.80	47.00
11.1 Catering services	29.10	28.70	33.60	30.90	30.00	31.80	37.30
11.1.1 Restaurant and café meals	9.80	10.70	12.80	11.80	12.70	13.50	15.20
11.1.2 Alcoholic drinks (away from home)	9.60	7.40	10.00	9.10	8.20	7.30	8.70
11.1.3 Take away meals eaten at home	4.20	3.90	4.20	4.00	3.60	3.90	4.10
11.1.4 Other take-away and snack food	4.00	3.90	4.00	3.80	3.50	4.20	6.40
11.1.5 Contract catering (food) and canteens	1.40	2.90	2.60	2.10	2.00	2.90	2.90
11.2 Accommodation services	3.30	4.90	6.00	5.90	4.40	7.00	9.70
11.2.1 Holiday in the UK	1.50	2.20	3.10	3.20	2.40	3.00	2.60
11.2.2 Holiday abroad	[1.70]	2.70	2.90	2.70	2.00	4.00	7.10
11.2.3 Room hire	[0.00]	[0.00]	–	[0.00]	–	[0.00]	–

Note: The commodity and service categories are not comparable to those in publications before 2001–02.
The numbering system is sequential, it does not use actual COICOP codes.

Table **A37** Detailed household expenditure by UK countries and Government Office Regions, 2006 (cont.)

based on weighted data and including children's expenditure

Commodity or service	South East	South West	England	Wales	Scotland	Northern Ireland	United Kingdom
			Average weekly household expenditure (£)				
9 Recreation & culture	64.40	60.20	58.60	52.60	63.70	47.50	58.50
9.1 Audio-visual, photographic and information processing equipment	8.30	6.40	7.00	5.40	9.60	5.70	7.10
9.1.1 Audio equipment and accessories, CD players	2.00	1.80	2.00	1.60	1.40	1.30	1.90
9.1.2 TV, video and computers	5.10	3.60	4.40	3.30	7.80	3.80	4.60
9.1.3 Photographic, cine and optical equipment	1.10	1.00	0.70	[0.40]	0.40	[0.40]	0.60
9.2 Other major durables for recreation and culture	1.90	[0.90]	1.80	[0.40]	[1.70]	[0.50]	1.70
9.3 Other recreational items and equipment, gardens and pets	12.50	11.80	10.30	10.40	9.20	10.50	10.30
9.3.1 Games, toys and hobbies	2.10	1.90	1.90	2.20	2.20	2.60	2.00
9.3.2 Computer software and games	1.10	1.10	1.10	[1.50]	1.00	0.90	1.10
9.3.3 Equipment for sport, camping and open-air recreation	1.20	1.90	1.10	0.90	0.90	2.80	1.20
9.3.4 Horticultural goods, garden equipment and plants	3.40	3.30	2.60	1.60	2.70	2.20	2.60
9.3.5 Pets and pet food	4.80	3.50	3.60	4.20	2.40	2.00	3.50
9.4 Recreational and cultural services	20.70	17.40	18.90	17.70	18.90	14.50	18.70
9.4.1 Sports admissions, subscriptions, leisure class fees and equipment hire	6.60	5.00	5.80	5.30	5.70	3.70	5.80
9.4.2 Cinema, theatre and museums etc.	1.90	2.30	2.10	1.80	1.90	1.40	2.00
9.4.3 TV, video, satellite rental, cable subscriptions, TV licences and the Internet	5.80	5.40	5.80	6.20	6.20	5.10	5.80
9.4.4 Miscellaneous entertainments	1.10	1.60	1.10	0.80	0.80	1.00	1.10
9.4.5 Development of film, deposit for film development, passport photos, holiday and school photos	0.40	0.30	0.40	[0.10]	0.30	0.40	0.40
9.4.6 Gambling payments	4.90	2.80	3.60	3.40	4.00	2.80	3.60
9.5 Newspapers, books and stationery	7.70	6.40	6.60	6.00	6.90	6.80	6.60
9.5.1 Books	1.90	1.30	1.60	1.30	1.60	1.30	1.60
9.5.2 Diaries, address books, cards etc.	2.60	2.10	2.00	1.90	1.60	1.70	2.00
9.5.3 Newspapers	2.00	1.90	2.00	1.80	2.50	2.60	2.00
9.5.4 Magazines and periodicals	1.20	1.00	1.00	1.00	1.10	1.20	1.00
9.6 Package holidays	13.20	17.30	14.00	12.70	17.40	9.50	14.10
9.6.1 Package holidays – UK	0.60	[0.50]	1.00	[0.70]	[0.60]	[0.20]	0.90
9.6.2 Package holidays – abroad	12.60	16.80	13.00	12.00	16.80	9.20	13.20
10 Education	8.30	7.00	7.70	3.70	5.70	3.80	7.20
10.1 Education fees	7.80	6.50	7.30	[3.50]	5.40	3.20	6.90
10.2 Payments for school trips, other ad-hoc expenditure	0.40	[0.40]	[0.40]	[0.20]	[0.30]	0.60	0.40
11 Restaurants & hotels	37.60	34.60	37.70	35.40	40.30	40.70	37.90
11.1 Catering services	30.10	28.00	31.20	32.70	35.80	37.40	31.90
11.1.1 Restaurant and café meals	13.50	12.60	12.80	12.10	12.30	15.00	12.80
11.1.2 Alcoholic drinks (away from home)	7.60	8.10	8.30	10.00	8.60	8.10	8.40
11.1.3 Take away meals eaten at home	3.50	2.90	3.80	4.00	4.20	6.20	3.90
11.1.4 Other take-away and snack food	3.80	3.10	4.10	4.60	4.60	5.10	4.20
11.1.5 Contract catering (food) and canteens	1.90	1.30	2.30	2.10	6.00	2.90	2.60
11.2 Accommodation services	7.40	6.60	6.50	2.60	4.50	3.30	6.00
11.2.1 Holiday in the UK	3.20	3.30	2.80	[0.80]	2.20	[0.50]	2.60
11.2.2 Holiday abroad	4.20	3.20	3.70	[1.80]	2.20	2.70	3.40
11.2.3 Room hire	[0.00]	[0.00]	[0.00]	[0.00]	0.10	[0.00]	[0.00]

Note: The commodity and service categories are not comparable to those in publications before 2001–02.
The numbering system is sequential, it does not use actual COICOP codes.

Table A37 Detailed household expenditure by UK countries and Government Office Regions, 2006 (cont.)

based on weighted data and including children's expenditure

Commodity or service	North East	North West	Yorkshire and The Humber	East Midlands	West Midlands	East	London
	Average weekly household expenditure (£)						
12 Miscellaneous goods & services	27.60	33.50	32.30	34.00	33.10	44.00	38.00
12.1 Personal care	8.80	8.80	10.00	10.10	8.80	10.80	10.90
12.1.1 Hairdressing, beauty treatment	3.40	3.00	3.20	3.00	2.80	3.80	3.40
12.1.2 Toilet paper	0.70	0.60	0.70	0.80	0.70	0.70	0.80
12.1.3 Toiletries and soap	1.50	1.70	2.30	2.20	1.90	2.20	2.10
12.1.4 Baby toiletries and accessories (disposable)	0.40	0.50	0.50	0.70	0.70	0.70	0.70
12.1.5 Hair products, cosmetics and electrical personal appliances	2.90	3.00	3.30	3.30	2.70	3.40	3.80
12.2 Personal effects	2.80	2.90	3.20	2.10	4.50	2.30	4.00
12.3 Social protection	[1.90]	1.80	2.10	[2.10]	2.40	3.90	2.50
12.4 Insurance	11.80	14.80	13.90	15.00	14.30	16.40	15.90
12.4.1 Household insurances – structural, contents and appliances	4.40	4.90	5.30	4.80	4.60	5.20	5.50
12.4.2 Medical insurance premiums	0.50	1.60	1.40	1.30	1.60	1.90	2.40
12.4.3 Vehicle insurance including boat insurance	6.80	8.20	7.00	8.80	7.90	9.20	8.10
12.4.4 Non-package holiday, other travel insurance	[0.00]	[0.00]	[0.20]	[0.00]	[0.20]	[0.10]	[0.10]
12.5 Other services n.e.c	2.30	5.20	3.00	4.80	3.10	10.50	4.60
12.5.1 Moving house	[1.00]	1.40	1.50	1.60	1.90	6.30	2.80
12.5.2 Bank, building society, post office, credit card charges	0.30	0.30	0.20	0.30	0.30	0.40	0.50
12.5.3 Other services and professional fees	1.00	3.50	1.30	2.80	0.90	3.90	1.30
1–12 All expenditure groups	**305.20**	**348.70**	**365.90**	**369.90**	**347.40**	**403.10**	**422.50**
13 Other expenditure items	54.30	72.90	58.50	68.60	64.90	84.10	115.50
13.1 Housing: mortgage interest payments, council tax etc.	38.80	43.50	43.90	52.10	47.10	60.70	64.40
13.2 Licences, fines and transfers	2.50	2.60	2.50	3.20	2.90	3.30	2.70
13.3 Holiday spending	[2.90]	18.60	3.40	[5.50]	[5.60]	8.50	32.70
13.4 Money transfers and credit	10.10	8.20	8.60	7.70	9.20	11.70	15.60
13.4.1 Money, cash gifts given to children	[0.00]	[0.00]	[0.10]	[0.00]	[0.30]	[0.10]	[0.10]
13.4.2 Cash gifts and donations	8.60	7.00	7.10	5.70	7.60	9.60	13.20
13.4.3 Club instalment payments (child) and interest on credit cards	1.50	1.20	1.40	2.00	1.40	2.00	2.30
Total expenditure	**359.50**	**421.70**	**424.40**	**438.50**	**412.30**	**487.20**	**538.00**
14 Other items recorded							
14.1 Life assurance, contributions to pension funds	16.30	17.80	18.90	21.40	21.00	23.50	27.20
14.2 Other insurance inc. Friendly Societies	0.50	1.20	1.80	1.20	1.30	1.40	1.00
14.3 Income tax, payments less refunds	59.40	71.10	70.70	78.90	84.90	86.50	134.00
14.4 National insurance contributions	24.50	21.80	22.40	25.80	25.30	25.80	32.90
14.5 Purchase or alteration of dwellings, mortgages	59.70	81.00	49.50	36.10	35.40	42.70	43.10
14.6 Savings and investments	3.70	2.80	3.80	7.60	3.90	6.80	7.10
14.7 Pay off loan to clear other debt	[1.60]	2.30	2.90	2.90	3.10	4.10	2.00
14.8 Windfall receipts from gambling etc.	2.00	3.20	1.40	1.80	1.60	1.90	0.90

Note: The commodity and service categories are not comparable to those in publications before 2001–02.
The numbering system is sequential, it does not use actual COICOP codes.

Table A37 Detailed household expenditure by UK countries and Government Office Regions, 2006 (cont.)

based on weighted data and including children's expenditure

Commodity or service	South East	South West	England	Wales	Scotland	Northern Ireland	United Kingdom
			Average weekly household expenditure (£)				
12 Miscellaneous goods & services	42.90	34.50	36.50	30.50	34.50	34.60	36.00
12.1 Personal care	10.10	8.80	9.80	9.60	10.20	11.20	9.80
12.1.1 Hairdressing, beauty treatment	3.50	2.80	3.20	3.00	3.30	3.70	3.20
12.1.2 Toilet paper	0.70	0.70	0.70	0.70	0.70	0.90	0.70
12.1.3 Toiletries and soap	2.10	1.90	2.00	2.10	2.00	2.40	2.00
12.1.4 Baby toiletries and accessories (disposable)	0.60	0.50	0.60	0.60	0.50	0.60	0.60
12.1.5 Hair products, cosmetics and electrical personal appliances	3.20	2.80	3.20	3.30	3.60	3.70	3.20
12.3 Personal effects	2.90	3.40	3.20	2.60	3.20	2.90	3.10
12.3 Social protection	4.00	[1.70]	2.60	[1.10]	3.60	2.50	2.60
12.4 Insurance	17.70	15.20	15.40	13.10	12.80	15.30	15.10
12.4.1 Household insurances – structural, contents and appliances	5.90	4.90	5.20	4.90	5.30	4.30	5.10
12.4.2 Medical insurance premiums	2.80	2.50	1.90	0.70	1.10	0.70	1.80
12.4.3 Vehicle insurance including boat insurance	8.60	7.40	8.10	7.50	6.20	10.20	8.00
12.4.4 Non-package holiday, other travel insurance	[0.40]	[0.40]	0.20	[0.10]	[0.20]	–	0.20
12.5 Other services n.e.c	8.20	5.40	5.60	4.10	4.80	2.70	5.40
12.5.1 Moving house	6.70	3.00	3.20	2.60	3.00	1.30	3.10
12.5.2 Bank, building society, post office, credit card charges	0.40	0.40	0.30	0.30	0.40	0.60	0.40
12.5.3 Other services and professional fees	1.00	2.00	2.00	1.20	1.30	0.80	1.90
1–12 All expenditure groups	**417.80**	**373.00**	**380.30**	**346.40**	**375.40**	**384.50**	**378.30**
13 Other expenditure items	94.00	73.20	80.10	58.30	68.60	63.00	77.60
13.1 Housing: mortgage interest payments, council tax etc.	64.90	51.50	53.60	40.20	47.20	35.90	52.00
13.2 Licences, fines and transfers	3.70	3.20	3.00	2.80	2.50	2.70	2.90
13.3 Holiday spending	13.50	9.00	12.80	[8.30]	8.20	9.80	12.10
13.4 Money transfers and credit	12.00	9.40	10.60	7.00	10.80	14.60	10.50
13.4.1 Money, cash gifts given to children	0.10	[0.00]	0.10	[0.10]	[0.10]	[0.20]	0.10
13.4.2 Cash gifts and donations	9.60	7.00	8.60	6.10	8.50	13.30	8.60
13.4.3 Club instalment payments (child) and interest on credit cards	2.20	2.40	1.90	0.80	2.10	1.10	1.80
Total expenditure	**511.80**	**446.20**	**460.30**	**404.70**	**444.00**	**447.50**	**455.90**
14 Other items recorded							
14.1 Life assurance, contributions to pension funds	23.20	23.70	22.00	19.50	22.30	17.10	21.70
14.2 Other insurance inc. Friendly Societies	1.60	1.30	1.30	0.80	1.30	1.00	1.30
14.3 Income tax, payments less refunds	128.50	85.20	94.20	64.20	83.70	60.00	91.00
14.4 National insurance contributions	27.30	24.00	25.90	22.50	23.50	20.80	25.40
14.5 Purchase or alteration of dwellings, mortgages	60.00	42.50	51.10	37.00	74.40	26.60	51.70
14.6 Savings and investments	7.50	12.10	6.30	4.90	5.70	11.30	6.30
14.7 Pay off loan to clear other debt	3.10	2.70	2.80	[2.50]	1.60	[0.30]	2.60
14.8 Windfall receipts from gambling etc.	3.90	1.20	2.10	1.60	3.00	1.90	2.20

Note: The commodity and service categories are not comparable to those in publications before 2001–02.
The numbering system is sequential, it does not use actual COICOP codes.

Table **A38** Household expenditure by urban/rural areas (GB)[1], 2006

based on weighted data and including children's expenditure

	Urban	Rural
Weighted number of households (thousands)	19,380	4,770
Total number of households in sample	4,780	1,280
Total number of persons in sample	11,300	3,010
Total number of adults in sample	8,560	2,320
Weighted average number of persons per household	2.4	2.3
Commodity or service	Average weekly household expenditure (£)	
1 Food & non-alcoholic drinks	46.10	49.00
2 Alcoholic drinks, tobacco & narcotics	10.70	12.40
3 Clothing & footwear	23.10	22.50
4 Housing (net)[2], fuel & power	47.20	49.00
5 Household goods & services	28.70	36.50
6 Health	5.30	8.60
7 Transport	59.70	71.40
8 Communication	11.80	11.00
9 Recreation & culture	57.10	65.40
10 Education	6.90	8.90
11 Restaurants & hotels	38.00	37.20
12 Miscellaneous goods & services	35.10	40.10
1–12 All expenditure groups	369.80	412.00
13 Other expenditure items	76.90	82.10
Total expenditure	**446.70**	**494.20**
Average weekly expenditure per person (£)		
Total expenditure	**189.20**	**211.30**

Note: The commodity and service categories are not comparable to those in publications before 2001–02.

1 Combined urban/rural classification for England & Wales and Scotland – see definitions in Appendix B.

2 Excludes mortgage interest payments and council tax.

Table A39 Government Office Regions of the United Kingdom

Table **A40** Income and source of income by household composition, 2006
based on weighted data

Composition of household	Weighted number of house-holds	Number of house-holds in the sample	Weekly household income Dispo-sable	Gross	Wages and salaries	Self employ-ment	Invest-ments	Annuities and pensions[1]	Social security benefits[2]	Other sources
	(000s)	Number	£	£	Percentage of gross weekly household income					
All households	24,790	6,650	521	642	67	9	3	7	12	1
One adult	6,940	1,820	277	333	52	6	6	12	23	1
Retired households mainly dependent on state pensions[3]	680	190	150	151	–	–	2	3	95	[0]
Other retired households	2,500	670	214	233	–	–	9	38	53	[0]
Non-retired households	3,760	960	341	432	74	9	5	3	7	1
One adult, one child	760	230	267	304	57	[10]	1	[0]	29	3
One adult, two or more children	700	220	316	349	44	[6]	1	[0]	43	6
One man and one woman	7,630	2,090	560	693	62	8	5	13	13	0
Retired households mainly dependent on state pensions[3]	500	150	226	228	[0]	–	2	7	91	[0]
Other retired households	2,080	620	403	444	4	[1]	10	42	42	0
Non-retired households	5,050	1,320	657	841	76	9	3	7	4	0
Two men or two women	570	140	535	648	72	[7]	2	6	12	2
Two men or two women with children	110	30	423	481	71	[1]	[0]	–	25	[2]
One man one woman, one child	1,770	490	682	865	84	8	[1]	1	5	1
One man one woman, two children	2,080	610	716	914	80	11	[2]	0	6	1
One man one woman, three children	620	190	816	1,023	75	12	[2]	0	9	1
Two adults, four or more children	230	70	539	641	[58]	9	[3]	0	29	2
Three adults	1,700	360	728	893	73	9	[3]	5	8	2
Three adults, one or more children	720	190	736	898	68	18	2	2	10	1
Four or more adults	680	130	926	1,135	79	9	2	3	5	2
Four or more adults, one or more children	270	70	826	985	[67]	9	3	[3]	13	[5]

1 Other than social security benefits.
2 Excluding housing benefit and council tax benefit (rates rebate in Northern Ireland) – see definitions in Appendix B.
3 Mainly dependent on state pension and not economically active – see defintions in Appendix B.

Table **A41** Income and source of income by age of household reference person, 2006
based on weighted data

Age of household reference person	Weighted number of house-holds	Number of house-holds in the sample	Weekly household income Dispo-sable	Gross	Wages and salaries	Self employ-ment	Invest-ments	Annuities and pensions[1]	Social security benefits[2]	Other sources
	(000s)	Number	£	£	Percentage of gross weekly household income					
Less than 30	2,450	610	460	569	83	7	1	[0]	7	3
30 to 49	9,610	2,580	632	801	81	9	2	1	7	1
50 to 64	6,430	1,710	576	713	68	11	4	8	8	1
65 to 74	3,190	940	374	424	15	5	9	32	39	0
75 or over	3,100	810	263	282	4	[2]	8	31	55	[0]

1 Other than social security benefits.
2 Excluding housing benefit and council tax benefit (rates rebate in Northern Ireland) – see definitions in Appendix B.

Table A42 Income and source of income by gross income quintile group, 2006

based on weighted data

Gross income quintile group	Weighted number of house-holds	Number of house-holds in the sample	Weekly household income		Source of income					
			Dispo-sable	Gross	Wages and salaries	Self employ-ment	Invest-ments	Annuities and pensions[1]	Social security benefits[2]	Other sources
	(000s)	Number	£	£	Percentage of gross weekly household income					
Lowest twenty per cent	4,950	1,360	138	140	6	3	2	9	77	2
Second quintile group	4,960	1,390	270	295	32	4	4	16	43	2
Third quintile group	4,960	1,370	427	501	61	7	3	11	17	2
Fourth quintile group	4,960	1,300	624	770	75	8	3	7	7	1
Highest twenty per cent	4,950	1,230	1,147	1,503	79	11	4	4	2	1

1 Other than social security benefits.
2 Excluding housing benefit and council tax benefit (rates rebate in Northern Ireland) – see definitions in Appendix B.

Table A43 Income and source of income by household tenure, 2006

based on weighted data

Tenure of dwelling[3]	Weighted number of house-holds	Number of house-holds in the sample	Weekly household income		Source of income					
			Dispo-sable	Gross	Wages and salaries	Self employ-ment	Invest-ments	Annuities and pensions[1]	Social security benefits[2]	Other sources
	(000s)	Number	£	£	Percentage of gross weekly household income					
Owners										
Owned outright	7,830	2,170	475	569	44	8	8	20	19	1
Buying with a mortgage	9,850	2,630	689	879	82	10	2	2	5	1
All	17,690	4,800	594	741	69	9	4	8	10	1
Social rented from										
Council	2,680	730	260	286	45	3	0	4	47	1
Registered social landlord[4]	1,610	420	250	274	42	[4]	1	4	48	1
All	4,290	1,150	256	281	44	4	1	4	47	1
Private rented										
Rent free	310	90	368	423	52	[16]	5	6	19	[3]
Rent paid, unfurnished	1,830	460	449	550	76	9	2	1	11	1
Rent paid, furnished	670	150	561	676	74	[13]	0	[0]	4	8
All	2,810	700	467	566	74	11	2	1	10	3

1 Other than social security benefits.
2 Excluding housing benefit and council tax benefit (rates rebate in Northern Ireland) – see definitions in Appendix B.
3 See footnotes in Table A34.
4 Formerly housing association.

Table A44 Income and source of income by UK countries and Government Office Regions, 2006
based on weighted data

	Weighted number of house-holds	Total number house-holds	Weekly household income		Source of income					
			Dispo-sable	Gross	Wages and salaries	Self employ-ment	Invest-ments	Annuities and pensions[1]	Social security benefits[2]	Other sources
Government Office Regions	(000s)	Number	£	£	Percentage of gross weekly household income					
United Kingdom	24,790	6,650	521	642	67	9	3	7	12	1
North East	1,100	280	415	500	70	[4]	2	7	18	0
North West	2,810	700	452	547	64	8	2	7	17	1
Yorkshire and The Humber	2,110	550	468	566	65	8	3	7	15	1
East Midlands	1,720	500	494	604	68	8	3	7	13	2
West Midlands	2,180	540	486	598	68	9	2	7	14	1
East	2,260	590	530	646	67	9	3	8	12	1
London	2,950	540	647	818	75	9	3	4	8	1
South East	3,490	890	613	775	66	10	6	8	9	1
South West	2,220	580	515	627	63	10	5	9	12	1
England	20,830	5,170	528	652	68	9	3	7	12	1
Wales	1,230	310	451	547	70	5	2	5	16	1
Scotland	2,090	580	505	618	64	9	3	8	15	2
Northern Ireland	640	590	472	562	66	9	2	5	16	1

1 Other than social security benefits.
2 Excluding housing benefit and council tax benefit (rates rebate in Northern Ireland) – see definitions in Appendix B.

Table A45 Income and source of income by GB urban/rural area, 2006
based on weighted data

	Weighted number of house-holds	Total number house-holds	Weekly household income		Source of income					
			Dispo-sable	Gross	Wages and salaries	Self employ-ment	Invest-ments	Annuities and pensions[1]	Social security benefits[2]	Other sources
GB urban rural areas	(000s)	Number	£	£	Percentage of gross weekly household income					
Urban	19,380	4,780	514	635	69	8	3	6	13	1
Rural	4,770	1,280	555	679	60	12	6	10	12	1

1 Other than social security benefits.
2 Excluding housing benefit and council tax benefit (rates rebate in Northern Ireland) – see definitions in Appendix B.

Table A46 Income and source of income by socio-economic classification, 2006
based on weighted data

| NS–SEC Group[5] | Weighted number of house-holds | Number of house-holds in the sample | Weekly household income | | Source of income | | | | | |
			Dispo-sable	Gross	Wages and salaries	Self employ-ment	Invest-ments	Annuities and pensions[1]	Social security benefits[2]	Other sources
	(000s)	Number	£	£	Percentage of gross weekly household income					
Large employers/higher managerial	1,200	310	1,084	1,465	92	2	2	2	2	0
Higher professional	1,820	470	918	1,206	76	17	3	2	2	0
Lower managerial and professional	4,520	1,170	728	937	85	6	3	3	3	1
Intermediate	1,460	380	529	656	85	3	1	3	7	2
Small employers	1,560	430	572	648	21	63	4	4	7	1
Lower supervisory	1,580	420	520	650	90	[1]	1	2	6	1
Semi-routine	1,810	490	424	511	80	[2]	1	3	12	1
Routine	1,570	430	468	564	83	3	1	3	10	1
Long-term unemployed[3]	480	130	225	241	27	[1]	4	[6]	59	[2]
Students	310	70	304	334	47	[1]	2	–	[6]	44
Occupation not stated[4]	8,460	2,360	290	318	12	[1]	8	29	48	1

1 Other than social security benefits.
2 Excluding housing benefit and council tax benefit (rates rebate in Northern Ireland) – see definitions in Appendix B.
3 Includes those who have never worked.
4 Includes those who are economically inactive – see definitions in Appendix B.
5 National Statistics Socio-economic classification (NS-SEC) – see definitions in Appendix B.

Table A47 Income and source of income, 1970 to 2006

| | Weighted number of house-holds | Number of house-holds in the sample | Weekly household income[1] | | | | Source of income | | | | | |
| | | | Current prices | | Constant prices | | Wages and salaries | Self employ-ment | Invest-ments | Annuities and pensions[2] | Social security benefits[3] | Other sources |
			Dispo-sable	Gross	Dispo-sable	Gross						
	(000s)	Number	£	£	£	£	Percentage of gross weekly household income					
1970		6,390	28	34	304	367	77	7	4	3	9	1
1980		6,940	115	140	340	416	75	6	3	3	13	1
1990		7,050	258	317	405	498	67	10	6	5	11	1
1995–96		6,800	307	381	405	503	64	9	5	7	14	2
1996–97		6,420	325	397	419	512	65	9	4	7	14	1
1997–98		6,410	343	421	428	525	67	8	4	7	13	1
1998–99[4]	24,660	6,630	371	457	449	553	68	8	4	7	12	1
1999–2000	25,340	7,100	391	480	466	572	66	10	5	7	12	1
2000–01	25,030	6,640	409	503	473	581	67	9	4	7	12	1
2001–02[5]	24,450	7,470	442	541	504	616	68	8	4	7	12	1
2002–03	24,350	6,930	453	552	506	616	68	8	3	7	12	1
2003–04	24,670	7,050	464	570	504	619	67	9	3	7	13	1
2004–05	24,430	6,800	489	601	515	632	68	8	3	7	13	1
2005–06	24,800	6,790	500	616	513	632	67	8	3	7	13	1
2006	24,790	6,650	521	642	521	642	67	9	3	7	12	1

1 Does not include imputed income from owner-occupied and rent-free households.
2 Other than social security benefits.
3 Excluding housing benefit and council tax benefit (rates rebate in Northern Ireland) and their predecessors in earlier years – see Appendix B.
4 Based on weighted data from 1998–99.
5 From 2001–02 onwards, weighting is based on the population figures from the 2001 Census.

Table A48 Characteristics of households, 2006

based on weighted data

	%* of all house- holds	Weighted number of house- holds (000s)	House- holds in sample (number)		%* of all house- holds	Weighted number of house- holds (000s)	House- holds in sample (number)
Total number of households	100	24,790	6,650	Composition of household (cont)			
				Four adults	2	610	120
Size of household							
One person	28	6,940	1,820	Four adults, one child	1	130	30
Two persons	36	8,960	2,460	Four adults, two or more children	0	80	30
Three persons	16	4,060	1,030				
Four persons	13	3,310	890	Five adults	[0]	60	10
Five persons	4	1,040	300				
Six persons	1	320	100	Five adults, one or more children	[0]	50	10
Seven persons	0	100	30				
Eight persons	[0]	30	10	All other households without children	[0]	10	–
Nine or more persons	[0]	30	–	All other households with children	[0]	10	–
Composition of household				Number of economically active persons in household			
One adult	28	6,940	1,820				
Retired households mainly							
dependent on state pensions[1]	3	680	190	No person	32	7,980	2,230
Other retired households	10	2,500	670	One person	28	7,030	1,940
Non-retired households	15	3,760	960	More than one person	39	9,770	2,480
One man	12	2,940	740	Two persons	31	7,710	2,030
Aged under 65	8	2,080	500	Three persons	6	1,550	340
Aged 65 and over	3	850	240	Four persons	2	460	100
One woman	16	4,010	1,080	Five persons	[0]	40	10
Aged under 60	6	1,400	380	Six or more persons	[0]	–	–
Aged 60 and over	11	2,610	700				
One adult, one child	3	760	230	Households with married women	50	12,330	3,380
One man, one child	0	100	30	Households with married women			
One woman, one child	3	660	200	economically active	28	6,880	1,820
One adult, two or more children	3	700	220	With no dependent children	15	3,780	930
One man, two or more children	[0]	60	20	With dependent children	12	3,090	890
One woman, two or more children	3	640	210	One child	5	1,340	360
				Two children	5	1,350	400
One man, one woman	31	7,630	2,090	Three children	1	350	110
Retired households mainly				Four or more children	0	50	20
dependent on state pensions[1]	2	500	150				
Other retired households	8	2,080	620	Households with married women			
Non-retired households	20	5,050	1,320	not economically active	22	5,450	1,560
Two men or two women	2	570	140	With no dependent children	16	4,050	1,150
				With dependent children	6	1,400	400
Two adults with children	19	4,810	1,390	One child	2	470	130
One man one woman, one child	7	1,770	490	Two children	2	560	160
Two men or two women, one child	0	100	30	Three children	1	200	70
One man one woman, two children	8	2,080	610	Four or more children	1	160	50
Two men or two women, two children	[0]	–	–				
One man one woman, three children	2	620	190	Economic activity status of household reference person			
Two men or two women, three children	[0]	–	–	Economically active	63	15,510	4,060
Two adults, four children	1	160	50	Employee at work	52	12,970	3,390
Two adults, five children	[0]	30	10	Full-time	44	10,830	2,810
Two adults, six or more children	[0]	30	–	Part-time	9	2,150	580
Three adults	7	1,700	360	Government-supported training	[0]	20	–
				Unemployed	2	450	120
Three adults with children	3	720	190	Self-employed	8	2,060	550
Three adults, one child	2	460	120				
Three adults, two children	1	160	50	Economically inactive	37	9,280	2,580
Three adults, three children	0	60	20				
Three adults, four or more children	[0]	30	–				

* Based on weighted number of households.

Table **A48** Characteristics of households, 2006 (cont.)
based on weighted data

	%* of all house- holds	Weighted number of house- holds (000s)	House- holds in sample (number)		%* of all house- holds	Weighted number of house- holds (000s)	House- holds in sample (number)
Age of household reference person				**GB urban/rural areas**			
15 and under 20 years	[0]	50	10	GB Urban	80	19,380	4,780
20 and under 25 years	3	830	190	GB rural	20	4,770	1,280
25 and under 30 years	6	1,560	400				
30 and under 35 years	8	1,980	520				
35 and under 40 years	10	2,470	660	**Tenure of dwelling**[4]			
40 and under 45 years	11	2,770	730	Owners			
				Owned outright	32	7,830	2,170
45 and under 50 years	10	2,390	670	Buying with a mortgage	40	9,850	2,630
50 and under 55 years	9	2,210	570	All	71	17,690	4,800
55 and under 60 years	9	2,280	600	Social rented from			
				Council	11	2,680	730
60 and under 65 years	8	1,940	540	Registered social landlord	7	1,610	420
65 and under 70 years	6	1,590	470	All	17	4,290	1,150
70 and under 75 years	6	1,610	470	Private rented			
				Rent free	1	310	90
75 and under 80 years	5	1,310	380	Rent paid, unfurnished	7	1,830	460
80 and under 85 years	4	1,080	270	Rent paid, furnished	3	670	150
85 and under 90 years	2	510	110	All	11	2,810	700
90 years or more	1	210	50				
				Households with durable goods			
				Car/van	76	18,740	5,050
Government Office Regions and Countries				One	44	10,850	2,960
United Kingdom	100	24,790	6,650	Two	26	6,380	1,720
				Three or more	6	1,510	370
North East	4	1,100	280				
North West	11	2,810	700	Central heating, full or partial	95	23,570	6,340
Yorkshire and The Humber	8	2,110	550	Fridge-freezer or deep freezer	97	23,960	6,430
				Washing machine	96	23,820	6,400
East Midlands	7	1,720	500	Tumble dryer	59	14,690	4,000
West Midlands	9	2,180	540	Dishwasher	38	9,310	2,560
East	9	2,260	590	Microwave oven	91	22,630	6,090
London	12	2,950	540	Telephone	91	22,630	6,080
South East	14	3,490	890	Mobile phone	80	19,760	5,180
South West	9	2,220	580	Video recorder	83	20,400	5,530
				DVD player	83	20,650	5,510
England	84	20,830	5,170	Satellite receiver[5]	71	17,550	4,730
Wales	5	1,230	310	Compact disc player	88	21,710	5,810
Scotland	8	2,090	580	Home computer	67	16,710	4,420
Northern Ireland	3	640	590	Internet connection	59	14,640	3,860
Socio-economic classification							
of household reference person							
Higher managerial and professional	12	3,020	780				
Large employers/higher managerial	5	1,200	310				
Higher professional	7	1,820	470				
Lower managerial and professional	18	4,520	1,170				
Intermediate	6	1,460	380				
Small employers	6	1,560	430				
Lower supervisory	6	1,580	420				
Semi-routine	7	1,810	490				
Routine	6	1,570	430				
Long-term unemployed[2]	2	480	130				
Students	1	310	70				
Occupation not stated[3]	34	8,460	2,360				

* Based on weighted number of households.
1 Mainly dependent on state pensions and not economically active – see definitions in Appendix B.
2 Includes those who have never worked.
3 Includes those who are economically inactive – see definitions in Appendix B.
4 See footnotes in Table A34.
5 Includes digital and cable receivers.

Table A49 Characteristics of persons, 2006
based on weighted data

	Males				Females				All persons		
	Percentage* of		Weighted number of persons (000s)	Persons in the sample (number)	Percentage* of		Weighted number of persons (000s)	Persons in the sample (number)	%* of	Weighted number of persons (000s)	Persons in the sample (number)
	all males	all persons			all females	all persons			all persons		
All persons	100	49	28,550	7,650	100	51	30,050	8,190	100	58,600	15,850
Adults	77	37	21,960	5,680	79	40	23,710	6,330	78	45,670	12,000
Persons aged under 60	57	28	16,320	4,080	56	29	16,890	4,440	57	33,220	8,520
Persons aged 60 or under 65	6	3	1,590	430	6	3	1,720	500	6	3,320	920
Persons aged 65 or under 70	4	2	1,250	370	4	2	1,330	390	4	2,580	760
Persons aged 70 or over	10	5	2,790	800	13	6	3,760	1,000	11	6,560	1,800
Children	23	11	6,590	1,980	21	11	6,340	1,870	22	12,930	3,840
Children under 2 years of age	2	1	690	210	2	1	610	180	2	1,300	390
Children aged 2 or under 5	4	2	1,040	320	3	2	1,020	310	4	2,070	630
Children aged 5 or under 16	14	7	4,070	1,210	13	7	3,930	1,180	14	8,000	2,390
Children aged 16 or under 18	3	1	800	230	3	1	770	200	3	1,570	430
Economic activity											
Persons active (aged 16 or over)	55	27	15,720	3,970	45	23	13,510	3,490	50	29,220	7,470
Persons not active	45	22	12,840	3,680	55	28	16,540	4,700	50	29,380	8,380
Men 65 or over and women 60 or over	13	6	3,660	1,060	20	10	6,040	1,680	17	9,690	2,740
Others (Including children under 16)	32	16	9,180	2,630	35	18	10,510	3,020	34	19,690	5,650

* Based on weighted number of households

Table A50 Percentage of households with durable goods, 1970 to 2006

	Car/ van	Central heating[1]	Washing machine	Tumble dryer	Dish- washer	Micro- wave	Tele- phone	Mobile phone	Video recorder	DVD Player	Satellite receiver[2]	Cd player	Home computer	Internet connection
1970	52	30	65	–	–	–	35	–	–	–	–	–	–	–
1975	57	47	72	–	–	–	52	–	–	–	–	–	–	–
1980	60	59	79	–	–	–	72	–	–	–	–	–	–	–
1985	63	69	83	–	–	–	81	–	30	–	–	–	13	–
1990	67	79	86	–	–	–	87	–	61	–	–	–	17	–
1994–95	69	84	89	50	18	67	91	–	76	–	–	46	–	–
1995–96	70	85	91	50	20	70	92	–	79	–	–	51	–	–
1996–97	69	87	91	51	20	75	93	16	82	–	19	59	27	–
1997–98	70	89	91	51	22	77	94	20	84	–	26	63	29	–
1998–99	72	89	92	51	24	80	95	26	86	–	27	68	32	9
1998–99*	72	89	92	51	23	79	95	27	85	–	28	68	33	10
1999–2000*	71	90	91	52	23	80	95	44	86	–	32	72	38	19
2000–01*	72	91	92	53	25	84	93	47	87	–	40	77	44	32
2001–02[3]*	74	92	93	54	27	86	94	64	90	–	43	80	49	39
2002–03*	74	93	94	56	29	87	94	70	90	31	45	83	55	45
2003–04*	75	94	94	57	31	89	92	76	90	50	49	86	58	49
2004–05*	75	95	95	58	33	90	93	78	88	67	58	87	62	53
2005–06*	74	94	95	58	35	91	92	79	86	79	65	88	65	55
2006*	76	95	96	59	38	91	91	80	82	83	71	88	67	59

– Data not available.
* Based on weighted data and including children's expenditure.
1 Full or partial.
2 Includes digital and cable receivers.
3 From 2001–02 onwards, weighting is based on the population figures from the 2001 Census.

Table A51 Percentage[1] of households with durable goods by income group and household composition, 2006

based on weighted data

	Central heating[2]	Washing machine	Tumble dryer	Micro-wave	Dish-washer	CD player
All households	95	96	59	91	38	88
Gross income decile group						
Lowest ten per cent	92	83	35	85	10	69
Second decile group	94	91	41	88	12	72
Third decile group	95	95	50	91	22	81
Fourth decile group	94	97	56	90	28	86
Fifth decile group	91	98	58	94	30	88
Sixth decile group	94	99	66	92	37	94
Seventh decile group	95	100	69	94	43	96
Eighth decile group	97	99	68	91	54	96
Ninth decile group	98	100	73	93	64	97
Highest ten per cent	99	100	75	94	75	98
Household composition						
One adult, retired households[3]	90	86	30	84	[8]	51
One adult, non-retired households	93	91	43	87	22	87
One adult, one child	93	98	54	94	21	90
One adult, two or more children	97	99	69	94	32	90
One man and one woman, retired households[3]						
One man and one woman, non-retired households	95	99	65	93	46	94
One man and one woman, one child	95	99	71	94	47	95
One man and one woman, two or more children	98	100	79	96	57	95
All other households without children	97	98	60	91	40	91
All other households with children	95	100	71	97	53	91

	Home computer	Internet connection	Tele-phone	Mobile phone	Satellite receiver[4]	DVD Player
All households	67	59	91	80	71	83
Gross income decile group						
Lowest ten per cent	31	21	77	56	50	62
Second decile group	35	24	87	59	57	63
Third decile group	45	34	91	70	60	73
Fourth decile group	55	44	90	80	69	80
Fifth decile group	69	60	91	86	72	87
Sixth decile group	79	68	92	87	76	90
Seventh decile group	85	77	95	89	80	92
Eighth decile group	87	80	95	89	78	96
Ninth decile group	92	88	98	89	83	94
Highest ten per cent	96	94	98	92	82	96
Household composition						
One adult, retired households[3]	12	8	97	28	40	33
One adult, non-retired households	59	49	81	82	62	83
One adult, one child	66	50	73	87	74	94
One adult, two or more children	77	60	82	88	79	96
One man and one woman, retired households[3]	32	19	100	60	59	59
One man and one woman, non-retired households	81	73	95	89	77	93
One man and one woman, one child	88	82	91	90	84	96
One man and one woman, two or more children	91	85	95	89	85	97
All other households without children	81	71	85	87	72	89
All other households with children	90	77	93	84	82	96

1 See Table A52 for number of recording households.
2 Full or partial.
3 Mainly dependent on state pensions and not economically active – see Appendix B.
4 Includes digital and cable receivers.

Table A52 Percentage of households with cars by income group, tenure and household composition, 2006
based on weighted data

	One car/van	Two cars/vans	Three or more cars/vans	All with cars/vans	Weighted number of house-holds (000s)	House-holds in the sample (number)
All households	44	26	6	76	24,790	6,650
Gross income decile group						
Lowest ten per cent	28	[3]	[0]	31	2,480	680
Second decile group	37	4	[1]	42	2,480	680
Third decile group	55	8	[1]	65	2,480	700
Fourth decile group	63	9	[2]	74	2,480	690
Fifth decile group	60	19	4	83	2,480	690
Sixth decile group	54	30	4	87	2,480	680
Seventh decile group	48	37	6	92	2,480	660
Eighth decile group	37	47	10	93	2,480	630
Ninth decile group	30	52	13	95	2,480	640
Highest ten per cent	25	48	21	94	2,480	590
Tenure of dwelling[1]						
Owners						
Owned outright	51	22	7	80	7,830	2,170
Buying with a mortgage	43	41	8	92	9,850	2,630
All	47	32	8	87	17,690	4,800
Social rented from						
Council	29	6	[1]	36	2,680	730
Registered social landlord[2]	32	7	[1]	39	1,610	420
All	30	6	[1]	38	4,290	1,150
Private rented						
Rent free	46	[11]	[4]	60	310	90
Rent paid, unfurnished	46	19	[3]	68	1,830	460
Rent paid, furnished	38	[4]	[1]	43	670	150
All	44	14	[3]	62	2,810	700
Household composition						
One adult, retired mainly dependent on state pensions[3]	29	[1]	–	30	680	190
One adult, other retired	39	[2]	[0]	41	2,500	670
One adult, non-retired	58	4	[1]	63	3,760	960
One adult, one child	50	[4]	[1]	55	760	230
One adult, two or more children	57	[1]	–	58	700	220
One man and one woman, retired mainly dependent on state pensions[3]	66	[7]	–	73	500	150
One man and one woman, other retired	62	19	[2]	84	2,080	620
One man and one woman, non-retired	41	43	5	90	5,050	1,320
One man and one woman, one child	37	47	5	89	1,770	490
One man and one woman, two children	36	53	5	93	2,080	610
One man and one woman, three children	35	48	[6]	89	620	190
Two adults, four or more children	44	28	[7]	79	230	70
Three adults	32	35	21	88	1,700	360
Three adults, one or more children	28	36	22	87	720	190
All other households without children	32	21	26	79	1,250	270
All other households with children	39	25	[17]	81	390	100

1 See footnotes in Table A34.
2 Formerly housing association.
3 Mainly dependent on state pensions and not economically active – see Appendix B.

Table A53 Percentage of households with durable goods
by UK countries and Government Office Regions, 2006
based on weighted data

	North East	North West	Yorkshire and The Humber	East Midlands	West Midlands	East	London
Weighted number of households (thousands)	1,100	2,810	2,110	1,720	2,180	2,260	2,950
Total number of households in sample	280	700	550	500	540	590	540
Percentage of households by Government Office Region and country							
Car/van	65	71	77	82	76	84	63
One	41	43	48	42	42	45	43
Two	20	23	25	33	27	32	17
Three or more	4	5	4	7	7	7	3
Central heating full or partial	100	94	94	96	93	95	95
Fridge-freezer or deep freezer	98	96	96	97	97	97	96
Washing machine	95	95	98	97	96	96	94
Tumble dryer	50	60	62	61	63	62	48
Dishwasher	24	30	33	39	32	45	38
Microwave	91	94	94	93	93	90	88
Telephone	89	88	92	94	90	92	90
Mobile phone	74	77	86	86	86	84	78
DVD player	82	84	84	84	83	84	83
Satellite receiver[1]	76	76	74	71	67	70	65
CD player	85	86	89	89	89	91	83
Home computer	60	64	65	72	68	66	70
Internet connection	51	54	57	66	57	59	62

	South East	South West	England	Wales	Scotland	Northern Ireland	United Kingdom
Weighted number of households (thousands)	3,490	2,220	20,830	1,230	2,090	640	24,790
Total number of households in sample	890	580	5,170	310	580	590	6,650
Percentage of households by Government Office Region and country							
Car/van	82	83	76	76	70	76	76
One	42	48	44	44	44	46	44
Two	31	27	26	27	21	23	26
Three or more	9	8	6	4	5	7	6
Central heating full or partial	96	94	95	95	96	98	95
Fridge-freezer or deep freezer	98	95	97	97	97	96	97
Washing machine	96	96	96	98	97	98	96
Tumble dryer	58	63	58	65	64	61	59
Dishwasher	47	39	37	35	37	46	38
Microwave	89	90	91	94	92	92	91
Telephone	92	94	91	89	93	89	91
Mobile phone	79	84	81	60	84	48	80
DVD player	85	82	84	80	84	79	83
Satellite receiver[1]	69	68	70	77	73	72	71
CD player	90	89	88	86	89	79	88
Home computer	72	65	68	69	66	62	67
Internet connection	66	57	59	59	57	52	59

1 Includes digital and cable receivers.

Table **A54** Percentage of households by size, composition and age in each gross income decile group, 2006
based on weighted data

	Lowest ten per cent	Second decile group	Third decile group	Fourth decile group	Fifth decile group	Sixth decile group
Lower boundary of group (£ per week)		143	215	293	384	497
Weighted number of households (thousands)	2,480	2,480	2,480	2,480	2,480	2,480
Number of households in the sample	680	680	700	690	690	680
Size of household						
One person	75	54	38	36	25	18
Two persons	18	27	46	41	41	39
Three persons	4	12	8	10	18	17
Four persons	[1]	6	5	7	10	17
Five persons	[0]	[1]	[2]	3	3	6
Six or more persons	[1]	[0]	[1]	4	[2]	[2]
All sizes	100	100	100	100	100	100
Household composition						
One adult, retired mainly dependent on state pensions[1]	15	9	[2]	[0]	[0]	–
One adult, other retired	28	33	19	11	5	[2]
One adult, non-retired	32	12	16	25	20	16
One adult, one child	10	4	4	4	2	[2]
One adult, two or more children	3	9	4	4	3	3
One man and one woman, retired mainly dependent on state pensions[1]	[2]	8	8	[2]	[0]	[0]
One man and one woman, other retired	[0]	6	20	20	15	8
One man and one woman, non-retired	5	7	13	11	21	25
One man and one woman, one child	[1]	[3]	3	4	8	8
One man and one woman, two children	[1]	[2]	[2]	5	7	12
One man and one woman, three children	[0]	[0]	[1]	[2]	[2]	4
Two adults, four or more children	[1]	[0]	[0]	[2]	[1]	[1]
Three adults	[1]	[2]	[3]	[3]	7	7
Three adults, one or more children	[0]	[1]	[1]	[2]	3	3
All other households without children	[1]	[2]	[3]	3	[3]	6
All other households with children	[0]	[1]	[0]	[1]	[2]	[2]
All compositions	100	100	100	100	100	100
Age of household reference person						
15 and under 20 years	[1]	[1]	[0]	–	[0]	–
20 and under 25 years	5	4	3	4	[3]	7
25 and under 30 years	6	5	4	5	6	8
30 and under 35 years	4	5	5	6	7	10
35 and under 40 years	5	5	5	10	10	11
40 and under 45 years	6	4	5	9	10	13
45 and under 50 years	5	5	4	6	8	12
50 and under 55 years	8	5	5	5	8	8
55 and under 60 years	9	5	7	8	12	8
60 and under 65 years	8	7	10	9	10	7
65 and under 70 years	7	10	11	10	7	6
70 and under 75 years	9	12	13	9	7	6
75 and under 80 years	9	13	12	7	5	3
80 and under 85 years	10	11	8	7	3	[2]
85 and under 90 years	5	6	5	[2]	[1]	[1]
90 years or more	[2]	[3]	[2]	[1]	[1]	–
All ages	100	100	100	100	100	100

1 Mainly dependent on state pensions and not economically active – see Appendix B.

Table A54 Percentage of households by size, composition and age in each gross income decile group, 2006 (cont.)
based on weighted data

	Seventh decile group	Eighth decile group	Ninth decile group	Highest ten per cent	All house-holds
Lower boundary of group (£ per week)	624	763	939	1,274	
Weighted number of households (thousands)	2,480	2,480	2,480	2,480	24,790
Number of households in the sample	660	630	640	590	6,650
Size of household					
One person	13	9	7	5	28
Two persons	43	36	34	36	36
Three persons	19	26	26	24	16
Four persons	18	19	25	25	13
Five persons	5	7	6	8	4
Six or more persons	[3]	3	2	[2]	2
All sizes	100	100	100	100	100
Household composition					
One adult, retired mainly dependent on state pensions[1]	–	–	–	–	3
One adult, other retired	[1]	[1]	[0]	[0]	10
One adult, non-retired	12	8	7	4	15
One adult, one child	[2]	[1]	[1]	[0]	3
One adult, two or more children	[1]	[1]	[1]	[1]	3
One man and one woman, retired mainly dependent on state pensions[1]	–	–	–	–	2
One man and one woman, other retired	7	3	[2]	[2]	8
One man and one woman, non-retired	31	30	29	32	20
One man and one woman, one child	11	11	13	10	7
One man and one woman, two children	13	13	17	13	8
One man and one woman, three children	3	4	4	4	2
Two adults, four or more children	[1]	[1]	[1]	[1]	1
Three adults	7	14	12	13	7
Three adults, one or more children	4	5	4	5	3
All other households without children	6	6	8	12	5
All other households with children	[2]	3	[1]	[3]	2
All compositions	100	100	100	100	100
Age of household reference person					
15 and under 20 years	–	–	–	–	[0]
20 and under 25 years	[3]	[4]	[1]	[1]	3
25 and under 30 years	9	8	7	6	6
30 and under 35 years	11	10	10	11	8
35 and under 40 years	12	14	13	14	10
40 and under 45 years	16	16	19	13	11
45 and under 50 years	12	12	17	15	10
50 and under 55 years	9	13	11	16	9
55 and under 60 years	11	11	9	13	9
60 and under 65 years	6	5	8	6	8
65 and under 70 years	4	4	[3]	[2]	6
70 and under 75 years	4	[2]	[2]	[1]	6
75 and under 80 years	[2]	[1]	[0]	[1]	5
80 and under 85 years	[1]	[0]	[1]	[0]	4
85 and under 90 years	[1]	[0]	–	–	2
90 years or more	–	[0]	–	–	1
All ages	100	100	100	100	100

1 Mainly dependent on state pensions and not economically active – see Appendix B.

Table A55 Percentage of households by, economic activity, tenure and socio-economic classification in each gross income decile group, 2006

based on weighted data

	Lowest ten per cent	Second decile group	Third decile group	Fourth decile group	Fifth decile group	Sixth decile group
Lower boundary of group (£ per week)		143	215	293	384	497
Weighted number of households (thousands)	2,480	2,480	2,480	2,480	2,480	2,480
Number of households in the sample	680	680	700	690	690	680
Number of economically active persons in household						
No person	81	80	61	41	24	13
One person	17	17	31	48	48	43
Two persons	[2]	[3]	6	10	26	41
Three persons	[0]	[0]	[1]	[1]	[3]	4
Four or more persons	–	–	–	[0]	[0]	[0]
All economically active persons	100	100	100	100	100	100
Tenure of dwelling[1]						
Owners						
Owned outright	26	39	50	41	38	27
Buying with a mortgage	8	8	13	26	38	50
All	34	47	63	68	76	77
Social rented from						
Council	31	25	16	13	8	6
Registered social landlord[2]	21	14	8	7	4	4
All	52	39	25	20	13	10
Private rented						
Rent free	[2]	[3]	[1]	[2]	[1]	[1]
Rent paid, unfurnished	11	8	8	9	8	9
Rent paid, furnished	[2]	[2]	[3]	[2]	[2]	[2]
All	15	13	12	12	12	12
All tenures	100	100	100	100	100	100
Socio-economic classification						
Higher managerial and professional						
Large employers/higher managerial	–	–	[1]	–	[1]	[3]
Higher professional	[0]	[0]	[1]	[1]	[2]	6
Lower managerial and professional	[1]	[2]	4	11	15	20
Intermediate	[1]	[1]	4	8	9	9
Small employers	5	4	5	6	9	8
Lower supervisory	[1]	[2]	3	8	9	10
Semi-routine	5	4	9	11	13	11
Routine	3	[3]	6	7	11	12
Long-term unemployed[3]	6	5	4	[1]	[1]	[1]
Students	[3]	[3]	[2]	[1]	[2]	[1]
Occupation not stated[4]	75	76	63	46	29	19
All occupational groups	100	100	100	100	100	100

1 See footnotes in Table A34.
2 Formerly Housing Association.
3 Includes those who have never worked.
4 Includes those who are economically inactive – see definitions in Appendix B.

Table A55 Percentage of households by, economic activity, tenure and socio-economic classification in each gross income decile group, 2006 (cont.)

based on weighted data

	Seventh decile group	Eighth decile group	Ninth decile group	Highest ten per cent	All house-holds
Lower boundary of group (£ per week)	624	763	939	1,274	
Weighted number of households (thousands)	2,480	2,480	2,480	2,480	24,790
Number of households in the sample	660	630	640	590	6,650
Number of economically active persons in household					
No person	11	6	4	[2]	32
One person	28	20	17	15	28
Two persons	53	56	59	56	31
Three persons	7	16	14	17	6
Four or more persons	[1]	[2]	6	10	2
All economically active persons	100	100	100	100	100
Tenure of dwelling[1]					
Owners					
Owned outright	25	24	21	25	32
Buying with a mortgage	57	61	70	65	40
All	82	85	91	91	71
Social rented from					
Council	4	[2]	[1]	[1]	11
Registered social landlord [2]	[3]	[2]	[1]	–	7
All	7	4	[2]	[1]	17
Private rented					
Rent free	[1]	[1]	[0]	[0]	1
Rent paid, unfurnished	6	6	4	5	7
Rent paid, furnished	[3]	[4]	[2]	[3]	3
All	11	11	7	8	11
All tenures	100	100	100	100	100
Socio-economic classification					
Higher managerial and professional					
Large employers/higher managerial	5	8	11	20	5
Higher professional	9	14	15	24	7
Lower managerial and professional	25	32	37	35	18
Intermediate	10	7	7	[4]	6
Small employers	8	7	7	4	6
Lower supervisory	11	10	8	[2]	6
Semi-routine	8	6	[3]	[3]	7
Routine	8	6	5	[2]	6
Long-term unemployed [3]	[0]	[0]	[0]	[0]	2
Students	[1]	[0]	[0]	[0]	1
Occupation not stated [4]	15	9	6	5	34
All occupational group	100	100	100	100	100

1 See footnotes in Table A34.
2 Formerly Housing Association.
3 Includes those who have never worked.
4 Includes those who are economically inactive – see definitions in Appendix B.

Methodology

Appendix B

Description and response rate of the survey

The survey

A household expenditure survey has been conducted each year in the UK since 1957. From 1957 to March 2001, the Family Expenditure and National Food Surveys (FES and NFS) provided information on household expenditure patterns and food consumption. In April 2001 these surveys were combined to form the Expenditure and Food Survey (EFS). In anticipation of the introduction of the Continuous Population Survey (CPS) in January 2008, from January 2006 the survey has been conducted on a calendar-year basis.

The EFS is a voluntary sample survey of private households. The basic unit of the survey is the household. The EFS (in line with other Government household surveys) uses the harmonised definition of a household: a group of people living at the same address with common housekeeping, that is sharing household expenses such as food and bills, or sharing a living room (see 'Definitions'). The previous definition (used on the FES) differed from the harmonised definition by requiring both common housekeeping **and** a shared living room.

Each individual aged 16 or over in the household visited is asked to keep diary records of daily expenditure for two weeks. Information about regular expenditure, such as rent and mortgage payments, is obtained from a household interview along with retrospective information on certain large, infrequent expenditures such as those on vehicles. Since 1998–99 the results have also included information from simplified diaries kept by children aged between 7 and 15. The effects of including children's expenditure were shown in Appendix F of *Family Spending* for 1998–99 and again for 1999–2000. The analysis is not repeated this year as inclusion of the data is now a standard feature of the survey.

Detailed questions are asked about the income of each adult member of the household. In addition, personal information such as age, sex and marital status is recorded for each household member. Paper versions of the computerised household and income questionnaires can be obtained from ONS at the address given in the Introduction.

The survey is continuous, interviews being spread evenly over the year to ensure that seasonal effects are covered. From time to time changes are made to the information sought. Some changes reflect new forms of expenditure or new sources of income, especially benefits. Others are the result of new requirements by the survey's users. An important example is the re-definition of housing costs for owner occupiers in 1992 (see 'Changes in definitions, 1991 to 2006').

The sample design

The EFS sample for Great Britain is a multi-stage stratified random sample with clustering. It is drawn from the Small Users file of the Postcode Address File – the Post Office's list of addresses. All Scottish offshore islands and the Isles of Scilly are excluded from the sample because of excessive interview travel costs. Postal sectors are the primary sample unit. Six hundred and seventy two postal sectors are randomly selected during the year after being arranged in strata defined by Government Office Regions (sub-divided into metropolitan and non-metropolitan areas) and two 1991 Census variables – socio-economic group and ownership of cars. These were new stratifiers introduced for the 1996–97 survey. The Northern Ireland sample is drawn as a random sample of addresses from the Land and Property Services Agency list.

Response to the survey

Great Britain

Around 12,096 households are selected each year for the EFS in Great Britain, but it is never possible to get full response. A small number cannot be contacted at all, and in other households one or more members decline to co-operate. Five thousand nine hundred and twenty-seven households in Great Britain co-operated fully in the survey in 2006; that is they answered the household questionnaire and all adults in the household answered the full income questionnaire and kept the expenditure diary. A further 131 households provided sufficient information to be included as valid responses. The overall response rate for the 2006 EFS was 55 per cent in Great Britain. This represented a 2% decrease in response from the 2005–06 survey year.

Details of response are shown in the following table.

Response in 2006 – Great Britain

	No of households or addresses	Percentage of effective sample
i. Sampled addresses	12,096	–
ii. Ineligible addresses: businesses, institutions, empty, demolished/derelict	1,260	–
iii. Extra households (multi-household addresses)	93	–
iv. Total eligible (i.e. i less ii, plus iii)	10,929	100.0
v. Co-operating households (which includes 131 partials)	6,058	55.4
vi. Refusals	3,790	34.7
vii. Households at which no contact could be obtained	1081	9.9

Northern Ireland

In the Northern Ireland survey, the eligible sample was 1,081 households. The number of co-operating households who provided usable data was 586, giving a response rate of 54 per cent. Northern Ireland is over-sampled in order to provide a large enough sample for some separate analysis. The re-weighting procedure compensates for the over-sampling.

The fieldwork

The fieldwork is conducted by the Office for National Statistics (ONS) in Great Britain, and by the Northern Ireland Statistics and Research Agency of the Department of Finance and Personnel (NISRA) in Northern Ireland, using almost identical questionnaires. Households at the selected addresses are visited and asked to co-operate in the survey. In order to maximise response, interviewers make at least four separate calls, and sometimes many more, at different times of day on households which are difficult to contact. Interviews are conducted by Computer Assisted Personal Interviewing (CAPI) using portable computers. During the interview, information is collected about the household, about certain regular payments such as rent, gas, electricity and telephone accounts, about expenditure on certain large items (for example vehicle purchases over the previous 12 months), and about income. Each individual aged 16 or over in the household is asked to keep a detailed record of expenditure every day for two weeks. Children aged between 7 and 15 are also asked to keep a simplified diary of daily expenditure. In 2006 a total of 2,013 children aged between 7 and 15 in responding households in the UK were asked to complete expenditure diaries; 228 or about 11 per cent did not do so. This number includes both refusals and children who had no expenditure during the two weeks. Information provided by all members of the household is kept strictly confidential. Each person aged 16 and over in the household who keeps a diary (and whose income information is collected) is subsequently paid £10, as a token of appreciation. Children who keep a diary are given a £5 payment.

In the last two months of the 1998–99 survey, as an experiment, a small book of postage stamps was enclosed with the introductory letter sent to every address. It seemed to help with response and the measure has become a permanent feature of the survey. It is difficult to quantify the exact effect on response but the cognitive work that was carried out as part of the EFS development indicated that it was having a positive effect.

A new strategy for reissues was adopted in 1999–2000 and has continued since. Addresses where there had been no contact or a refusal, but were judged suitable for reissue, were accumulated to form complete batches consisting only of reissues. The interviewers dealing with them were specially selected and given extra briefing. In 2006 some 995 addresses were reissued, of which 73 were converted into responding households. This added 0.6 percentage points to the response rate.

Eligible response

Under EFS rules, a refusal by just one person to respond to the income section of the questionnaire invalidates the response of the whole household. Similarly, a refusal by the household's main shopper to complete the two-week expenditure diary also results in an invalid response.

Proxy Interviews – while questions about general household affairs are put to all household members or to a main household informant, questions about work and income are put to the individual members of the household. Where a member of the household is not present during the household interview, another member of the household (e.g. spouse) may be able to provide information about the absent person. The individual's interview is then identified as a proxy interview.

In 2001–02, the EFS began including households that contained a proxy interview. In that year, 12 per cent of all responding households contained at least one proxy interview. In 2006, the percentage of responding households with a proxy interview was 14 per cent. Analysis of the 2002–03 data revealed that the inclusion of proxy interviews increased response from above average income households. For the 2002–03 survey, the average gross normal weekly household income was some 3 per cent higher than it would have been if proxy interviews had not been accepted. The analysis showed a similar difference for average total expenditure.

Short Income – all adult members of a household must supply information about their income. This information is quite detailed, and a small number of respondents are reluctant to provide it. For these people, we accept responses to a reduced set of questions, called short income.

From 2001–02, the EFS began including households that contained a short income section. In that year, 0.5 per cent of households contained at least one short income response. In 2006, 0.2 per cent did so.

Reliability

Great care is taken in collecting information from households and comprehensive checks are applied during processing, so that errors in recording and processing are minimised. The main factors that affect the reliability of the survey results are sampling variability, non-response bias and some incorrect reporting of certain items of expenditure and income. Measures of sampling variability are given alongside some results in this report and are discussed in detail in 'Standard errors and estimates of precision'.

The households which decline to respond to the survey tend to differ in some respects from those which co-operate. It is therefore possible that their patterns of expenditure and income also differ. A comparison was made of the households responding in the 1991 FES with those not responding, based on information from the 1991 Census of Population (*A comparison of the Census characteristics of respondents and non-respondents to the 1991 FES* by K Foster, ONS Survey Methodology Bulletin No. 38, Jan 1996). Results from the study indicate that response was lower than average in Greater London, higher in non-metropolitan areas and that non-response tended to increase with increasing age of the head of the household, up to age 65. Households that contained three or more adults, or where the head was born outside the United Kingdom or was classified to an ethnic minority group, were also more likely than others to be non-responding. Non-response was also above average where the head of the household had no post-school qualifications, was self-employed, or was in a manual social class group. The data are now re-weighted to compensate for the main non-response biases identified from the 1991 Census comparison, as described in 'Weighting'. ONS has recently completed a similar comparative exercise, with the 2001 Census data, which will result in an update of the non-response weights for the 2007 calendar year EFS estimates.

Checks are included in the CAPI program, which are applied to the responses given during the interview. Other procedures are also in place to ensure that users are provided with high quality data. For example, quality control is carried out to ensure that any outliers are genuine, and checks are made on any unusual changes in average spending compared with the previous year.

When aspects of the survey change, rigorous tests are used to ensure the proposed changes are sensible and work both in the field and on the processing system. For example, in 1996–97 an improved set of questions was introduced on income from self-employment. This was developed by focus groups and then tested by piloting before being introduced into the main survey.

Income and expenditure balancing

The EFS is designed primarily as a survey of household expenditure on goods and services. It also gathers information about the income of household members, and is an important and detailed source of income data. However, it is not possible to draw up a balance sheet of income and expenditure either for individual households or groups of households.

The majority of expenditure information collected relates to the two week period immediately following the interview, whereas income components can refer to a much longer period (the most recent 12 months). EFS income does not include withdrawal of savings, loans and money received in payment of loans, receipts from maturing insurance policies, proceeds from the sale of assets (e.g. a car) and winnings from betting or windfalls, such as legacies. Despite this, recorded expenditure might reflect these items, as well as the effects of living off savings, using capital, borrowing money or income – either recent or from a previous period.

Hence, there is no reason why income and expenditure should balance. In fact measured expenditure exceeds measured income at the bottom end of the income distribution. However, this difference cannot be regarded as a reliable measure of savings or dis savings.

For further information of what is included in income on the EFS see Income headings on page 187.

Imputation of missing information

Although EFS response is generally based on complete households responding, there are areas in the survey for which missing information is imputed. This falls into two broad categories:

(i)   Specific items of information missing from a response. These missing values are imputed on a case by case basis using other information collected in the interview. The procedure is used, for example, for council tax payments and for interest received on savings.

(ii) Imputation of a complete diary case. Where a response is missing a diary from a household member, this information is imputed using information from respondents with similar characteristics.

Uses of the survey

EFS Expenditure data

Retail Prices Index – The main reason, historically, for instituting a regular survey on expenditure by households has been to provide information on spending patterns for the Retail Prices Index (RPI). The RPI plays a vital role in the uprating of state pensions and welfare benefits and in general economic policy and analysis. The RPI measures the change in the cost of a selection of goods and services representative of the expenditure of the vast majority of households. The pattern of expenditure gradually changes from one year to the next, and the composition of the basket needs to be kept up-to-date. Accordingly, regular information is required on spending patterns and much of this is supplied by the EFS. The expenditure weights for the general RPI need to relate to people within given income limits, for which the EFS is the only source of information.

Household expenditure and GDP – EFS data on spending are an important source used in compiling national estimates of household final consumption expenditure which are published regularly in United Kingdom National Accounts (ONS Blue Book). Household final consumption expenditure estimates feed into the National Accounts and estimates of GDP. They will also provide the weights for the Consumer Price Index (CPI), and for Purchasing Power Parities (PPPs) for international price comparisons. EFS data are also used in the estimation of taxes on expenditure, in particular VAT.

Regional accounts – EFS expenditure information is one of the sources used by ONS to derive regional estimates of consumption expenditure. It is also used in compiling some of the other estimates for the regional accounts.

Pay Review Bodies governing the salaries of HM Armed Forces and the medical and dental professions receive estimates of the minimum valuation of the benefit of a company car. This is based on EFS data on the cost of buying and running private cars.

The Statistical Office of the European Communities (Eurostat) collates information from family budget surveys conducted by the member states. The EFS is the UK's contribution to this. The UK is one of only a few countries with such a regular, continuous and detailed survey.

Other Government uses – The Department of Trade and Industry and the Department for Transport, both use EFS expenditure data in their own fields, e.g. – relating to energy, housing, cars and transport. Several other Government publications include EFS expenditure data, such as *Social Trends, Regional Trends and the Social Focus series.*

Non-Government uses – There are also numerous users outside Central Government, including academic researchers and business and market researchers.

EFS Income data

Redistribution of income – EFS information on income and expenditure is used to study how Government taxes and benefits affect household income. The Government's interdepartmental tax benefit model is based on the EFS and enables the economic effects of policy measures to be analysed across households. This model is used by HM Treasury and HM Revenue and Customs to estimate the impact on different households of possible changes in taxes and benefits.

Non-Government users – As with the expenditure data, EFS income data are also studied extensively outside Government. In particular, academic researchers in the economic and social science areas of many universities use the EFS. For example the Institute for Fiscal Studies uses EFS data in research it carries out both for Government and on its own account to inform public debate.

Other EFS data

The Department for Environment, Food and Rural Affairs (DEFRA) publishes separate reports using EFS data on food expenditure to estimate consumption and nutrient intake.

The Department for Transport uses EFS data to monitor and forecast levels of car ownership and use, and in studies on the effects of motoring taxes.

Note: Great care is taken to ensure complete confidentiality of information and to protect the identity of EFS households. Only anonymised data are supplied to users.

Standard errors and estimates of precision

Because the EFS is a sample of households and not a census of the whole population, the results are liable to differ to some degree from those that would have been obtained if every single household had been covered. Some of the differences will be systematic, in that lower proportions of certain types of household respond than of others. That aspect is discussed in 'Description and response rate of the survey' and 'Weighting'. This section discusses the effect of sampling variability that is the differences in expenditure and income between the households in the sample and in the whole population that arise from random chance. The degree of variability will depend on the sample size and how widely particular categories of expenditure (or income) vary between households. The sampling variability is smallest for the average expenditure of large groups of households on items purchased frequently and when the level of spending does not vary greatly between households. Conversely, it is largest for small groups of households, and for items purchased infrequently or for which expenditure varies considerably between households. A numerical measure of the likely magnitude of such differences (between the sample estimate and the value of the entire population) is provided by the quantity known as the standard error.

The calculation of standard errors takes into account the fact that the EFS sample is drawn in two stages, first a sample of areas (primary sampling units) then a sample of addresses within each of these areas. The main features of the sample design are described in 'Description and response rate of the survey'. The calculation also takes account of the effect of weighting. The two-stage sample increases sampling variability slightly, but the weighting reduces it for some items.

Standard errors for detailed expenditure items are presented in relative terms in Table A1 (standard error as a percentage of the average to which it refers). As the calculation of full standard errors is complex, this is the only table where they are shown. Tables B1 and B2 in this section show the design factor (DEFT), a measure of the efficiency of the survey's sample design. The DEFT is calculated by dividing the 'full' standard error by the standard error that would have applied if the survey had used a simple random sample ('simple method').

Table **B1** Percentage standard errors of expenditure of households and number of recording households, 2006

| Commodity or service | Weighted average weekly household expenditure (£) | Percentage standard error | | Percentage standard error | Households recording expenditure | |
		Simple method	Design factor (DEFT)	Full method	Recording households in sample	Percentage of all households
All expenditure groups	378.30	1.0	1.2	1.1	6,645	100
Food and non-alcoholic drinks	46.90	0.8	1.0	0.8	6,601	99
Alcoholic drink, tobacco & narcotics	11.10	1.9	1.0	1.9	4,207	63
Clothing and footwear	23.20	2.1	1.2	2.4	4,608	69
Housing, fuel and power	47.60	1.5	1.2	1.8	6,623	100
Household goods and services	30.30	2.7	1.1	2.8	6,130	92
Health	5.90	7.6	1.1	8.4	3,476	52
Transport	62.00	2.0	1.1	2.2	5,709	86
Communication	11.70	1.3	1.1	1.5	6,366	96
Recreation and culture	58.50	2.0	1.0	2.0	6,575	99
Education	7.20	9.4	1.2	11.3	576	9
Restaurants and hotels	37.90	1.8	1.1	2.1	5,912	89
Miscellaneous goods and services	36.00	1.7	1.1	1.9	6,514	98

Table **B2** Percentage standard errors of income of households and numbers of recording households, 2006

| Source of income | Weighted average weekly household income (£) | Percentage standard error | | Percentage standard error | Households recording income | |
		Simple method	Design factor (DEFT)	Full method	Recording households in sample	Percentage of all households
Gross household income	642	1.2	1.2	1.4	6,636	100
Wages and salaries	432	1.7	1.1	1.8	3,973	60
Self-employment	56	5.7	1.1	6.0	790	12
Investments	21	6.0	1.1	6.5	3,533	53
Annuities and pensions (other than social security benefits)	45	3.5	0.9	3.0	1,870	28
Social security benefits	80	1.4	0.8	1.1	4,820	73
Other sources	7	9.1	0.9	8.5	973	15

Using the standard errors – confidence intervals

A good way of using standard errors is to calculate 95% confidence intervals from them. Simplifying a little, these can be taken to mean that there is only a 5% chance that the true population value lies outside that confidence interval. The 95% confidence interval is calculated as 1.96 times the standard error on either side of the mean. For example the average expenditure on food and non-alcoholic drinks is £46.90 and the corresponding percentage standard error (full method) is 0.8%. The amount either side of the mean for 95% confidence is then:

1.96 x (0.8 ÷100) x £46.90 = £0.70 (rounded to nearest 10p)
Lower limit is 46.90 – 0.70 = £46.20 (rounded to nearest 10p)
Upper limit is 46.90 + 0.70 = £47.60 (rounded to nearest 10p)

Similar calculations can be carried out for other estimates of expenditure and income. The 95% confidence intervals for main expenditure categories are given in Table B3.

Table **B3** 95 per cent confidence intervals for average household expenditure, 2006

Commodity or service	Weighted average weekly household expenditure (£)	95% confidence interval	
		Lower limit	Upper limit
All expenditure groups	**378.30**	**369.80**	**386.80**
Food and non-alcoholic drinks	46.90	46.10	47.60
Alcoholic drink, tobacco & narcotics	11.10	10.70	11.50
Clothing and footwear	23.20	22.10	24.40
Housing, fuel and power	47.60	45.90	49.20
Household goods and services	30.30	28.60	31.90
Health	5.90	4.90	6.80
Transport	62.00	59.40	64.70
Communication	11.70	11.40	12.10
Recreation and culture	58.50	56.20	60.80
Education	7.20	5.60	8.80
Restaurants and hotels	37.90	36.30	39.40
Miscellaneous goods and services	36.00	34.70	37.40

Calculation of standard errors

Simple method

This formula treats the EFS sample as though it had arisen from a much simpler design with no multi-stage sampling, stratification, nor differential sampling and no non-response weights. The weights are used but only to estimate the true population standard deviation in what is, in fact, a weighted

design. The method of calculation is as follows: Let n be the total number of responding households in the survey, x_r the expenditure on a particular item of the r-th household, w_r be the weight attached to household r, and $\bar{x}$ the average expenditure per household on that item (averaged over the n households). Then the standard error $\bar{x}$, $sesrs$ is given by:

$$ sesrs = \sqrt{\frac{\sum_{r=1}^{n} w_r (x_r - \bar{x})^2}{(n-1)\sum_{r=1}^{n} w_r}} $$

Full method

In fact, the sample in Great Britain is a multi-stage, stratified, random sample described further in 'Description and response rate of the survey'. First a sample of areas, the Primary Sampling Units (PSUs), is drawn from an ordered list. Then within each PSU a random sample of households is drawn. In Northern Ireland, however, the sample is drawn in a single stage and there is no clustering. The results are also weighted for non-response and calibrated to match the population separately by sex, by 5–year age ranges, and by region, as described in 'Weighting'.

The method for calculating complex standard errors for the weighted estimates used on this survey is quite complex. First, we apply methods that take account of the clustering, stratification and differential sampling (and initial non-response weights) used in the design. Then we modify these to allow for the calibration weighting used on the survey. The exact formulae also depend on whether we are estimating standard errors for an estimated total or a mean or proportion. Here we outline the method for a total.

Consecutive PSUs in the ordered list are first grouped up into pairs, or triples at the end of a regional stratum. The standard error of a weighted total is estimated by:

$$ sedes = \sqrt{\sum_{h} \frac{k_h}{k_h - 1} \sum_{i} (x_{hi} - \bar{x}_h)^2} $$

where the h denotes the stratum (PSU pairs or triples), k_h is the number of PSUs in the stratum h (either 2 or 3), the x_{hi} is the weighted total in PSU i and the $\bar{x}_h$ is the mean of these totals in stratum h. Further details of this method of estimating sampling errors are described in *A Sampling Errors Manual* (B Butcher and D Elliot, ONS 1987).

The effect of the calibration weighting is calculated using a jackknife linearisation estimator. It uses the formula given above but with each household's expenditure, x_r, replaced by a residual from a linear regression of expenditure on the number of people in each household in each of the regions and age by sex categories used in the weighting.

The formulae have been expressed in terms of expenditures on a particular item, but of course they can also be applied to expenditures on groups of items, commodity groups and incomes from particular sources.

Definitions

Major changes in definitions since 1991 are described in 'Changes to definitions, 1991 to 2006'. Changes made between 1980 and 1990 are summarised in Appendix E of *Family Spending* 1994–95. For earlier changes see Annex 5 of Family Expenditure Survey 1980.

Household

A household comprises one person or a group of people who have the accommodation as their only or main residence and (for a group):

> share the living accommodation, that is a living room or sitting room, or
>
> share meals together or have common housekeeping

Resident domestic servants are included. The members of a household are not necessarily related by blood or marriage. As the survey covers only private households, people living in hostels, hotels, boarding houses or institutions are excluded. Households are not excluded if some or all members are not British subjects, but information is not collected from households containing members of the diplomatic service of another country or members of the United States armed forces.

Retired households

Retired households are those where the household reference person is retired. The household reference person is defined as retired if 65 years of age or more and male or 60 years of age or more and female, and economically inactive. Hence if, for example, a male household reference person is over 65 years of age, but working part-time or waiting to take up a part-time job, this household would not be classified as a retired household. For analysis purposes two categories are used in this report:

a. 'A retired household mainly dependent upon state pensions' is one in which at least three-quarters of the total income of the household is derived from national insurance retirement and similar pensions, including housing and other benefits paid in supplement to or instead of such pensions. The term 'national insurance retirement and similar pensions' includes national insurance disablement and war disability pensions, and income support in conjunction with these disability payments.

b. 'Other retired households' are retired households which do not fulfil the income conditions of 'retired household mainly dependent upon state pensions' because more than a quarter of the household's income derives from occupational retirement pensions and/or income from investments, annuities etc.

Household reference person (HRP)

From 2001–02, the concept of household reference person (HRP) was adopted on all government-sponsored surveys, in place of head of household. The household reference person is the householder, i.e. the person who:

a. owns the household accommodation, or

b. is legally responsible for the rent of the accommodation, or

c. has the household accommodation as an emolument or perquisite, or

d. has the household accommodation by virtue of some relationship to the owner who is not a member of the household.

If there are joint householders the household reference person will be the one with the higher income. If the income is the same, then the eldest householder is taken.

Members of household

In most cases the members of co-operating households are easily identified as the people who satisfy the conditions in the definition of a household, above, and are present during the record-keeping period. However difficulties of definition arise where people are temporarily away from the household or else spend their time between two residences. The following rules apply in deciding whether or not such persons are members of the household:

a. married persons living and working away from home for any period are included as members provided they consider the sampled address to be their main residence; in general, other people (e.g. relatives, friends, boarders) who are either temporarily absent or who spend their time between the sampled address and another address, are included as members if they consider the sampled address to be their main residence. However, there are exceptions which override the subjective main residence rule:

    i. Children under 16 away at school are included as members;

    ii. Older persons receiving education away from home, including children aged 16 and 17, are excluded unless they are at home for all or most of the record-keeping period;

    iii. Visitors staying temporarily with the household and others who have been in the household for only a short time are treated as members provided they will be staying with the household for at least one month from the start of record-keeping.

Household composition

A consequence of these definitions is that household compositions quoted in this report include some households where certain members are temporarily absent. For example, 'two adult and children' households will contain a few households where one parent is temporarily away from home.

Adult

In the report, persons who have reached the age of 18 are classed as adults. In addition, those aged 16–18 who are not in full-time education, or who are married, are classed as adults.

Children

In the report, persons who are under 18 years of age, in full-time education and have never been married are classed as children.

However, in the definition of clothing, clothing for persons aged 16 years and over is classified as clothing for men and women; clothing for those aged five but under 16 as clothing for boys and girls; and clothing for those under five as babies clothing.

Main Diary Keeper (MDK)

The MDK is the person in the household who is normally responsible for most of the food shopping. This includes people who organise and pay for the shopping although they do not physically do the shopping themselves.

Spenders

Members of households who are aged 16 or more, excluding those who for special reasons are not capable of keeping diary record-books, are described as spenders.

Absent Spenders

If a spender is absent for longer than 7 days they are defined as an 'absent spender'. Absent spenders do not keep a diary and consequently are not eligible for the monetary gift that is paid to diary keepers.

Non-Spenders

If a household member is completely incapable of contributing to the survey by answering questions or keeping a diary, then they are defined as a 'non-spender'. However, incapable people living on their own cannot be designated as non-spenders as they comprise the whole expenditure unit. If this is the case, the interviewer should enlist the help of the person outside of the household who looks after their interests. If there is no-one able or willing to help, the address should be coded as incapable.

Economically active

These are persons aged 16 or over who fall into the following categories:

a. *Employees at work* – those who at the time of interview were working full-time or part-time as employees or were away from work on holiday. Part-time work is defined as normally working 30 hours a week or less (excluding meal breaks) including regularly worked overtime.

b. *Employees temporarily away from work* – those who at the time of interview had a job but were absent because of illness or accident, temporary lay-off, strike etc.

c. *Government supported training schemes* – those participating in government programmes and schemes who in the course of their participation receive training, such as Employment Training, including those who are also employees in employment.

d. *Self-employed* – those who at the time of interview said they were self-employed.

e. *Unemployed* – those who at time of interview were out of employment, and have sought work within the last four weeks and were available to start work within two weeks, or were waiting to start a job already obtained.

f. *Unpaid family workers* – those working unpaid for their own or a relative's business. In this report, unpaid family workers are included under economically inactive in analyses by economic status (Tables A19 and A48) because insufficient information is available to assign them to an economic status group.

Economically inactive

a. *Retired* – persons who have reached national insurance retirement age (60 and over for women, 65 and over for men) and are not economically active.

b. *Unoccupied* – persons under national insurance retirement age who are not working, nor actively seeking work. This category includes certain self-employed persons such as mail order agents and baby-sitters who are not classified as economically active.

In this report, unpaid family workers are classified as economically inactive in analyses by economic status, although they are economically active by definition. This is because insufficient information is available to assign them to an economic status group.

National Statistics Socio-economic classification (NS–SEC)

From 2001, the National Statistics Socio-economic classification (NS–SEC) was adopted for all official surveys, in place of Social Class based on Occupation and Socio-economic group. NS–SEC is itself based on the Standard Occupational Classification 2000 (SOC2000) and details of employment status. Although NS–SEC is an occupationally based classification, there are procedures for classifying those not in work.

The main categories used for analysis in *Family Spending* are:

1 Higher managerial and professional occupations, sub-divided into:

1.1 Large employers and higher managerial occupations

1.2 Higher professional occupations

2 Lower managerial and professional occupations
3 Intermediate occupations
4 Small employers and own account workers
5 Lower supervisory and technical occupations
6 Semi-routine occupations
7 Routine occupations
8 Never worked and long-term unemployed
9 Students
10 Occupation not stated
11 Not classifiable for other reasons

The long-term unemployed are defined as those unemployed and seeking work for 12 months or more. Members of the armed forces, who were assigned to a separate category in Social Class, are included within the NS–SEC classification. Individuals that have retired within the last 12 months are classified according to their employment. Other retired individuals are assigned to the 'Not classifiable for other reasons' category.

Regions

These are the Government Office Regions as defined in 1994. See the region map on page 155 for more details.

Urban and rural areas

This classification replaces the previous Department for Transport, Local Government and the Regions (DTLR) 1991 Census-based urban and rural classification, which was used in previous editions of *Family Spending*. The new classification is applied across Great Britain (GB) and is an amalgamation of the Rural and Urban Classification 2004 for England and Wales and the Scottish Executive Urban Rural Classification. These classifications are based on 2001 Census data and have been endorsed as the standard National Statistics Classifications for identifying urban and rural areas across GB.

It should be noted that the Rural and Urban Classification 2004 for England and Wales and the Scottish Executive Urban Rural Classification use different definitions, as the nature of rurality is different in these countries. Within Tables A38, A45 and A48 of this publication, households in Scotland have been classified using the Scottish Classification for rural and urban areas and households in England and Wales have been classified using the England and Wales Classification. Nonetheless, in broad terms, both classifications define an area as urban or rural depending on whether the population falls inside a settlement of population 10,000 or more. For further details concerning these classifications please refer to the National Statistics website: http://www.statistics.gov.uk/ geography/nrudp.asp.

Expenditure

Any definition of expenditure is to some extent arbitrary, and the inclusion of certain types of payment is a matter of convenience or convention depending on the purpose for which the information is to be used. In the tables in this report, total expenditure represents current expenditure on goods and services. Total expenditure, defined in this way, excludes those recorded payments which are really savings or investments (e.g. purchases of national savings certificates, life assurance premiums, contributions to pension funds). Similarly, income tax payments, national insurance contributions, mortgage capital repayments and other payments for major additions to dwellings are excluded. Expenditure data are collected in the diary record-book and in the household schedule. Informants are asked to record in the diary any payments made during the 14 days of record-keeping, whether or not the goods or services paid for have been received. Certain types of expenditure which are usually regular though infrequent, such as insurance, licences and season tickets, and the periods to which they relate, are recorded in the household schedule as well as regular payments such as utility bills.

The cash purchase of motor vehicles is also entered in the household schedule. In addition, expenditure on some items purchased infrequently (thereby being subject to high sampling errors) has been recorded in the household schedule using a retrospective recall period of either three or 12 months. These items include carpets, furniture, holidays and some housing costs. In order to avoid duplication, all payments shown in the diary record-book which relate to items listed in the household or income schedules are omitted in the analysis of the data irrespective of whether there is a corresponding entry on the latter schedules. Amounts paid in respect of periods longer than a week are converted to weekly values.

Expenditure tables in this report show the 12 main commodity groups of spending and these are broken down into items which are numbered hierarchically (see 'Changes to definitions, 1991 to 2006' which details a major change to the coding frame used from 2001–02). Table A1 shows a further breakdown in the items themselves into components which can be separately identified. The items are numbered as in the main expenditure tables and against each item or component

are shown the average weekly household expenditure and percentage standard error.

Qualifications which apply to this concept of expenditure are described in the following paragraphs:

a. *Goods supplied from a household's own shop or farm*

Spenders are asked to record and give the value of goods obtained from their own shop or farm, even if the goods are withdrawn from stock for personal use without payment. The value is included as expenditure.

b. *Hire purchase and credit sales agreements, and transactions financed by loans repaid by instalments*

Expenditure on transactions under hire purchase or credit sales agreements, or financed by loans repaid by instalments, consists of all instalments which are still being paid at the date of interview, together with down payments on commodities acquired within the preceding three months. These two components (divided by the periods covered) provide the weekly averages which are included in the expenditure on the separate items given in the tables in this report.

c. *Club payments and budget account payments, instalments through mail order firms and similar forms of credit transaction*

When goods are purchased by forms of credit other than hire purchase and credit sales agreement, the expenditure on them may be estimated either from the amount of the instalment which is paid or from the value of the goods which are acquired. Since the particular commodities to which the instalment relates may not be known, details of goods ordered through clubs, etc. during the month prior to the date of interview are recorded in the household schedule. The weekly equivalent of the value of the goods is included in the expenditure on the separate items given in the tables in this report. This procedure has the advantage of enabling club transactions to be related to specific articles. Although payments into clubs, etc. are shown in the diary record-book, these entries are excluded from expenditure estimates.

d. *Credit card transactions*

From 1988 purchases made by credit card or charge card have been recorded in the survey on an acquisition basis rather than the formerly used payment basis. Thus, if a spender acquired an item (by use of credit/ charge card) during the two week survey period, the value of the item would be included as part of expenditure in that period whether or not any payment was made in this period to the credit card account.

Payments made to the card account are ignored. However any payment of credit/charge card interest is included in expenditure if made in the two week period.

e. *Income Tax*

Amounts of income tax deducted under the PAYE scheme or paid directly by those who are employers or self-employed are recorded (together with information about tax refunds). For employers and the self-employed the amounts comprise the actual payments made in the previous twelve months and may not correspond to the tax due on the income arising in that period, e.g. if no tax has been paid but is due or if tax payments cover more than one financial year. However, the amounts of tax deducted at source from some of the items which appear in the Income Schedule are not directly available. Estimates of the tax paid on bank and building society interest and amounts deducted from dividends on stocks and shares are therefore made by applying the appropriate rates of tax. In the case of income tax paid at source on pensions and annuities, similar adjustments are made. These estimates mainly affect the relatively few households with high incomes from interest and dividends, and households including someone receiving a pension from previous employment.

f. *Rented dwellings*

Expenditure on rented dwellings is taken as the sum of expenditure on rent, rates, council tax, water rates etc. For local authority tenants the expenditure is gross rent less any rebate (including rebate received in the form of housing benefit), and for other tenants gross rent less any rent allowance received under statutory schemes including the Housing Benefit Scheme. Rebate on Council Tax or rates (Northern Ireland) is deducted from expenditure on Council Tax or rates. Receipts from sub-letting part of the dwelling are not deducted from housing costs but appear (net of the expenses of the sub-letting) as investment income. Average payments by households renting accommodation for repairs, maintenance and decorations are shown separately in the estimates of expenditure by such households in table A34 which gives housing expenditure by tenure type. Accommodation rented from a housing association is shown separately.

g. *Rent-free dwellings*

Rent-free dwellings are those owned by someone outside the household and where either no rent is charged or the rent is paid by someone outside the household. Households whose rent is paid directly to the landlord by the DWP do not live rent-free. Payments

for Council Tax, water rates etc., are regarded as the cost of housing. Rebate on rates (Northern Ireland)/ Council Tax/water rates(Scotland) (including rebate received in the form of housing benefit), is deducted from expenditure on rates/Council Tax/water rates. Receipts from sub-letting part of the dwelling are not deducted from housing costs but appear (net of the expenses of the sub-letting) as investment income.

h. *Owner-occupied dwellings*

In the EFS payments for water rates, ground rent, fuel, maintenance and repair of the dwelling, and other miscellaneous services related to the dwelling etc., are regarded as the cost of housing. Receipts from letting part of the dwelling are not deducted from housing costs but appear (net of the expenses of the letting) as investment income. Mortgage capital repayments and amounts paid for the outright purchase of the dwelling or for major structural alterations are not included as housing expenditure, but are entered under 'other items recorded', as are Council Tax, rates (Northern Ireland), and mortgage interest payments. Structural insurance is included in Miscellaneous goods and services.

i. *Second-hand goods and part-exchange transactions*

The survey expenditure data are based on information about actual payments and therefore include payments for second-hand goods and part-exchange transactions. New payments only are included for part-exchange transactions, i.e. the costs of the goods obtained less the amounts allowed for the goods which are traded in. Receipts for goods sold or traded in are not included in income.

j. *Business expenses*

The survey covers only private households and is concerned with payments made by members of households as private individuals. Spenders are asked to state whether expenditure which has been recorded on the schedules includes amounts which will be refunded as expenses from a business or organisation or which will be entered as business expenses for income tax purposes, e.g. rent, telephone charges, travelling expenses, meals out. Any such amounts are deducted from the recorded expenditure.

Income

The standard concept of income in the survey is, as far as possible, that of gross weekly cash income current at the time of interview, i.e. before the deduction of income tax actually paid, national insurance contributions and other deductions at source. However, for a few tables a concept of disposable income is used, defined as gross weekly cash income less the statutory deductions and payments of income tax (taking refunds into account) and national insurance contributions. Analysis in Chapter 3 of this volume and some other analyses of EFS data use 'equivalisation' of incomes – i.e. adjustment of household income to allow for the different size and composition of each household. For more information see Chapter 3 of this volume. The cash levels of certain items of income (and expenditure) recorded in the survey by households receiving supplementary benefit were affected by the Housing Benefit Scheme introduced in stages from November 1982. From 1984 housing expenditure is given on a strictly net basis and all rent/council tax rebates and allowances and housing benefit are excluded from gross income.

Although information about most types of income is obtained on a current basis, some data, principally income from investment and from self-employment, are estimated over a 12–month period.

The following are excluded from the assessment of income:

a. money received by one member of the household from another (e.g. housekeeping money, dress allowance, children's pocket money) other than wages paid to resident domestic servants;

b. withdrawals of savings, receipts from maturing insurance policies, proceeds from sale of financial and other assets (e.g. houses, cars, furniture, etc.), winnings from betting, lump-sum gratuities and windfalls such as legacies;

c. the value of educational grants and scholarships not paid in cash;

d. the value of income in kind, including the value of goods received free and the abatement in cost of goods received at reduced prices, and of bills paid by someone who is not a member of the household;

e. loans and money received in repayment of loans.

Details are obtained of the income of each member of the household. The income of the household is taken to be the sum of the incomes of all its members. The information does not relate to a common or a fixed time period. Items recorded for periods greater than a week are converted to a weekly value.

Particular points relating to some components of income are as follows:

a. *Wages and salaries of employees*

   The normal gross wages or salaries of employees are taken to be their earnings. These are calculated by adding to the normal 'take home' pay amounts deducted at source, such as income tax payments,

national insurance contributions and other deductions, e.g. payments into firm social clubs, superannuation schemes, works transport, benevolent funds etc. Employees are asked to give the earnings actually received including bonuses and commission the last time payment was made and, if different, the amount usually received. It is the amount usually received which is regarded as the normal take home pay. Additions are made so as to include in normal earnings the value of occasional payments, such as bonuses or commissions received quarterly or annually. One of the principal objects in obtaining data on income is to enable expenditure to be classified in ranges of normal income. Average household expenditure is likely to be based on the long-term expectations of the various members of the household as to their incomes rather than be altered by short-term changes affecting individuals. Hence if employees have been away from work without pay for 13 weeks or less they are regarded as continuing to receive their normal earnings instead of social security benefits, such as unemployment or sickness benefit, that they may be receiving. Otherwise, normal earnings are disregarded and current short-term social security benefits taken instead. Wages and salaries include any earnings from subsidiary employment as an employee and the earnings of HM Forces.

b. *Income from self-employment*

   Income from self-employment covers any personal income from employment other than as an employee; for example, as a sole trader, professional or other person working on his own account or in partnership, including subsidiary work on his own account by a person whose main job is as an employee. It is measured from estimates of income or trading profits, after deduction of business expenses but before deduction of tax, over the most recent 12–month period for which figures can be given. Should either a loss have been made or no profit, income would be taken as the amounts drawn from the business for own use or as any other income received from the job or business. Persons working as mail order agents or baby-sitters, with no other employment, have been classified as unoccupied rather than as self-employed, and the earnings involved have been classified as earnings from "other sources" rather than self-employment income.

c. *Income from investment*

   Income from investments or from property, other than that in which the household is residing, is the amount received during the 12 months immediately prior to the date of the initial interview. It includes receipts from sub-letting part of the dwelling (net of the expenses of the sub-letting). If income tax has been deducted at source the gross amount is estimated by applying a conversion factor during processing.

d. *Social security benefits*

Income from social security benefits does not include the short-term payments such as unemployment or sickness benefit received by an employee who has been away from work for 13 weeks or less, and who is therefore regarded as continuing to receive his normal earnings as described on page 188.

Quantiles

The quantiles of a distribution, e.g. of household expenditure or income, divide it into a number of equal parts; each of which contains the same number of households.

For example, the median of a distribution divides it into two equal parts, so that half the households in a distribution of household income will have income more than the median, and the other half will have income less than the median. Similarly, quartiles, quintiles and deciles divide the distribution into four, five and ten equal parts respectively.

Most of the analysis in *Family Spending* is done in terms of quintile groups and decile groups.

In the calculation of quantiles for this report, zero values are counted as part of the distribution.

Income headings

Headings used for identifying 2006 income information

Source of income

References in tables	Components separately identified	Explanatory notes
a. Wages and salaries	Normal 'take-home' pay from main employment 'Take-home' pay from subsidiary employment Employees' income tax deduction Employees' National Insurance contribution Superannuation contributions deducted from pay Other deductions	(i) In the calculation of household income in this report, where an employee has been away from work without pay for 13 weeks or less his normal wage or salary has been used in estimating his total income instead of social security benefits, such as unemployment or sickness benefits that he may have received. Otherwise such benefits are used in estimating total income (see notes at reference e) (ii) Normal income from wages and salaries is estimated by adding to the normal 'take-home' pay deductions made at source last time paid, together with the weekly value of occasional additions to wages and salaries (see page 185) (iii) The components of wages and salaries for which figures are separately available amount in total to the normal earnings of employees, regardless of the operation of the 13 week rule in note (i) above. Thus the sum of the components listed here does not in general equal the wages and salaries figure in tables of this report
b. Self-employment	Income from business or profession, including subsidiary self-employment	The earnings or profits of a trade or profession, after deduction of business expenses but before deduction of tax
c. Investments	Interest on building society shares and deposits Interest on bank deposits and savings accounts including National Savings Bank Interest on ISAs Interest on TESSAs Interest on Gilt-edged stock and War Loans Interest and dividends from stocks, shares, bonds, trusts, PEPs, debentures and other securities Rent or income from property, after deducting expenses but inclusive of income tax (including receipts from letting or sub-letting part of own residence, net of the expenses of the letting or sub-letting) Other unearned Income	

Income headings (cont.)

Headings used for identifying 2006 income information

Source of income

d. Annuities and pensions,other than social security	Annuities and income from trust or covenant Pensions from previous employers Personal pensions	

e. Social security benefits	Child benefit
	Guardian's allowance
	Carer's allowance (formerly Invalid care allowance)
	Retirement pension (National Insurance) or
	    old person's pension
	Pension credit
	Widow's pension/bereavement allowance or
	    widowed parent's allowance
	War disablement pension or war widow/widower's
	    pension
	Severe disablement allowance
	Care component of disability living allowance
	Mobility component of disability living allowance
	Attendance allowance
	Job seekers allowance
	Winter fuel allowance
	Income support
	Working tax credit
	Child tax credit
	Incapacity benefit
	Statutory sick pay (from employer)
	Industrial injury disablement benefit
	Maternity allowance
	Statutory maternity pay
	Statutory paternity pay
	Statutory adoption pay
	Any other benefit including lump sums and grants
	Social security benefits excluded from income
	    calculation by 13 week rule
		(i) The calculation of household income in this report takes account of the 13 week rule described at reference a, note (i)
		
		(ii) The components of social security benefits for which figures are separately available amount in total to the benefits received in the week before interview. That is to say, they include amounts that are discounted from the total by the operation of the 13 week rule in note i. Thus the sum of the components listed here differs from the total of social security benefits used in the income tables of this report
		
		(iii) Housing Benefit is treated as a reduction in housing costs and not as income

f. Other sources	Married person's allowance from husband/wife
	    temporarily away from home
	Alimony or separation allowances;
	    allowances for foster children, allowances from
	    members of the Armed Forces or Merchant Navy,
	    or any other money from friends or relatives,
	    other than husband outside the household
	Benefits from trade unions, friendly societies etc.,
	    other than pensions
	Value of meal vouchers
	Earnings from intermittent or casual work over
	    12 months, not included in a or b above
	Student loans and money scholarships received by
	    persons aged 16 and over and aged under 16.
	Other income of children under 16
		
		e.g. from spare-time jobs or income from Trusts or investments

STANDARD STATISTICAL REGION   **GOVERNMENT OFFICE REGION**

NORTH	Cleveland Durham Northumberland Tyne and Wear	**NORTH EAST**
	Cumbria	
NORTH WEST	Cheshire Greater Manchester Lancashire Merseyside	**NORTH WEST**
YORKSHIRE AND HUMBERSIDE	Humberside North Yorkshire South Yorkshire West Yorkshire	**YORKSHIRE AND THE HUMBER**
EAST MIDLANDS	Derbyshire Leicestershire Lincolnshire Northamptonshire Nottinghamshire	**EAST MIDLANDS**
WEST MIDLANDS	Hereford and Worcester Shropshire Staffordshire Warwickshire West Midlands	**WEST MIDLANDS**
EAST ANGLIA	Cambridgeshire Norfolk Suffolk	**EAST OF ENGLAND**
	Bedfordshire Essex Hertfordshire	
	Greater London	**LONDON**
SOUTH EAST	Berkshire Buckinghamshire East Sussex Hampshire Isle of Wight Kent Oxfordshire Surrey West Sussex	**SOUTH EAST**
SOUTH WEST	Avon Cornwall Devon Dorset Gloucestershire Somerset Wiltshire	**SOUTH WEST**

Changes in definitions, 1991 to 2006

1991

No significant changes.

1992

Housing – Imputed rent for owner occupiers and households in rent-free accommodation was discontinued. For owner occupiers this had been the rent they would have had to pay themselves to live in the property they own, and for households in rent-free accommodation it was the rent they would normally have had to pay. Up to 1990 these amounts were counted both as income and as a housing cost. Mortgage interest payments were counted as a housing cost for the first time in 1991.

1993

Council Tax – Council Tax was introduced to replace the Community Charge in Great Britain from April 1993.

1994–95

New expenditure items – The definition of expenditure was extended to include two items previously shown under 'other payments recorded'. These were:

> gambling payments;
> mortgage protection premiums.

Expenditure classifications – A new classification system for expenditures was introduced in April 1994. The system is hierarchical and allows more detail to be preserved than the previous system. New categories of expenditure were introduced and are shown in detail in Table 7.1. The 14 main groups of expenditure were retained, but there were some changes in the content of these groups.

Gambling Payments – data on gambling expenditure and winnings are collected in the expenditure diary. Previously these were excluded from the definition of household expenditure used in the FES. The data are shown as memoranda items under the heading 'Other payments recorded' on both gross and net bases. The net basis corresponds approximately to the treatment of gambling in the National Accounts. The introduction of the National Lottery stimulated a reconsideration of this treatment. From April 1994, (gross) gambling payments have been included as expenditure in 'Leisure Services'. Gambling winnings continued to be noted as a memorandum item under 'Other items recorded'. They are treated as windfall income. They do not form a part of normal household income, nor are they

subtracted from gross gambling payments. This treatment is in line with the PRODCOM classification of the Statistical Office of the European Communities (SOEC) for expenditure in household budget surveys.

1995–96

Geographical coverage – The FES geographical coverage was extended to mainland Scotland north of the Caledonian Canal.

Under 16s diaries – Two-week expenditure diaries for 7–15 year olds were introduced following three feasibility pilot studies which found that children of that age group were able to cope with the task of keeping a two-week expenditure record. Children are asked to record everything they buy with their own money but to exclude items bought with other people's money. Purchases are coded according to the same coding categories as adult diaries except for meals and snacks away from home which are coded as school meals, hot meals and snacks, and cold meals and snacks. Children who keep a diary are given a £5 incentive payment. A refusal to keep an under 16's diary does not invalidate the household from inclusion in the survey.

Pocket money given to children is still recorded separately in adult diaries; and money paid by adults for school meals and school travel is recorded in the Household Questionnaire. Double counting is eliminated at the processing stage.

Tables in *Family Spending* reports did not include the information from the children's diaries until the 1998–99 report. Appendix F in the 1998–99 and 1999–2000 reports show what difference the inclusion made.

1996–97

Self-employment – The way in which information about income from self-employment is collected was substantially revised in 1996–97 following various tests and pilot studies. The quality of such data was increased but this may have lead to a discontinuity. Full details are shown in the Income Questionnaire, available from the address in the introduction.

Cable/satellite television – Information on cable and satellite subscriptions is now collected from the household questionnaire rather than from the diary, leading to more respondents reporting this expenditure.

Mobile phones – Expenditure on mobile phones was previously collected through the diary. From 1996/97 this has been included in the questionnaire.

Job seekers allowance (JSA) – Introduced in October 1996 as a replacement for Unemployment Benefit and any Income Support associated with the payment of Unemployment

Benefit. Receipt of JSA is collected with NI Unemployment Benefit and with Income Support. In both cases the number of weeks a respondent has been in receipt of these benefits is taken as the number of weeks receiving JSA in the last 12 months and before that period the number of weeks receiving Unemployment Benefit/Income Support.

Retrospective recall – The period over which information is requested has been extended from 3 to 12 months for vehicle purchase and sale. Information on the purchase of car and motorcycle spare parts is no longer collected by retrospective recall. Instead expenditure on these items is collected through the diary.

State benefits – The lists of benefits specifically asked about was reviewed in 1996–97. See the Income Questionnaire for more information.

Sample stratifiers – New stratifiers were introduced in 1996–97 based on standard regions, socio-economic group and car ownership.

Government Office Regions – Regional analyses are now presented using the Government Office Regions (GORs) formed in 1994. Previously all regional analyses used Standard Statistical Regions (SSRs). For more information see Appendix F in the 1996–97 report.

1997–98

Bank/Building society service charges – Collection of information on service charges levied by banks has been extended to include building societies.

Payments from unemployment/redundancy insurances – Information is now collected on payments received from private unemployment and redundancy insurance policies. This information is then incorporated into the calculation of income from other sources.

Retired households – The definition of retired households has been amended to exclude households where the head of the household is economically active.

Rent-free tenure – The definition of rent-free tenure has been amended to include those households for which someone outside the household, except an employer or an organisation, is paying a rent or mortgage on behalf of the household.

National Lottery – From February 1997, expenditure on National lottery tickets was collected as three separate items: tickets for the Wednesday draw only, tickets for the Saturday draw only and tickets for both draws.

1998–99

Children's income – Three new expenditure codes were introduced: pocket money to children; money given to children for specific purposes and cash gifts to children. These replaced a single code covering all three categories.

Main job and last paid job – Harmonised questions were adopted.

1999–2000

Disabled Persons Tax Credit replaced Disability Working Allowance and Working Families Tax Credit replaced Family Credit from October 1999.

2000–01

Household definition – the definition was changed to the harmonised definition which has been in use in the Census and nearly all other government household surveys since 1981. The effect is to group together into a single household some people who would have been allocated to separate households on the previous definition. The effect is fairly small but not negligible.

Up to 1999–2000 the FES definition was based on the pre–1981 Census definition and required members to share eating and budgeting arrangements as well as shared living accommodation.

The definition of a household was:

One person or a group of people who have the accommodation as their only or main residence

and (for a group)

    share the living accommodation, that is a living or sitting room
    and   share meals together (or have common housekeeping).

The harmonised definition is less restrictive:

One person or a group of people who have the accommodation as their only or main residence and (for a group)

    share the living accommodation, that is a living or sitting room
    or   share meals together or have common housekeeping.

The effect of the change is probably to increase average household size by 0.6 per cent.

Question reductions – A thorough review of the questionnaire showed that a number of questions were no longer needed by government users. These were cut from the 2000–01 survey to reduce the burden on respondents. The reduction was fairly small but it did make the interview flow better. All the questions needed for a complete record of expenditure and income were retained.

Redesigned diary – The diary was redesigned to be easier for respondents to keep and to look cleaner. The main change of substance was to delete the column for recording whether each item was purchased by credit, charge or shop card.

Ending of MIRAS – Tax relief on interest on loans for house purchase was abolished from April 2000. Questions related to MIRAS were therefore dropped. They included some that were needed to estimate the amount if the respondent did not know it. A number were retained for other purposes, however, such as the amount of the loan still outstanding which is still asked for households paying a reduced rate of interest because one of them works for the lender.

2001–02

Expenditure and Food Survey (EFS) introduced, replacing the Family Expenditure and National Food Surveys (FES and NFS)

Household reference person – this replaced the previous concept of head of household. The household reference person is the householder, i.e. the person who:

a. owns the household accommodation, or

b. is legally responsible for the rent of the accommodation, or

c. has the household accommodation as an emolument or perquisite, or

d. has the household accommodation by virtue of some relationship to the owner who is not a member of the household.

If there are joint householders the household reference person is the one with the higher income. If the income is the same, then the eldest householder is taken.

A key difference between household reference person and head of household is that the household reference person must always be a householder, whereas the head of household was always the husband, who might not even be a householder himself.

National Statistics Socio-economic classification (NS–SEC) – the National Statistics Socio-economic classification (NS–SEC) was adopted for all official surveys, in place of Social Class based on Occupation and Socio-economic group. NS–SEC is itself based on the Standard Occupational Classification 2000 (SOC2000) and details of employment status.

The long-term unemployed, which fall into a separate category, are defined as those unemployed and seeking work for 12 months or more. Members of the armed forces, who were assigned to a separate category in Social Class, are included within the NS–SEC classification. Residual groups that remain unclassified include students and those with inadequately described occupations.

COICOP – From 2001–02, the Classification Of Individual COnsumption by Purpose (COICOP/HBS, referred to as COICOP in this volume) was introduced as a new coding frame for expenditure items. COICOP has been adapted to the needs of Household Budget Surveys (HBS) across the EU and, as a consequence, is compatible with similar classifications used in national accounts and consumer price indices. This allows the production of indicators which are comparable Europe-wide, such as the Harmonised Indices of Consumer Prices (computed for all goods as well as sub-categories such as food and transport). The main categorisation of spending used in this volume (namely 12 categories relating to food and non-alcoholic beverages; alcoholic beverages, tobacco and narcotics; clothing and footwear; housing, fuel and power; fhousehold goods and services; health, transport; communication; recreation and culture; education; restaurants and hotels; and miscellaneous goods and services) is only comparable between the two frames at a broad level. Table 4.1 in this volume has been produced by mapping COICOP to the FES 14 main categories. However the two frames are not comparable for any smaller categories, leading to a break in trends between 2000–01 and 2001–02 for any level of detail below the main 12–fold categorisation. A complete listing of COICOP and COICOP plus (an extra level of detail added by individual countries for their own needs) is available on request from the address in the introduction.

Proxy interviews – While questions about general household affairs are put to all household members or to a main household informant, questions about work and income are put to the individual members of the household. Where a member of the household is not present during the household interview, another member of the household (e.g. spouse) may be able to provide information about the absent person. The individual's interview is then identified as a proxy interview. From 2001–02, the EFS began accepting responses that contained a proxy interview.

Short income – From 2001–02, the EFS accepted responses from households that answered the short income section. This was designed for respondents who were reluctant to provide more detailed income information.

2002–03

Main shopper – At the launch of the EFS in April 2001, the respondent responsible for buying the household's main shopping was identified as the 'Main Diary Keeper''. From 2002–03, this term has been replaced by the 'Main Shopper'.

The importance of the Main Shopper is to ensure that we have obtained information on the bulk of the shopping in the household. Without this person's co-operation we have insufficient information to use the other diaries kept by members of the household in a meaningful way. The main shopper must therefore complete a diary for the interview to qualify as a full or partial interview. Without their participation, the outcome will be a refusal no matter who else is willing to complete a diary.

2003–04

Working Tax Credit replaced Disabled Persons Tax Credit and Working Families Tax Credit from April 2003.

Pension Credit replaced Minimum Income Guarantee from October 2003.

Child Tax Credit replaced Children's Tax Credit and Childcare Tax Credit from April 2003.

2004–05

No significant changes.

2005–06

Urban and rural definition – A new urban and rural area classification based on 2001 Census data has been introduced onto the EFS dataset and is presented in Tables A38, A45 and A48 of this publication. The classification replaces the Department for Transport, Local Government and the Regions (DTLR) 1991 Census-based urban and rural classification that was used in previous editions of *Family Spending*. The new classification is the standard National Statistics classification for identifying urban and rural areas in England and Wales, and Scotland. Please refer to 'Definitions' for further details.

Motor vehicle road taxation refunds – Questions on road tax refunds were inadvertently omitted from the 2005–06 questionnaire. Within the Appendix A tables of the 2005–06 report, the heading for category 13.2.3 'Motor vehicle road taxation payments less refunds', has been changed to reflect this omission.

Purchase of vehicles – During April to December 2005, respondents who had sold a vehicle were not asked whether they had bought that same vehicle in the previous year. This was corrected from January 2006, but means that some expenditure on vehicles may have been missed.

2006

No significant changes.

Weighting

Since 1998–99 the FES/EFS has been weighted to reduce the effect of non-response bias. The weights are produced in two stages. First, the data are weighted to compensate for non-response (sample-based weighting). Second, the sample distribution is weighted so that it matches the population distribution in terms of region, age group and sex (population-based weighting).

Sample-based weighting using the Census

Weighting for non-response involves giving each respondent a weight so that they represent the non-respondents that are similar to them in terms of the survey characteristics. The EFS uses results from the Census-linked study of non-respondents to carry out non-response weighting[1].

The Census-linked study matched Census addresses with the sampled addresses of some of the large continuous surveys, of which the FES was one. In this way it was possible to match the address details of the FES respondents as well as the non-respondents with corresponding information gathered from the Census for the same address. The information collected during the 1991 Census/FES matching work was then used to identify the types of households that were being under-represented in the survey. A combination of household variables were analysed using the software package Answer Tree (using the chi-squared statistics CHAID)[2], to identify which characteristics were most significant in distinguishing between responding and non-responding households. These characteristics were sorted by the program to produce ten weighting classes with different response rates. For the 2006 EFS, households within each of the weighting classes were assigned a non-response weight, based on the inverse of their response rate. A group with a low response rate was therefore given a high initial weight.

ONS is currently analysing data from the 2001 Census; this will result in an update to the non-response weights.

Table **B4** The effect of weighting on expenditure, 2006

Commodity or service	Average weekly household expenditure		Absolute difference	Percentage difference
	Unweighted	Weighted as published		
All expenditure groups	**373.90**	**378.30**	**4.43**	*1.2*
Food and non-alcoholic drinks	47.40	46.90	-0.48	*-1.0*
Alcoholic drink and tobacco	11.10	11.10	0.04	*0.3*
Clothing and footwear	23.20	23.20	0.02	*0.1*
Housing (net), fuel and power	45.80	47.60	1.81	*4.0*
Household goods and services	30.40	30.30	-0.18	*-0.6*
Health	5.80	5.90	0.11	*1.9*
Transport	60.60	62.00	1.43	*2.4*
Communication	11.50	11.70	0.23	*2.0*
Recreation and culture	58.40	58.50	0.05	*0.1*
Education	7.00	7.20	0.18	*2.5*
Restaurants and hotels	36.90	37.90	0.99	*2.7*
Miscellaneous	35.80	36.00	0.24	*0.7*
Weekly household income:				
Disposable	510	521	11	*2.1*
Gross	627	642	15	*2.5*

Population-based weighting

The second stage of the weighting adjusts the non-response weights so that weighted totals match population totals. As the EFS sample is based on private households, the population totals used in the weighting need to relate to people living in private households. For 2006, the EFS used population projections from the 2001 Census. These estimates exclude residents of institutions not covered by the EFS, i.e. those living in bed-and-breakfast accommodation, hostels, residential homes and other institutions.

The existing non-response weights were calibrated[3], so that weighted totals matched population totals, for males and females in different age groups and for regions. An important feature of the population-based weighting is that it is done by adjusting the factors for households not individuals.

The weighting is carried out separately for each quarter of the survey. The main reason is that sample sizes vary from quarter to quarter more than in the past. This is due to re-issuing addresses where there had been no contact or a refusal to a new interviewer after an interval of a few months, which results in more interviews in the later quarters of the year than in the first quarter. Quarterly weighting therefore counteracts any bias from the uneven spread of interviews through the

year. Quarterly weighting also results in small sample numbers in some of the age/sex categories that were used in previous years. The categories have therefore been widened slightly to avoid this.

Effects of weighting on the data

Table B4 shows the effects of the weighting by comparing unweighted and weighted data from 2006.

Weighting increased the estimate of total average expenditure by £4.43 a week; that is by 1.2 per cent. It had the largest impact on average weekly expenditure on housing, fuel and power, increasing the estimate by 4 per cent; on restaurants and hotels, increasing the estimate by 2.7 per cent; and on transport, increasing the estimate by 2.4 per cent. It reduced the estimate of spending on food and non-alcoholic drinks by 1 per cent. Weighting also increased the estimates of average income, by £11 a week (2.1 per cent) for disposable household income and by £15 a week (2.5 per cent) for gross household income, which is the income used in most tables in the report.

Re-weighting also has an effect on the variance of estimates. In an analysis on the 1999–2000 data, weighting increased variance slightly for some items and reduced for others. Overall the effect was to reduce variance slightly.

Further information

Further information on the method used to produce the weights is available from the contacts given on page ii of this publication.

Notes

1   See Foster, K. (1994) *Weighting the FES to compensate for non-response, Part 1: An investigation into Census-based weighting schemes*, London: OPCS.

2   CHAID is an acronym that stands for Chi-squared Automatic Interaction Detection. As is suggested by its name, CHAID uses chi-squared statistics to identify optimal splits or groupings of independent variables in terms of predicting the outcome of a dependent variable, in this case response.

3   Implemented by the CALMAR software package.

Index to tables in reports on the Family Expenditure Survey in 1997–98 to 2000–01 and the Expenditure and Food Survey 2001–02 to 2006

2006 tables		2005–06	2004–05	2003–04	2002–03	2001–02[1]	2000–01	1999–2000	1998–99	1997–98
						Table numbers in reports for				
Detailed expenditure and place of purchase										
A1	Detailed expenditure with full-method standard errors	A1	A1	A1	7.1	7.1	7.1	7.1	7.1	7.1
A2	expenditure on alcoholic drink by type of premises	A2	A2	A2	7.2	7.2	7.2	7.2	7.2	7.2
A3	expenditure on food by place of purchase	A3	A3	A3	7.3	7.3	7.3	7.3	7.3	7.3
..	expenditure on alcoholic drink by place of purchase	..	..	..	–	–	–	7.4	7.4	7.4
A4	expenditure on selected items by place of purchase	A4	A4	A4	7.4	7.4	7.4	–	–	–
..	expenditure on petrol, diesel and other motor oils by place of purchase	..	..	..	–	–	–	7.5	7.5	7.5
..	selected household goods and personal goods and services by place of purchase				–	–	–	7.6	7.6	7.6
..	selected regular purchases by place of purchase	..	..	..	–	–	–	7.7	7.7	7.7
A5	expenditure on clothing and footwear by place of purchase	A5	A5	A5	7.5	7.5	7.5	7.8	7.8	7.8
Expenditure by income										
A6	main items by gross income decile	A6	A6	A6	1.1	1.1	1.1	1.1	1.1	1.1
A7	percentage on main items by gross income decile	A7	A7	A7	1.2	1.2	1.2	1.2	1.2	1.2
A8	detailed expenditure by gross income decile	A8	A8	A8	1.3	1.3	1.3	1.3	1.3	1.3
..	(housing expenditure in each tenure group)	..	..	..	–	–	–	–	–	–
A9	main items by disposable income decile	A9	A9	A9	1.4	1.4	1.4	1.4	–	–
A10	percentage on main items by disposable income decile	A10	A10	A10	1.5	1.5	1.5	1.5	–	–
Expenditure by age and income										
A11	main items by age of HRP	A11	A11	A11	2.1	2.1	2.9	–	–	–
..	main items by age of head of household	..	..	..	–	–	2.1	2.1	2.1	2.1
A12	main items as a percentage by age of HRP	A12	A12	A12	2.2	2.2	2.2	2.2	2.2	2.2
A13	detailed expenditure by age of HRP	A13	A13	A13	2.3	2.3	2.3	2.3	2.3	2.3
A14	aged under 30 by income	A14	A14	A14	2.4	2.4	2.4	2.4	2.4	2.4
A15	aged 30 and under 50 by income	A15	A15	A15	2.5	2.5	2.5	2.5	2.5	2.5
A16	aged 50 and under 65 by income	A16	A16	A16	2.6	2.6	2.6	2.6	2.6	2.6
A17	aged 65 and under 75 by income	A17	A17	A17	2.7	2.7	2.7	2.7	2.7	2.7
A18	aged 75 or over by income	A18	A18	A18	2.8	2.8	2.8	2.8	2.8	2.8
Expenditure by socio-economic characteristics										
A19	by economic activity status of HRP	A19	A19	A19	3.1	3.1	3.9	–	–	–
..	by economic activity status of HoH	..	..	..	–	–	3.1	3.1	3.1	3.1
..	by occupation	..	..	..	–	–	3.2	3.2	3.2	3.2
A20	HRP is a full-time employee by income	A20	A20	A20	3.2	3.2	3.3	3.3	3.3	3.3
A21	HRP is self-employed by income	A21	A21	A21	3.3	3.3	3.4	3.4	3.4	3.4
..	by social class	..	..	..	–	–	3.5	3.5	3.5	3.5
A22	by number of persons working	A22	A22	A22	3.4	3.4	3.6	3.6	3.6	3.6
A23	by age HRP completed continuous full-time education	A23	A23	A23	3.5	3.5	3.7	3.7	3.7	3.7
..	by occupation of HRP	..	..	..	–	–	3.8	–	–	–
A24	by socio-economic class of HRP	A24	A24	A24	3.6	3.6	–	–	–	–
Expenditure by composition, income and tenure										
A25	expenditure by household composition	A25	A25	A25	4.1	4.1	4.1	4.1	4.1	4.1
A26	one adult retired households mainly dependent on state pensions	A26	A26	A26	4.2	4.2	4.2	4.2	4.2	4.2
A27	one adult retired households not mainly dependent on state pensions	A27	A27	A27	4.3	4.3	4.3	4.3	4.3	4.3
A28	one adult non-retired	A28	A28	A28	4.4	4.4	4.4	4.4	4.4	4.4
A29	one adult with children	A29	A29	A29	4.5	4.5	4.5	4.5	4.5	4.5
A30	two adults with children	A30	A30	A30	4.6	4.6	4.6	4.6	4.6	4.6

.. Tables do not appear in these publications.

1 Household Reference Person (HRP) replaced Head of Household (HoH) in 2001–02.

Index to tables in reports on the Family Expenditure Survey in 1997–98 to 2000–01 and the Expenditure and Food Survey 2001–02 to 2006 (cont.)

2006 tables	2005–06	2004–05	2003–04	2002–03	2001–02[1]	2000–01	1999–2000	1998–99	1997–98
				Table numbers in reports for					
Expenditure by composition, income and tenure (cont.)									
A31 one man one woman non-retired	A31	A31	A31	4.7	4.7	4.7	4.7	4.7	4.7
A32 one man one woman retired mainly dependent on state pensions	A32	A32	A32	4.8	4.8	4.8	4.8	4.8	4.8
A33 one man one woman retired not mainly dependent on state pensions	A33	A33	A33	4.9	4.9	4.9	4.9	4.9	4.9
A34 household expenditure by tenure	A34	A34	A34	4.10	4.10	4.10	4.10	4.10	4.10
.. household expenditure by type of dwelling	..	..	..	–	–	–	–	4.11	4.11
Expenditure by region									
A35 main items of expenditure by GOR	A35	A35	A35	5.1	5.1	5.1	5.1	5.1	5.1
A36 main items as a percentage of expenditure by GOR	A36	A36	A36	5.2	5.2	5.2	5.2	5.2	5.2
A37 detailed expenditure by GOR	A37	A37	A37	5.3	5.3	5.3	5.3	5.3	5.3
.. (housing expenditure in each tenure group)	..	..	..	–	–	–	–	–	–
.. expenditure by type of administrative area	..	..	..	–	–	5.4	5.4	5.4	5.4
A38 expenditure by urban/rural areas (GB only)	A38	A38	A38	5.4	5.4	5.5	–	–	–
Household income									
A40 Income by household composition	A40	A40	A40	8.1	8.1	8.1	8.1	8.1	8.1
A41 Income by age of HRP	A41	A41	A41	8.2	8.2	8.10	–	–	–
.. by age of head of household	..	..	..	–	–	8.2	8.2	8.2	8.2
A42 Income by income group	A42	A42	A42	8.3	8.3	8.3	8.3	8.3	8.3
A43 Income by household tenure	A43	A43	A43	8.4	8.4	8.4	8.4	8.4	8.4
.. Income by economic status of HoH	..	..	..	–	–	8.5	8.5	8.5	8.5
.. Income by occupational grouping of HoH	..	..	..	–	–	8.6	8.6	8.6	8.6
A44 Income by Region	A44	A44	A44	8.5	8.5	8.7	8.7	8.7	8.7
A45 Income by GB urban/rural areas	A45	A45	A45	8.6	8.6	8.8	–	–	–
A46 Income by socio-economic class	A46	A46	A46	8.7	–	–	–	–	–
A47 Income 1970 to 2004–05	A47	A47	A47	8.8	8.7	8.9	8.8	8.8	8.8
.. Income by economic activity status of HRP	..	..	..	–	–	8.11	–	–	–
.. Income by occupation of HRP	..	..	..	–	–	8.12	–	–	–
Households characteristics and ownership of durable goods									
A48 Household characteristics	A48	A48	A48	9.1	9.1	9.1	9.1	9.1	9.1
A49 Person characteristics	A49	A49	A49	9.2	9.2	9.2	9.2	9.2	9.2
A50 percentage with durable goods 1970 to 2003–04	A50	A50	A50	9.3	9.3	9.3	9.3	9.3	9.3
A51 percentage with durable goods by income group & household composition	A51	A51	A51	9.4	9.4	9.4	9.4	9.4	9.4
A52 percentage with cars	A52	A52	A52	9.5	9.5	9.5	9.5	9.5	9.5
A53 percentage with durable goods by UK Countries and Government Office Regions	A53	A53	A53	9.6	9.6	9.6	9.6	9.6	9.6
A54 percentage by size, composition, age, in each income group	A54	A54	A54	9.7	9.7	9.7	9.7	9.7	9.7
.. percentage by occupation, economic activity, tenure in each income group	..	..	..	–	–	9.8	9.8	9.8	9.7
A55 percentage by economic activity, tenure and socio-economic class in each income group	A55	A55	A55	9.8	9.8	–	–	–	–
Trends in household expenditure (moved to Chapter 4)									
4.1 FES main items 1984–2006	4.1	4.1	4.1	6.1	6.1	6.1	6.1	–	–
4.2 FES as a percentage of total expenditure 1984 to 2006	4.2	4.2	4.2	6.2	6.2	6.2	6.2	6.1	6.1
.. by Region	..	..	..	–	–	6.3	6.3	6.2	–
4.3 COICOP main items 2001–02 to 2006	4.3	..	..	..	..	..	..	..	..
4.4 COICOP as a percentage of total expenditure 2001–02 to 2006	4.4	..	..	..	..	..	..	..	..

.. Tables do not appear in these publications.

1 Household Reference Person (HRP) replaced Head of Household (HoH) in 2001–02.